# The Shipmans

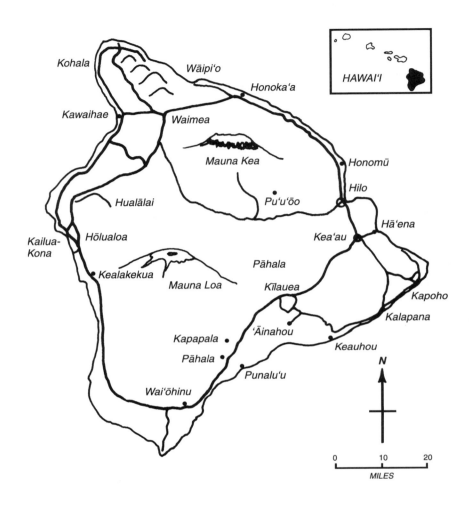

Kohala

Wāipi'o

Honoka'a

Kawaihae

Waimea

Mauna Kea

Honomū

Hilo

Hualālai

Pu'u'ōo

Hā'ena

Hōlualoa

Kea'au

Kailua-
Kona

Pāhala

Kealakekua

Mauna Loa

Kīlauea

Kapoho

Kalapana

Kapapala

'Āinahou

Keauhou

Pāhala

Punalu'u

Wai'ōhinu

HAWAI'I

N

0        10        20
MILES

The island of Hawai'i

# The Shipmans of East Hawai'i

EMMETT CAHILL

University of Hawai'i Press
Honolulu

**Library of Congress Cataloging-in-Publication Data**

Cahill, Emmett.

The Shipmans of East Hawai'i / Emmett Cahill.

p.   cm.

Includes bibliographical references and index.

ISBN 0–8248–1680–3 (paper : alk. paper)

1. Shipman family.   2. Hawaii—Genealogy.   I. Title.

CS71.S55675   1996

929'.2'0973—dc20             95–47621

CIP

University of Hawai'i Press books are printed on acid-free paper and meet the guidelines for permanence and durability of the Council on Library Resources

Frontispiece map: The island of Hawai'i

Book design by Paula Newcomb

# CONTENTS

# FOREWORD

Through the ages, generations of families have come and gone, and unless someone takes time to record the family history it is lost forever. There are surely many families today who wonder where their ancestors came from, where and how they lived, whom they married, and what accomplishments and experiences they had that were worth recording.

For many years the history of the Shipman family has existed in bits and pieces—in letters, pictures, and documents kept in drawers and attics. Parts of the story have been told to each generation, but never the whole story. And, over time, as stories are retold, the facts inevitably become twisted and lost. When my generation was growing up we were all urged to listen to our grandparents' and parents' generations and write down the stories we heard. Fortunately, over the years the six children of William and Mary Shipman, whenever possible, saved important and interesting letters, papers, and photographs for posterity. So, with this book, posterity is being served.

During the latter part of 1989, my good friend Emmett Cahill asked me why the story of the Shipmans of Hawai'i had never been written. I told him it had been discussed but no one had ever gotten down to the task. As he seemed interested in the subject, I asked if he would like to take it on. Some prior research had convinced him that the material was there, just waiting to be used. With the blessing of the W. H. Shipman board of directors, Emmett began.

Emmett and I had worked together several years earlier at the Hawaiian Telephone Company, so we were good friends; we respected and understood one another. I knew Emmett would do a good job. That's when the major task began, for first it was necessary to seek out all the family material that had been preserved and accumulated somewhere. The initial mission was to assess it and put it in proper perspective and chronological order. Thanks to Aunty Carrie Shipman, Uncle Herbert, my mother, Florence Shipman Blackshear (who never threw anything away), and notes kept by my sister, Beryl Walter, and my nephew, Tom Walter, as well as information from the English and Fisher families, our job was made easier. In 1970, my Aunt Carrie Shipman decided that if she didn't write down what family history she had, it would be lost. She wrote in longhand a manuscript that when typed totaled eighteen pages. Each niece and nephew received a copy, which then became the nucleus of early Shipman history in Hawai'i.

Emmett and I early on spent many hours in the Shipman board-room poring over the original missionary and family letters dating back to the 1850s. There were over 250, and each one had to be taken from its envelope, smoothed out for copying, and often typed for better review. Many required the help of a magnifying glass. Eventually, Emmett had examined all the letters and had them catalogued and itemized; they now form the Shipman Letter Collection. So what follows is the story of the Shipmans of Hawai'i.

It tells how the young Reverend William Cornelius Shipman and his wife, Jane, sailed from Boston and the relative safety and comfort of Eastern living. It tells of the 135-day ocean voyage on the Atlantic, through the stormy Magellan Straits, and into the Pacific in order to preach the Christian gospel to the people of faraway Micronesia. We read of how their plans were changed due to the impending birth of young Willie when the vessel laid over at Lahaina, Maui, then of their move to the island of Hawai'i and all the trials and tribulations that followed. Revealed is the story of how Willie and his part-Hawaiian wife, Mary, became owners of the 64,275 acres (more or less) of the *ahupua'a* of Kea'au, purchased from the King Lunalilo Trust. The story is told of how the nene, the state bird of Hawai'i, was saved from extinction by Herbert Shipman, who owned the only flock in existence; also of Herbert's impact on bringing the orchid industry to Hawai'i and his being awarded the prestigious gold medal of the American Orchid Society. Little was known until now of Jane Shipman's second marriage to William Reed after the death of her missionary husband, or of Reed's own history, followed by the story of succeeding generations.

It is rare that so many facts about a family still exist, but it is even rarer that some of the buildings and lands so prominent in the Shipman history are still owned by members of the same family. On behalf of all the members of our widespread family, I hope that its readers will enjoy reading this book, which is truly a part of old Hawai'i.

ROY SHIPMAN BLACKSHEAR

# PREFACE

My introduction to the Shipmans of Hawai'i took place in 1975 while I was living in alleged retirement in the delightful small village of Wai'ōhinu. When Roy Blackshear, a friend from years past, learned where I was domiciled, he told me with pride that 120 years earlier his great-grandfather had had his pastorate on the site of "that little white New England style church near your side road. " That interested me, and my interest heightened over the next few years, for I had always found putting together pieces of Hawai'i's regional history an engaging pastime.

Ten years later, after a hiatus in Honolulu, my wife and I returned to make our home in Volcano, on the island of Hawai'i. Then, having ample hours to reflect, ponder, and wonder, I asked myself why no one had ever written a history of the Shipman family. I sensed that there was a story to be told and shared. My approach to Blackshear was to inquire if a full family history had ever been written, and if not, why not? I correctly anticipated his reply that the project had never been attempted, for I had already searched the state libraries. I did find numerous biographies of early missionary families in Hawai'i, but the Shipmans were conspicuous by their absence.

Blackshear and other Shipman descendants welcomed someone willing to undertake the task. The search for sufficient material began, and as the months lengthened into years, the completion date was advanced again and again, as new and worthwhile bits of related history surfaced. My search took me to the Hawaii State Archives time and time again; also to material in the Bishop Museum, to Hilo's Lyman House Museum, and to the files of the American Board of Commissions for Foreign Missions, both in the Hawaii Historical Society and the Houghton Library at Harvard University. Government land documents added grist to the mill, as did the Hawai'i section of the University of Hawai'i (Hilo) Library. A plethora of photographs dating back to 1855 removed any lingering doubts I had regarding insufficiency of material.

Only after I had started my research, and had overcome the mysteries of operating a word processor, did I find myself overwhelmed with newfound riches. For those old and weathered documents, especially correspondence, I am indebted to long-gone Shipmans who read, treasured, and saved them, especially Jane Stobie Shipman, who seems to have passed on to her many descendants the art of acquisition and preservation. I missed Jane when she left the frame of history, much as I missed her practical, sensible missionary husband when he was snatched from the field of his endeavors.

I refer to the reams of early letters as "riches" because there can be no more accurate or better picture of the past than the testimony of those who were writing of their own present. With those many resurrected letters I had struck a vein of gold. Besides the many personal letters, I was fortunate in obtaining copies of the "Station Reports" that the Reverend Shipman sent annually to his superiors in Honolulu and New England. They carried me into his personal missionary life in the isolated district of Ka'ū, with all his trials, struggles, successes, failures, hopes and aspirations.

With the passing of this man of God, whose company I enjoyed while it lasted, there were three more generations of Shipmans to bring to life. And life came from unexpected sources, such as acquaintances of earlier Shipmans more than willing to reminisce and provide anecdotal items.

This narrative of the Shipman family will, I hope, add worthwhile bytes and bits of information to the already rich history of the island of Hawai'i. But it will in no way alter its history; for this is, in the final analysis, the history of a family that contributed much to Hawai'i.

Those readers who may be looking for tidbits of sex, scandal, and sensationalism among the Shipmans, or even other *kamaaina* families, will be disappointed. I found nothing of the sort to enliven these pages. Those who assume that the Shipmans, like many old and established families, acquired their land and wealth by stealth and devious dealings with the Hawaiians will be quite wrong. The family's early history of honest transactions with their contemporaries, coupled with Yankee energy and a love of their home island, are valid sources of Shipman pride; and their community has long had reason to be grateful for the generous gifts it has received from Shipman benefactors.

# ACKNOWLEDGMENTS

Perhaps one reason the history of the Shipmans has not been written until now is because there was so much to write about. Faced with extensive research, prospective chroniclers may have blenched at the thought. Nor would I have tackled, much less completed, this work but for many individuals who provided not only gems of information but also encouragement, even directing me to other sources—which led to still others.

First I owe much to author and Pacific historian Gavan Daws, not only for guidance in style and content but for his suggestions and sharing of source material. I would still be laboring on this tome had it not been for archaeologist and historian Dorothy Barrere. Her wide and deep knowledge of Hawaiian history, lore, and language, her familiarity with early land laws and transactions, and her willingness to review my drafts have all contributed to the finished product.

Researching my subject chronologically took me first, by telephone and correspondence, to the Glastonbury Historical Society in Connecticut, whose Nancy Berlet filled me in on the history of early Shipmans. New England was also the birthplace of the American Board of Commissioners of Foreign Missions (ABCFM), which played a major role in the life of the lead character, the Reverend William Cornelius Shipman. I would still be plodding through ABCFM archives had it not been for the help of Melanie Wisner, Houghton College Librarian at Harvard University, the custodian of ABCFM records. By phone and letter she helped round out the relationship of the ABCFM to Hawai'i's missionary history, and in particular to William C. Shipman.

In my following that New England family to Illinois, Joe Conover, editor of the *Quincy Herald-Whig*, not only provided early Shipman census records but led me to Philip German of the Historical Society of Quincy and Adams Counties. Donna Pursley, clerk of the Pike County (Illinois) Records Office, was patient and productive in obtaining land and court matters involving Shipman families. So was Illinois genealogist Jean Kay, who filled in many blanks on two generations of Shipmans and Stobies. Ruth Hutchcraft of the Illinois State Archives was equally helpful.

On the local front, useful information came from Charlene Dahlquist, volunteer librarian at the Lyman House Memorial Museum. Junko

Nowaki, chief librarian for the University of Hawai'i (Hilo) special collections section, assisted by pointing me to several sources of pertinent Hawaiian history (also how to use a microfiche). The reference librarians at the Hilo Public Library made my searches easier by their willingness to produce rare resource material from their sanctum sanctorum, to which we great unwashed are denied access. Alberta Nathaniel, secretary for the Haili Church, has my gratitude for the gift of the book *The History of Haili Church: 1824–1974.*

I would never have been enriched by the history of Kapāpala Ranch had not ranch manager Gordon Cran and his wife, Jon, given me hours of their time as well as a four-wheel-drive tour of the green grasslands that carpet the slope of Mauna Loa. Helen Bevins deserves many thanks for researching Hawaii Volcanoes National Park involvement with 'Āinahou Ranch, as does former park staff member Dan Taylor.

In Honolulu, the Bishop Museum's archival staff, Lynn Davis, Betty Lou Kam, and Neena Sachdeva, showed personal interest in my project. Also, personnel of the Hawaii State Archives frequently came to my aid, first by walking me through their card files and then their computer system. Archaeologist Marian Kelly was always eager to share her wide knowledge of majestic Ka'ū. The same cooperation came from Barbara Dunn, librarian of the Hawaiian Historical Society, and Marilyn Reppun of the Hawaiian Mission Children's Society. Mary Rentz, a State of Hawaii librarian, was an able assistant, on her own time, in researching state library sources. Also, her reviewing and editing my text helped to improve it no little. Stanley Melman (Hawaii Maritime Museum), Roger Coryell, and Carol Silva contributed to many successful searches.

Several persons close to the Shipman family, especially to the late Herbert Shipman, gave of their time to be interviewed on tape. Particularly Richard Devine, former Shipman office manager, followed by persons with retentive memories like Yasuki Arakaki, Carl Roehner, Margaret Wessel Stearns, John Cross, Masaru and Yoshie Uchida, Bessie Morita, and Eldon English. Thurston Twigg-Smith shared nuggets about his grandfather Lorrin Thurston, and William Paris did the same about Lanakila Church. Russell Apple filled some of the voids, as did former Micronesia pastor, the Reverend Eldon Buck.

To Roy Shipman Blackshear, who gave this project the green light and agreed to write the Foreword, I am grateful for his ongoing support, his contributions, and his friendship. His sister, Beryl Blackshear Walter, furnished much of the Shipman, Kauwe, and Johnson genealogy.

Let me not overlook Ka'ū old-timers, Walter Wong-Yuen and Earnest Freitas, who took me to faraway meadows that are still referred to by local people as "Shipman's land." Much of my task was lightened by the willingness of my wife, Bernice, to spend hours of proofreading endless pages and offering valued suggestions. It is a very much appreciated labor of love.

To others whom I may have overlooked, my apologies and *mahalo*—thanks. Last but not least (excuse the cliché, Iris), to Iris Wiley, former University of Hawai'i Press executive editor, for her guidance and encouragement, and for steering me away from clichés.

Every effort has been made to credit pictures correctly. If errors or omissions remain, I would appreciate being informed so that correct attributions can be made in any future editions.

# 1

# *1854—A Year to Remember*

The respected Hawai'i historian R. S. Kuykendall has referred to the year 1854 as the start of a critical twenty-year period for the Hawaiian kingdom.[1] But 1854 was not only the beginning of a crucial period in Hawai'i; it also made history in many other parts of the world.[2] Back in New England it was significant for William Cornelius Shipman and his wife, Jane, for it was then that he was ordained and the couple set sail for the far-off missions of Micronesia. Instead, 1854 saw them land in Lahaina, Maui. It was a year that would change Shipman's plans and his life, and have aftereffects touching many lives in years to come.

In faraway England, Queen Victoria ruled Britannia and Britannia ruled the waves, as it had since the days of Elizabeth I and the Spanish Armada. In 1854 Victoria had been on the throne for seventeen years and would remain there for forty-seven more. It was with her navy that the Crimean War began in 1854. This was the same year in which Great Britain and France concluded a treaty with Turkey to curb the expanding empire of the tsar of Russia. In Rome, Pope Pius IX declared the dogma of the Immaculate Conception of the Blessed Virgin Mary to be an article of faith—an item of less than zero interest to New England Protestant missionaries in Hawai'i such as the Reverend William Shipman.

In Japan in 1854, Commodore Matthew Perry of the United States Navy negotiated the first trade treaty with the hitherto hidden empire of the mikado. This act not only swept Japan into a new and changing world, but would have far-reaching and long-lasting political, cultural, and economic effects on Hawai'i.

In that same year another important document, the Ostend Manifesto, was signed in Belgium by representatives of Great Britain, France, and the United States. It urged the acquisition of Cuba from Spain by the U.S.A., either by purchase or by force. This expansionist threat gladdened the hearts of Hawai'i annexationists and brought gloom to its loyalists.

# Shipman

Translated, the Shipman coat of arms reads: "Not for self but for the world."

In the United States, President Franklin Pierce was in mid-term as he occupied the White House; some of his contemporary detractors said that was *all* Pierce did. But in 1854 national events were seething to a point that would bring the country, seven years later, into a full-fledged civil war.[3] Abolitionists were a thorn in the side of the several slave states, and Pierce, a Democrat and a Northerner, was unable to please his supporters. His position on states' rights would prevent federal intervention and allow each state to make its own choice on slavery. His signing the controversial Kansas-Nebraska Act in 1854 hastened the advent of the Civil War and helped effect his own downfall.

In the same year the Grand Old Party was born in Ripon, Wisconsin, from the seeds of discontent sown by opponents of the Kansas-Nebraska Act. An 1854 preview of what would befall Hawai'i some forty years later was the ratification of the Gadsden Purchase, although in the case of Hawai'i no money changed hands. Mexico lost some of its northern territory to the United States, which gained what is now New Mexico and part of Arizona. On a much more restrained note, in Massachusetts, whence the Reverend and Mrs. William Cornelius Shipman would soon sail, Henry David Thoreau was living in a sylvan setting quietly writing *Walden: or Life in the Woods*.

Ties between the United States and the island kingdom of Hawai'i would shorten and tighten with the growth of mid-century ocean shipping. Not only was the U.S.A. Hawai'i's closest neighbor, but the wellspring of commerce would contribute to Hawai'i's prosperity, as well as its subsequent annexation. Shipping was the umbilical cord to the West Coast and also knit the islands more closely together. Foreign and interisland shipping served several needs in a period that marked the transition from sailing to steam-driven vessels. Foreign vessels registered in Hawai'i in 1855 numbered over sixty, and these were largely engaged in such Pacific basin trade as guano, whaling, sealing, and general merchandise, as well as traffic among the islands. Both Honolulu and Lahaina were endowed with good roadsteads (Honolulu means "fair haven"), and in 1854 Lahaina served as a convenient way station between Honolulu and the southern island of Hawai'i. Travel between any of the islands was a genuine discomfort, be it by sailing vessel or steamer. Limited space, crowded accommodations, decks shared with livestock, and often choppy channels added nothing to the comfort of passengers. Some interisland vessels took a week or more to complete their trip. With the entry of transpacific steam navigation around 1850, a couple of steam-powered interisland vessels plied Hawaiian waters.[4] These were the forerunners of what became the Interisland Steam Navigation Company, which served Hawai'i until the end of World War II, when air service proved more practical and economical.

As early as 1853, a year before the Shipmans arrived, Hawai'i's first steamship, the SS *Akamai*, traveled Hawaiian waters between Lahaina and Honolulu. She came to a sudden end a year later when a heavy squall crippled her. She limped back to Honolulu with her five hundred passengers, but the *Akamai* was reckoned a total loss.[5]

The year 1854 was not only critical for the Hawaiian monarchy, it was also the end of one era and the beginning of another. In 1825 Kauikeaouli, the eleven-year-old son of Kamehameha the Great, inherited the throne from his brother Liholiho and became King Kamehameha III. This longest reign of Hawaiian sovereigns also inherited the problems that came with an increasing foreign presence.[6]

During his early years, Kamehameha III was a mixture of weakness and strength. He had little opportunity to demonstrate the latter, for he was under the guidance and governance of the strong-willed and self-appointed regent, Queen Dowager Ka'ahumanu. She had been the favorite wife of Kamehameha the Great, and after his death and with the advent of the missionaries became a resolute and rigid convert to Protestantism.[7] Upon her death in 1832, the young king, still a considerable carouser, was saddled with yet another female regent. (Princess Kīna'u was every bit as determined a matriarchal ruler as her predecessor.) When the king finally did become a ruler in his own right, he had grown and matured. In his efforts to move his nation forward, he was faced with problems that sprang from a growing foreign population. Not the least of these was the pressure from foreign interests for laws more favorable to newcomers. As for annexation, by 1854 it had become a serious topic of discussion, and it was not about to disappear.[8]

By 1854 land reform, begun under Kamehameha III, had made great strides and brought many changes. The king earned his place in history for his 1848 Great *Mahele* (division), a royal decision that divided the land between the Crown, the government, and the chiefs, with precious little going to the commoners.[9] His tenure saw Hawai'i's entry into international affairs, which included an unauthorized and brief annexation by Great Britain and differences with France over threats from its visiting gunboats. Not to be overlooked was the 1854 act of the Hawai'i legislature providing for the improvement of Honolulu harbor in anticipation of trade with the Empire of Japan now that it was opened to the world of commerce. Kamehemeha III must get credit for replacing an absolute monarchy with a constitutional monarchy.[10]

In retrospect, it has been said that it all began with Captain Cook and his arrival in Hawai'i in 1778. Cook was followed shortly afterward by Captain George Vancouver, like Cook, a benevolent leader as well as a superb navigator. After these events, the Sandwich Islands (named after Cook's patron, the earl of Sandwich) became known and attractive to outsiders, who came to see, save souls, barter and trade, and establish residence. For the most part they were Americans; and the more they came, the longer they stayed, and the more they felt that Hawai'i's customs and ways of living could be improved by Western ways. Changes did come to pass, some of which did indeed benefit the Hawaiians, especially commoners, as well as foreigners. Although the inevitable result, annexation by the United States, did not occur for nearly a half-century, in 1854 American interests were already plotting, planning, and wooing powerful aiders and abetters.[11]

When the Shipmans arrived in Lahaina in October 1854 enroute to Micronesia, they came to a Pacific nation whose economy was on a sound basis and in which harmony prevailed despite the nagging possibility of annexation. The missionary couple's forced layover of nine months, due to Mrs. Shipman's pregnancy, came during a transition from one monarchy to another that would build on the progress of its predecessor.

The 1854 port town of Lahaina was not unlike its counterpart, Honolulu.[12] Both were experiencing growing pains and a cultural transition resulting from the emergence of sugar plantations, whaling, and missionary endeavors. Honolulu in 1854 was the established seat of operations for the widespread Protestant missions. By far the larger of the two communities, Honolulu had a population of about 11,000 in 1854

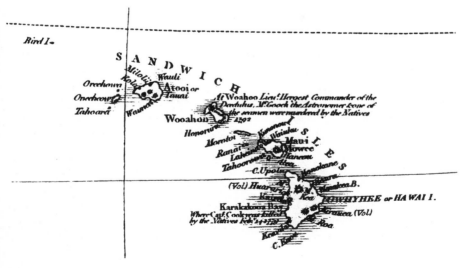

This 1855 map of the Hawaiian Islands was printed in London the year the Reverend William Cornelius Shipman, with his wife and baby, arrived in Waiohinu. (Editions Limited)

and had been recognized as a city for four years. By that time it had already been the capital of the kingdom for eleven years, replacing Lahaina. The latter had been the choice of King Kamehameha I when he moved from Kailua on Hawai'i Island to Maui. When his son, Liholiho, assumed the throne, he did nothing to change things. But pragmatism and destiny led to Honolulu's becoming the new seat of government, although the quasi-capital of Lahaina lingered on, with its uncompleted palace and residences for royalty. Diplomatic, political, and commercial activity began to focus more on Honolulu and soon relegated Lahaina to second place. Honolulu became the official capital in 1843,[13] the same year during which Herman Melville lolled in Lahaina before working for a short span in Honolulu,[14] while turning over in his mind the plot for *Moby Dick*.

The Lahaina that greeted the Shipmans was a community of contrasts with varied interests, activities, and occupations. A situation existed in which the missionaries, who had been established there since 1820, were in conflict with a way of life, brought by the whalers, that overwhelmed the village. Lahaina was transformed from a primeval village into a complex community. In 1854 there were an estimated 4,800 persons living in Lahaina district, and half of them probably lived in the village. It was a rapidly changing community, far from the complacent,

In 1848 Lahaina was the early capital of the Hawaiian Kingdom. It attracted ships and sailors from many lands. (BM)

relaxed coastal capital of eleven years earlier. The agent that let the genie out of the Lahaina bottle was the whaling industry. Lahaina's sister city, Honolulu, was likened to Sodom—which left Lahaina to be labeled as Gomorrah.

Whaling, which prospered mightily in 1854, entered the Pacific shortly after the War of 1812 once the fishing beds of New Bedford and Nantucket, and the general Atlantic area, had been depleted. The Pacific attracted whalers to come around the Horn by the hundreds. They sailed thousands of miles from New England to hunt whales that would provide whalebone for the corsets and oil for the lamps of many lands.[15]

The first whaling ship to arrive in Lahaina was the *Baelena*, in 1819. As early as 1822, thirty-four American whalers were in Hawai'i replenishing their supplies as they prepared to move north, where they capitalized on newly discovered fishing fields near Japan. As those became exhausted, they moved north to arctic seas around the Bering Strait and Alaska. But freezing winters were not conducive to successful whaling, and Hawai'i proved the ideal oasis for repairs, replenishing supplies, rest and recreation. Honolulu and Lahaina were sanctuaries welcomed by the hundreds of whalers, who were in turn eagerly welcomed by sailmakers, chandlers, and merchants dealing in food, grog, clothing, fresh fruits and vegetables, souvenirs for collectors, and provisions of every kind for coming months in northern seas. In this off-season, Lahaina was favored because of its broad and calm roadsteads. Here ships, sailors, and whalers luxuriated in Lahaina's warmth and worldly attractions.

The golden age of whaling in Hawai'i was approximately between 1843 and 1860. This would put the Shipmans' 1854 arrival in the middle of Lahaina's prosperity boom. Often as many as 75 to 100 vessels anchored in the Lahaina roadsteads during those years of plenty. A high point was 1859, when 549 whaling vessels visited the Islands.[16] It was said that a sober sailor could jump from one ship to another without so much as getting his shoes wet. It was also said—nay, boasted—that "There is no God west of the Horn."[17] And no small number of the men on leave would set out each day to prove it. Considering that each ship on a given day might have thirty men on leave, Lahaina could figure on having upward of two thousand visitors in a twenty-four-hour period. Lahaina merchants were as glad to see them as missionaries and many townspeople were not. Such interlopers roaming Lahaina's streets and byways with American dollars for booze, brothels, and even wild-horseback riding were bound to create conflict. Although welcomed by the merchants, sailors clashed with the authorities of law and order, and more so with a well- and long-established missionary element.

After all, in terms of residence, the missionaries could claim a quarter-century over the sailors of 1854. These missionaries of the Second Company, which departed Boston in 1822, were dedicated, Christ-committed, and energetic individuals. Succeeding missionaries were of the same ilk. They and their families left a mark on Lahaina that is still visible even today. They came to stay, and they brought their culture with them.[18] They built wood-frame houses to replace grass shacks. They built churches and, in Lahaina, the Dwight Baldwin Mission Home, where the Shipmans resided during their nine-month layover.[19] (It is today the home of the Lahaina Restoration Foundation and Museum.)

In 1831, a mile outside of town at the foot of the West Maui mountains, the missionaries started construction of Lahainaluna, the first school to be built west of the Rockies.[20] Only male students were

King Kamehameha III, the monarchy's longest-reigning sovereign, died on December 16, 1854, the day before the birth in Lahaina of the Shipmans' first child. (HSA)

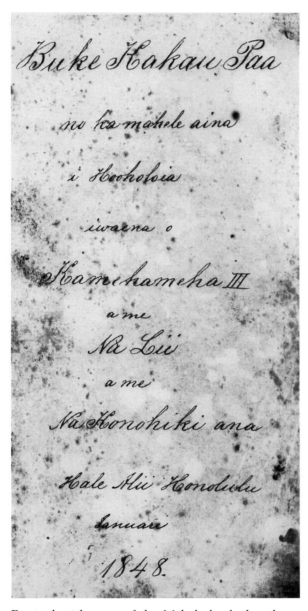

Facsimile title page of the Mahele book that documented the first distribution of lands under Kamehameha III. Translated it reads: "Book of the Land Division resolved between Kamehameha III and the chiefs and his land agents. Palace, Honolulu, January, 1848." (HSA)

enrolled, and they were taught algebra, geometry, trigonometry, and arithmetic—all prerequisites for young men determined to learn the art of land surveying. Others who showed promise of becoming good teachers and preachers of the Gospel were encouraged to take the courses necessary for such a calling. English was not taught until 1870. Another distinction of Lahainaluna is that in 1834 its printing presses ran off the first copy of *Ka Lama (The Lamp)*, the first Pacific newspaper west of the Rockies.

The New England families had, early on, solidly established themselves in a community of worldly values, and they had no intention of surrendering their well-rooted ideology to transient carousers. It was this turbulent environment which the young New England–bred William Shipman encountered. How he and his wife fared in the tumultuous town is unknown. But quartered as they were in the middle of the village, isolation from daily events was unlikely. They endured until mid-1855, meanwhile getting a firsthand taste of a side of missionary life they had hardly anticipated.

The year 1854 was the close of a historic era in Hawai'i, and with it came the demise of the progressive and popular Kamehameha III. The stress and strain of governing an emerging Hawai'i, combined with ill health resulting from earlier dissolute living, took its toll. Although only forty-one, this royal Hawaiian sovereign died on December 15, 1854.

The very day after the death of the ruler, the head of a somewhat lesser dynasty was born. In a letter (December 20, 1854) to her husband in Honolulu, Charlotte Baldwin wrote, "Mrs. Shipman has nice boy, weighed ten pounds, born last Saturday night, December 16 . . . ."[21]

Kauikeaouli, King Kamehameha III, son of Kamehameha the Great and the longest-reigning ruler in the history of the monarchy, had departed. And William Herbert Shipman, "Willie," founder of what would later become W. H. Shipman Limited, had arrived.

# 2

# *Who Were the Shipmans?*

The study of family names, or surnames, can be both fascinating and entertaining when applied to those who are bearers of the patronymic.[1] In centuries long past, a single or given name sufficed. Only when the world became more populated, and therefore more complex, was the surname born out of convenience, and probably as a matter of pride to the bearer. As a community grew and expanded, there could be several males within it carrying the given names of James, John, William, and so on; a way to distinguish among them became essential. Particular given names became more popular not only with the growth of communities but also with the advent of the Christian church and its use of Christian names. These not only identified a child but, by adding the surname, revealed whose it was, and often whence its parents came. For individuals having only a baptismal or given name, the addition of a surname would distinguish them from others in the area with the same name.

As a rule, surnames are divided into four categories. The first is that of the father, the patronymic. This yields such family names as Mac-Donald (son of Donald) and O'Neil (a descendant of the Neil clan). Johnson is obvious, as is any name with the suffix "son." The Gaelic name MacShane and the Russian name Ivanovitch both correspond to Johnson. Names such as Fitzgibbons came to the British Isles by way of the Norman conquest, when the prefix *fils*, "son," was carried across the Channel. For the same purpose the Welsh use the prefix *ap*. (An American naval officer, Captain Thomas ap Catesby Jones, had a hand in drawing up a Hawaiian trade agreement in 1826.)[2] The surname Apritchard is often shortened to Pritchard; anglicized it becomes Richardson.

The second classification of surnames relates to physical or personal characteristics. Very often names of colors were forced upon individuals by oppressive rulers or uncaring authorities. There is no end of Browns, Blacks, Whites, and Greens. The Irish, among others, had a penchant for glamorizing and glorifying their family names with qualities signifying valor, character, honor, and of course fearlessness in battle.

Many English families were given, or took, such descriptive appellations as Goodman, Wellman, Wiseman, and Truman—or Humphrey, from *homme vrai* (true man).

The third category comprises scores of surnames derived from the locale or one-time place of residence of the name holder. Milford, Bradford, Danford, and Redford—and the name Ford itself—indicate that a member of that family lived near a stream or river crossing. Lane came from a small byway. The North family came from somewhere in that direction, as Norton came from Northtown. Other points of the compass gave the surnames Easton, West/Weston, and Sutton. Men who were yeomen or freemen, and not of the gentry, might be known as James of the Woods, John of the Brook, and William of the North; and surely there was Andrew the Farmer. Their descendants are James Woods, John Brooks, William North, and Andrew Farmer.

The fourth classification of family names may also be the largest in English-speaking countries. These names evolve from the position or status of the male, be he an officer of rank, a tradesman, a craftsman—or a shipman. The English adopted the system of using such surnames as early as the thirteenth century. Many identified themselves by the office they held, and so we have Bishop, Judge, Mayor, Parson, Knight, Chamberlain, Marshall, Clarke (clerk), Parker, Sumner (summoner), and Constable. Even more common families identified themselves through occupations—for example, Baker, Barber, Brewer, Carter, Carpenter, Collier, Cooper, Draper, Farmer, Fisher, Gardner, Hunter, Merchant, Miller, and a host of others, including Seaman. Sequentially, logically, and alphabetically, this last is but a step away from another important surname, Shipman.

The first male to take the family name of Shipman did so to identify himself with the source of his livelihood. He was just what his name stated: a man connected with ships. He may have been a builder, or perhaps he owned one. He may have been a sailor, or perhaps a navigator. Maybe he was a ship's officer, a captain or first mate. He may have commanded a fleet of vessels or provided ships with such items as canvas, hardware, and other maritime necessities. He may have been any one of the above or a combination of them.

Spellings of Shipman include Schippmann, Schipman, Schypman, and Scipman. These point to Teutonic roots, particularly countries bordering the North Sea. The earliest English documentation of the family appears during the reign of King Henry III, who was on the throne from 1216 to 1272. On record is Hugh le Schipman, an indication of Norman origins. A William Schippeman appears in the Lincoln County rolls of 1273. That same year an Alexander Shipman was a member of Britain's Parliament.[3]

The first Shipman to leave for the English colonies in America was probably a twenty-two-year-old named William. He was a passenger in 1635 aboard the *Speedwell,* a ship out of London. William Shipman debarked in the Virginia Colony, where his trail ends. But another Shipman trail began four years later and continues to the present.[4]

Around 1626 Edward Shipman was born in the shipping city of Hull, England. One account states that "Edward, the orphan child of a religious refugee, came to America in 1639, sailing from Hull . . . in the care of George Fenwick." This Edward Shipman, looked upon as the father of the first generation of Shipmans in America, is also the progenitor of the branch of the family that produced the Hawai'i Shipmans.

Edward arrived during a period when a number of other English citizens, specifically the Puritans, were seeking religious refuge and freedom of worship. He settled in Saybrook (now Chester), Connecticut, and seems to have fared well. He became a selectman of Saybrook in 1672 and was an active member of the relatively new Congregational church. He also became a landowner of no small means. At one time he held title to about 3,000 acres of land "within sight of Hartford," nearly all virgin territory. Edward not only served his township but even the colony of Connecticut by his military service in the Narragansett War. For this, a grateful government awarded him five acres of land to add to his already large holdings. Upon his death in 1697 he bequeathed his many acres to his five sons.

It was with Edward's son William, of the second American generation, that the Hawai'i line of Shipman took shape and continued for the next 335 years. (The given name of William reappears with more frequency than any other Shipman first name. It shows up generation after generation, even down to the founding father of Hawai'i's William H. Shipman Ltd.).

William was a landowner by inheritance and also by land acquired as a gift from the town of Colchester, of which he was considered a founder. He died at the age of seventy-one, but not before his wife had given birth to twelve children. The fourth was the first white girl to be born in the town of Hebron, Connecticut.

The fathers of the third, fourth, and fifth generations were each given the Christian name Stephen. The fifth Stephen Shipman lived up to his surname. Annals of his life list him as a sea captain, a ship builder, and merchant—all of which enabled him to become one of the more affluent residents of Glastonbury, Connecticut. Captain Shipman was a soldier in the Revolutionary War and became a leading citizen and landowner. His wife was directly related to Hannibal Hamlin, Abraham Lincoln's first vice president. Well before his death in 1834, Captain Shipman bought and lived in one of Glastonbury's most attractive homes. Today it is one of New England's showpieces, a notable example of eighteenth-century residential architecture. It is listed in the National Register of Historic Places and has been cited by the U.S. Department of the Interior as possessing exceptional architectural interest.[5]

In that house Reuben, one of Stephen and Eunice's six children, was born. He was named after the captain's younger brother, who had died a captive in the Revolutionary War. Reuben, a sixth-generation Shipman, became a farmer and lived in Wethersfield and nearby Rocky Hill. There, in December 1818, he married Margaret Clarissa Bulkley (also given as Bliny and Buckley). Reuben and Margaret had five children. The second child was a boy; they named him William Cornelius. Thirty years later he would earn the title of Reverend, and in the same

Reuben Shipman, father of the missionary William Cornelius, was born in this Glastonbury, Connecticut, home in 1791. Built in 1755, it remains a showpiece as well as being on the National Register of Historic Buildings.

year this seventh generation of Shipmans would sail for the foreign missions in far-off Micronesia.

William Cornelius was a boy of eight in 1832 when Reuben, his wife, and five children forsook Connecticut for the fabled farmlands of western Illinois. It was a period of migration to what was considered the Far West, and the migrants were mostly New England and New York farmers who had wearied of scratching a living from their postage-stamp-thin soil. Fortunately the federal government, anxious to open up the West, was offering rich farmlands and forests in western Illinois at most attractive prices.

It was a long and tortuous journey for those families, who had to travel by wagon through miles of wilderness to reach the rich soil of the Mississippi or Illinois river basins. But with the opening of the Erie Canal in 1825, both distance and time were diminished, as travelers could cross New York State by boat. From Buffalo they could continue on the Great Lakes to the upper areas of Indiana and Illinois; even those states had waterways that often provided convenient transportation to inland destinations.

Also forsaking Connecticut for western Illinois were Reuben's nephew George and two of Reuben's brothers, William Henry and James Madison Shipman (after the president in office at James' birth). All the Shipmans chose well when they made the decision to stake their future in the fertile township of Hadley in Pike County, Illinois. A history of the locality in the last half of the nineteenth century describes it as a "magnificent township for agricultural purposes; surpassed by few in the area. The sight presented to the early settler must have been pleasant as he viewed nature's beautiful lawn, studded with houses, orchards, hedges, and all the insignia of a healthy cultivation."[6]

Two years after his arrival, Reuben purchased from the United States government one hundred acres of virgin land. Shortly afterward he made additional purchases near his original tract. By 1848 he had title to four hundred acres.[7] Pike County records show that in 1839 forty acres were purchased in the name of William Cornelius Shipman. As William was only fifteen at the time, the purchase was presumably made by his father, Reuben, as an enticement to keep his oldest son on the farm, as well as an investment. With this amount of acreage, Reuben would need all the help he could muster. A Hadley history records that Reuben Shipman was among the first settlers who "made good improvements and were good farmers."[8] He became not only a landowner of some substance but also a respected citizen. His name appears on an early Hadley docu-

ment affirming that he was one of three chairmen for a committee certi-
fying the plot plans for the proposed village of New Philadelphia.[9] The
project never got off the drawing board because the railroad bypassed the
desired site. When the railroad did come, it crossed Reuben's section and
the station was within walking distance of the Shipman homestead.

Reuben died in 1868 and his wife a year later. But both outlived
their son William, who forsook the farm for the missionary field. By this
time Reuben and other Shipmans had become well entrenched in the
rural township. Alfred, the youngest son, owned a sizable tract, as did the
middle son, James Henry. Reuben's brother, James Madison Shipman,
also appears on Hadley rolls as an early landowner. Another large farm
was owned by a cousin, George Shipman. An 1872 Hadley land map
shows George Conrad and Hector Brownell as owners of the land once
the property of Reuben. In that era it was not uncommon for rural
inhabitants to "marry within the smoke of their own chimney." Both men
had married daughters of Reuben and Margaret. The map also indicates
the farmhouse that Reuben built, high on fertile plateau land. Pike
County records of 1850 include a Henry, Eliza, and Frederick Shipman.
Later census rolls show still more Shipmans as residents of the Barry and
Hadley areas.

# 3

# *The Making of a Missionary*

The early life of William Cornelius Shipman might well be called the "hidden years"; all we know is that he spent his first eight years on the family farm in Rocky Hill, Connecticut. When in 1832 Reuben and his young family pulled up stakes to head for the greener pastures of western Illinois, William's farm experience was that of any other eight-year-old at the time: feeding chickens, gathering eggs, helping with the garden, and herding cows.

Like many of his New England neighbors, Reuben Shipman found scratching a living from the rough scrabble soil a hard existence. True, the federal government, eager to attract people to the West, was offering rich farmlands and forests in western Illinois at very low prices. But for early travelers the only available modes of transportation were horse or wagon trail, and the entire trip could take months.

The Erie Canal, opened one year after William was born, greatly eased the hardships of overland travel, usually made by covered wagon. The new canal offered an almost entire water route to the shores of the Mississippi. Starting near Albany, passengers reached Buffalo in a week or two, then transferred to a Great Lakes vessel that took them across Lake Erie and eventually deposited them on the Illinois shore of Lake Michigan. Another waterway, the Illinois River, carried the pioneers southwest to midland Illinois. From there it was an overland trip of perhaps two hundred miles to the Shipman destination of Hadley Township in Pike County.

Reuben Shipman soon had his "section," as the tracts were designated, sufficiently cleared for the crops and buildings necessary for family, harvests, livestock, and tools. As no school existed in their Illinois township of Hadley until 1836, when William was twelve, his early learning came from his parents.[1] In addition to the three R's there was still another: Religion. William's parents had been members of the Glastonbury Congregational Church and continued to attend church in the nearby Illinois village of Barry. The boy continued his education in the

Reuben and his wife, Margaret Clarissa, moved from New England to Illinois around 1832. Each enjoyed a long life and remained faithful correspondents with their faraway two missionaries.

local schools and as he grew older helped his father and younger brothers work the family farm. During his youth he was known by the given name William and also, by some, as Cornelius. This came to light years later when his Uncle George Conrad wrote: "I saw all the colored folks that used to know Cornelius. They all enquired about you and told me to give you their best respects."

Reuben took advantage of the government's reasonable prices to buy adjacent sections of farmland.[2] One of these was deeded in 1839 in the name of William C. Shipman, at the time only fifteen years old. It would later become part of an entangled case in the Illinois Chancery Court.

Those teenage years gave William time to ponder his future. He may not have realized it then, but his life on the farm was to prove an asset in his missionary years. It was when he was working the fields with his father and brothers that he came to the realization that his future would be in the service of Christ. This change in life direction, he wrote later, was brought about through the influence of a Christian neighbor. Whoever that neighbor was, he swayed William, directly or indirectly, to take the first step toward becoming a servant of the Master. It was with this vision of his future that, when he was twenty-two, he enrolled in Mission Institute in the nearby city of Quincy. The year was 1846, the same year that another young Illinois rural resident, Abraham Lincoln, won his first bid for the Congress of the United States.

The institute was founded about 1840, its object to "educate and qualify young people of both sexes for the duty of Christian missionaries in foreign lands." Its founder was Dr. David Nelson, a well-known abolitionist who had served prison time in Missouri for helping slaves to escape. During the Civil War the institute would become an important underground railroad station.[3] What little is known of William's four years at the institute is found in two letters of recommendation on his behalf for acceptance to Yale Divinity School. The first, dated August 20, 1850, was from a faculty member of Mission Institute and addressed to "The Professors of Yale Theological Seminary." It introduced

> Brother William C. Shipman who has attended a course of four years' study . . . with a view of preparing for the Missionary field. He wishes to attend a theological course at your Seminary as a further preparation. I therefore wish to state that he is a young gentleman of an excellent moral and religious character, of good natural and acquired abilities. . . . I would therefore cheerfully say that I verily believe that his zeal for the cause of Christ and his piety in general as well as his pecuniary circumstances . . . would recommend him to your special care if he should need aid in the further prosecution of his studies.[4]

The second letter, dated ten days later and cosigned by the superintendent of the institute and a faculty member, is briefer but equally supportive. Addressed "To whom It may concern," the letter testifies that "Wm. C. Shipman has been, for several years past, a member of Mission Institute, regular & faithful in the performance of his duties as a student, & of good moral religious habits. He is hereby, at his own request, dismissed from further connection with this Institution, with the hope that the fulness of the blessing of the gospel of Christ may ever dwell with him."[5]

Apparently, these favorable recommendations from respected sources opened Yale doors, for in 1850 he was enrolled. There is no documentation of his academic progress or performance during these years, but in May 1854 he was ordained a Congregational minister in New Haven's Howe Street Church.[6]

Before William left Mission Institute for New Haven, he had the option of studying for Protestant missionary work in the United States or abroad. He chose the latter, and in March 1854, two months before his ordination, wrote a letter of application to the American Board of Commissioners for Foreign Missions (ABCFM).[7]

The ABCFM had been in existence for fourteen years when William was born. Through his Congregationalist parents he would have heard of it at home, and later from the pulpit. Surely he learned more about it while at Mission Institute, which had already prepared other students for ABCFM assignments. He was also aware of the remote and distant posts staffed by ABCFM missionaries. When William applied for assignment just prior to his ordination, he literally went all out. Instead of seeking a station somewhat closer to home like the Marquesas, Hawai'i, or even Patagonia, he chose the Siam mission, half a world away.

In his letter (March 6, 1854) to the Reverend Rufus Anderson, an ABCFM executive, William made clear the serious consideration he had given to his chosen vocation.[8]

> "Permit me though a stranger to address you briefly. I graduated from the Theo. Seminary at N.H. last summer. After some deliberation I offered myself as a missionary to the American Missionary Association and was accepted and appointed to the Siam Mission with the expectation of sailing for that place as soon as Sept. 1st. Now it is thought by the committee not practicable to send a reinforcement to that station at all or at least for some time. . . . My object in addressing you now is to enquire . . . if you would receive me under the patronage of the American Board; and also if among your missions you have a place where you would be glad to send a young man immediately.

Less than a week later he pursued his aim in a letter to the Reverend Dr. Samuel Pomeroy, the ABCFM secretary who was then the decision maker for all applicants.[9] No clearer or more definitive picture of the budding missionary is on record. In four handwritten pages, dated March 12, 1854, William revealed for the first time in writing the event that had led him from the Hadley farm to Mission Institute. It is much more than a resumé, for he laid out his qualifications, desires, motives, and goals. He even went beyond, exhibiting spiritual conflict as well as ambitions that reflected the Calvinist influence of his earlier upbringing. He not only opened his heart but, almost on bended knee before his confessor, voiced his mea culpas.

It is not unreasonable to believe the applicant felt that by labeling himself a repentant sinner who wished to repent still further, he might receive favorable consideration. This is not to say that Shipman was less than sincere in his pursuit of a vocation as a servant of God. But his instinct told him what his earthly judges might well like to hear. As can be seen in his letters of later years, William was not the rigid and morose missionary that quite often personified Calvinist preachers of his era. His appeal to Pomeroy revealed much about the young man, whose sincerity and zeal cannot be doubted. He opened with a statement of testimonials yet to come and a mention of his years at Mission Institute. He then went to the heart of his case:

> I experienced a change of heart when I was about twenty years of age. I was favored with pious parents & in my younger days with good religious privileges in general. Living in Rocky Hill & enjoying the instructions of Dr. Calvin Chapin as a christian minister. When young, my parents moved to the west where the religious advantages were quite inferior & where for years I had very little religious instruction except for what was received at home. Yet I could not get away from the thought that I was a sinner. My convictions of sin commenced at an early age. For some 2 or 3 years before I gave my heart to God I was under [that] conviction most of the time.
>
> At the time when I met with the change there was no particular religious interests in these places but there was a man moved into the neighborhood who was a devoted and working christian; he soon found a way to me & through his influence I trust that I was led to Christ. Instead of seeking my own pleasures I resolved to seek & do the will of God, looking into Christ for pardon & salvation. There was a change in my affections so that the things I once hated I now loved. Previous to this I had set it in my mind that I would spend my days as a farmer, now I felt that I could do more in some other sphere & a sense of duty I trust led me to desire the ministry; and at the same time fixed my eye on the missionary work.
>
> My experience since has been various. Sometimes I have almost been discouraged & thought myself deluded; that I had never met with a change of heart; but I have never thought to give up the determination to be a christian. I think that I can safely say that I have made progress, though much slower than necessary. I believe that my faith in God and his promises has much increased in the past year or two; & that my determination to do his will whatever it may be & to trust alone in Jesus Christ for righteousness has also increased. Yet I cannot but at times . . . wonder that I can still be forgetful of my highest interests.
>
> My motives in desiring the missionary work are I trust those of benevolence—thinking that in this way I can better promote the glory of God & do good to the human family. There is in my mind no romance in a missionary life that I should for this desire it. Neither do I expect a life free of care or of worldly goods or riches, that I should be induced to leave the home & friends that I love, & the country which is so dear to me for a life among the heathen. I think that nothing but . . . the love which I bear for the cause of Christ would ever induce me to make the sacrifice required.

In looking at the wants of the West I have often thought that I might be useful there, & felt willing to labor if such were the will of God; but it seems to me that calls for the West are more frequently responded to than are those for the heathen, & that my efforts are more needed there than they are West. I trust that no worldly motives have influenced me to take the course which I have; with the view of the missionary work which I have, self would, I think, in every respect lead me to remain in my own country.

I neglected to say in my first communication to you, that I have a wife & that she is with me in New Haven. Certificates from the Professor of the Seminary & from the deacons of the church . . . you will receive soon. My prayer is that we may all be guided by the spirit & providences of God in that path which will be for his glory.

Young Shipman's casual and last-minute mention of the existence of a wife may have been either an oversight or intentional. In support of the latter view is the possibility that the delicate health of his wife, Jane Stobie, might well have prevented William's being accepted by the missions. The ABCFM desired not only married missionaries but ones whose wives were, if not robust, at least in good health. Stamina was vital for missionaries' wives, who not only had to endure a sea voyage of as much as six months, but also be capable of adapting to very different cultures, probably keeping house and raising a family under somewhat primitive conditions and in a climate quite unlike that of New England.

The eager young minister was not one to rely solely on his own two letters to the ABCFM. He had other stops to pull, and did so by soliciting support from four other respectable sources. Just one day after his diligent and revealing letter to Pomeroy, the latter received a two-paragraph testimonial signed "From four Trustees of the Howe Street Church," who gave their blessing to the candidate:

We most cheerfully recommend him to the ABCFM as a suitable person to improve every opportunity for doing good. He is of kind and amiable temperament . . . he will act wisely and with discretion, he is diligent and ready to improve every opportunity for doing good. Correct in his habits and good economy, his general deportment is such as will secure the friendship and respect . . . of the people with whom he dwells. He is of strong constitution and accustomed to labor. We have heard him preach and think he will be an acceptable and useful preacher wherever he may in the providence of God be called to labor.[10]

The very next day, March 14, another letter of a somewhat different but franker tone went to Pomeroy. At the request of Shipman, a Yale faculty member, C. A. Goodrich, wrote a letter in which he described the candidate as he saw him.[11]

He is a man of *medium* natural abilities. His early education was imperfect; his studies preparatory to entering the Theological Seminary were chiefly at the Quincy Institute; and his course of theological education was broken in upon, to some extent, by his desire to attend the College lectures in order to make up for early deficiencies. Besides this, he has always been poor, and has therefore worked to a very great disadvantage.

Mr. Shipman has good sense, great patience and perseverance, a self sacrificing spirit, & uncommon devotedness to the interests of Christ's kingdom. He has a perfect willingness to labor in any place he can do the most good. He has a great deal of the Western spirit of 'going ahead'; and if connected with older men he respects and loves, he will be useful in one of our missionary stations. Like most men of such temperament, he is tenacious of his opinions when he thinks himself right . . . I have no fears of his being an unpleasant member of a missionary station; on the contrary I think he will be found to be kind and useful. I should not think him fitted for service in the East [Asia], where difficult languages are to be mastered, & where a contest is to be carried on against the subtleties of a false philosophy. I think he might be a useful laborer in Africa or Micronesia, & . . . Mr. Sturges who knew him well, wrote to invite him, in urgent terms, to the field last mentioned. . . .

That same week Pomeroy, the high potentate of the ABCFM, received a letter from a G. Whipple,[12] an officer of the American Missionary Committee, who was quite willing to give William the necessary support in only three sentences: "There is nothing in Mr. Shipman's relations to us that should prevent his appointment by you, nor do we know of anything prejudicial to his christian character. The recommendations he brought to us have been returned to him and he will doubtless lay them before you. His intercourse with us has always been pleasant, and we shall always be glad to hear of his welfare."

One month later, on April 14, 1854, William acknowledged to another ABCFM executive that he had received an appointment to Strong Island in Micronesia. After expressing his pleasure in one opening sentence, the practical minister immediately moved on to the business of the day, which was to tell the Reverend Selak B. Treat what he needed in the way of clothing, furniture, and other necessities.[13] He pointed out that, "as my purse is low [I shall] be compelled to call on you for means to purchase materials." He related that "the ladies here will assist my wife in making up the clothing; but none have offered to do anything further towards our outfit, they probably may do something more. . . ." He then got down to the brass tacks of asking Treat how far Strong Island was from the next island, the number of its inhabitants, and whether the islands in the area were close enough to have communication. From that point on, Shipman's concerns were directed toward the important business of seeing that his wife would be well enough to embark on an early June sailing.

The Boston-based ABCFM that accepted William Shipman had been founded in 1810 by a small group of New England Congregationalist ministers for the purpose of fulfilling the mission of Christ: to preach the word of God to all nations. At that time much of the doctrine of John Calvin (1509–1564) influenced the Congregational church, as it would continue to do well into the nineteenth century. Its mission to spread the word of God to the heathen nations was carried out with zeal and dedication. Before it phased itself out a half-century later, the ABCFM had sent about 2,500 men and women to such non-Christian nations as India, Siam (Thailand), Japan, Ceylon, China, Syria, Turkey, Patagonia, and the Pacific islands of the Marquesas, far-flung Micronesia, and the then Sandwich Islands.[14]

In response to a request from a Hawaiian youth, Henry Obookiah, who had been transported to New England, the First Company of ABCFM missionaries arrived in Hawai'i on the brig *Thaddeus* in 1820.[15] Hawai'i was to change (some wonder whether for the better or the worse), as this brand of Christianity brought with it Western ways to replace the long-established Polynesian culture and religion.

Fortune smiled on these first missionaries, for King Kamehameha the Great had died only the year before, and as his successor son, King Liholiho, was not the enforcer of native religious customs that his father had been, a religious vacuum existed. The Reverend Hiram Bingham and his followers were not slow in filling it with Christian precepts heavily weighted with New England customs and values. Bingham was the leader of the First Company, and for more than twenty years he would fit the stereotype of the black-frocked, rigid preacher of salvation and damnation, a recognized leader well seasoned with bias and prone to political interference.[16]

Over the next thirty-four years the ABCFM sent eleven more companies, consisting of 185 missionaries, to Hawai'i.[17] They were ordained ministers, wives, and laymen skilled in crafts that would be helpful in the transition of cultures. The instructions given them were idealistic and practical:

Your views are not to be limited to a low, narrow scale: but you are to open your hearts wide and set your marks high. You are to aim at nothing short of covering these islands with fruitful fields, and pleasant dwellings and schools and churches, and of raising up the whole people to an elevated state of Christian civilization. You are to obtain an adequate knowledge of the language of the people, to make them acquainted with letters; to give them the Bible, with skill to read it . . . to introduce and get into extended operation and influence among them, the arts and institutions and usages of civilized life and society; and you are to abstain from all interference with local and political interests of the people and to inculcate the duties of justice, moderation, forbearance, truth and universal kindness. Do all in your power to make men of every class good, wise and happy.[18]

It was not until after 1854, the year William and Jane Shipman arrived with the twelfth and last company to Hawai'i, that the ABCFM began to withdraw its support and phase in the Hawaiian Evangelical Association.[19] When the ABCFM did finally relinquish its role, it left behind many native clergy, and had established mission stations, churches, and schools on most of the Islands. It had accomplished much. For the most part, its missionaries had faithfully carried out the instructions given them by ABCFM headquarters before they had sailed from New England to settle in Hawai'i.

# 4

# *Love and Commitment*

The woman William was to choose as his helpmate was born Jane Stobie, a native of Scotland. She was seven years old when, in 1834, with her father, James, her mother, Margaret Craigie, and at least three siblings, she left their Whitefield farm home in Aberdour parish, Fifeshire, to sail for America.[1] Unlike many immigrants to the New World who debarked either at Boston, New York, Philadelphia, or Charlestown, the Stobies traveled through the Gulf of Mexico to the port of New Orleans. There they transferred to a paddle-wheeler that took them up the Mississippi to Hannibal, Missouri, on the west side of the river and Quincy, Illinois, on the other. It was on the east side that the Stobies debarked and made their home inland.

Upon his departure from Scotland, James Stobie carried a letter from the minister and clerk of the Aberdour church. It testified that James and his wife had lived in the parish for twenty-five years, "and they leave the parish free of scandal or any ground of Church censure known to us and in full communion with the Established Church." It went on to affirm that Mr. Stobie's morals and religious character were such that "in the year 1816 he was ordained to the then office of an Elder of the Parish Church here and that of the Church of Scotland, which important and sacred office he has continued to hold and exercise up to this date."[2]

As a young woman Jane received her education at Quincy's Mission Institute, as did her sisters, Catherine and Jenette. The training she received prepared her not only to teach in the local schools but also for the mission field, if the future might so ordain. Testimonials on Jane's behalf show that she possessed many qualities necessary to a missionary wife. Motivation, education, dedication, and piety were among them; but vitality and good health were not.

It was at Mission Institute that Jane and her two sisters met their future husbands. Catherine was to marry the Reverend Samuel Jones, and that couple spent their missionary life in Jamaica. Jenette married James

These two 1853 certificates bear testimony to the marriage of William Shipman and Jane Stobie. The lower one is signed by Reverend James Weller, who performed the ceremony.

Weller, who became the pastor of the nearby Waverly Congregational Church.

Although the seeds of love between Jane and William had been sown while both were at the Institute, they grew, blossomed, and flourished while William was at Yale Divinity School beginning in September 1850. The couple was betrothed just prior to his departure for the East. Her very first letter to him began, "A week has passed since we bid each other adieu,—you are hundreds of miles from me tonight and I am in my own little room. Oh that I could see you for a little while, . . . but if I were granted this privilege I would not be satisfied with a little while." Jane

The Reverend James Weller, who officiated at the wedding of William and Jane, was a brother-in-law of Jane Stobie.

expressed concern that she had not heard from him and said she had been to the post office "this evening, but was disappointed. When you left this house more than a week ago to return to your family in Barry Grandma thought you might have got drowned in one of the creeks. I felt more afraid about you getting sick after riding late so wet and damp." She told him of her lonesomeness and prayed that it would not always be thus for the next three years. "At prayer meeting I could not hear that well-known voice. On the Sabbath I was again reminded of your absence by the vacant seat. So I stayed home from services that Sabbath evening."

In an early and lengthy surviving letter (June 1851) to "My very dear Friend," she told William: "The periods when I write you are always greeted with pleasure. Then I lay aside my other duties and think only of my best and far off Friend. . . . I imagine you in your snug little room, or engaged in such domestic duties as making oyster soup, washing your dishes, perhaps making mush. Oh! pardon me, hasty pudding, as you Yankee folk call it." She confessed to having periodic blues, so if he did, she could sympathize. "Last week they gave me a good shaking, I was blue even to my finger ends."

She filled him in on local disasters such as a serious flood that washed away homes, roads, and bridges in the area, followed by a cholera epidemic that carried off people they knew in great numbers. "Four have died in Mr. Comstock's family, his wife and three children in less than a week. . . . I suppose in your civilized area you are not troubled with such audacious calamities as we are in the far West." Jane related these disasters to God's judgment, but also saw Him as "a God of mercy as well as justice, and He may avert this disease from our midst."

Her letters to William, she felt, were far inferior to his. "Yours are always written in such good spirit. I write scattered thoughts, but it will be nonsense for you to expect any bright gems from one who is by no means romantic. Yet I will always try in my poor humble way. If you can receive my letters in kindness it is because you love me. Happy would it make me if we could see each other, when we could open to each other our hearts. To this I look forward and may we ever prove a blessing to each other if we are permitted to labor together. May we be a blessing to this world." Then, this twenty-four-year-old young lady who did not consider herself romantic closed by "wishing you refreshing sleep and pleasant dreams and may guardian angels watch round the bed."

In a subsequent letter to "My Ever Dear Jane," William expressed his love and longing in unmistakable terms. Their separation pained him, as he made clear when he wrote:

> Is it possible that 2 1/2 years have passed since we last saw each other? I have been thinking of you today and almost feel like flying to your blessed abode. I never came so near to knowing what homesickness is as I do now. Not really homesickness, but I long to see you. My heart is sworn to thee, and I *cannot help* it. But if the Lord is willing we shall meet again in a few months. I hope it is consistent with the will of God. . . . Sometimes I fear lest we may be disappointed. But God has dealt mercifully with us thus far and I will not doubt his benevolence now.
>
> Oh my Jane, my heart is bound up in thee, and I have sometimes feared lest I should love thee too much . . . but I hope to be guided and have grace to have my affection properly directed. How could I help but love you—one whom I have chosen to be a companion for life, one who has ever been so kind and affectionate. . . .

I often think of you as the one who shall accompany me in my labors and loneliness among the far and distant heathen. Yes, therefore far away from friends and from home, we are to be mutual comforts. Oh how sweet will be that affection and love then to be in our hearts. We may love each other above all earthly friends, it is lawful and right. I have not written half my feelings and what is more I cannot describe them. What I have written comes from the heart and needs no apology. It will be received into a heart, where pulse beats in unison with the love from whence it came. In a heart which is love, gentleness and kindness. May God spare us to great usefulness and happiness and prosperity.

Eleven months later, in November 1852, Jane received from her sweet William a letter that spoke to the realities of what a minister might and should face.

I am happy now for I think that I am in the path of duty. I think that a minister must have a very hard time if he does his duty. I can begin to see some of the labor which devolves upon a man who is settled over a church, and I do by no means expect an easy life. I wish to be used for the glory of God, and for the advancement of his Kingdom. I sometimes tremble but then I know that I must trust only in God and go forward and he will give me strength for all that he has for me to do.

The letter continued with mention of his visiting New England relatives whom he had never met before, and of preaching "some seven sermons and had not received but $15.00." Then came another declaration of love and the assurance that "my affection has not abated. I have seen many pretty girls here, but none of them are as my own dear Jane. I hope that in a few months we shall be together again."

Before that year was out, a long letter to Jane went into considerable detail about William's activities in the previous weeks. There he made mention for the first time, at least in writing, of his interest in becoming a missionary: "I had near concluded to offer myself to the committee [but] I did not feel quite ready to decide with a certainty about it. I want to hear from our folks first and also from yourself. I believe that you really have not said that you really thought it best to go to a foreign mission. I wish you to speak your mind fully on this point."

It is here that William first makes reference to Jane's health, a concern that would persist for many years. He wrote her:

I have no hesitation in saying we better go if your health is sufficiently good. I also want to hear from Brother and Sister Weller and learn what they think of your health. If you have any fears as to your health I hope you will not be backward to name it. . . . I very much wish to go on a mission if your health will permit. But don't fear to do what is right. You spoke in your last about leaving friends and then said the Lord would be with us. That is true and we need fear no evil. The glory of God is the only true consideration to guide us. I should love to go where our friends are but if for the glory of God we go elsewhere it is alright and I am satisfied.

A postscript reminds Jane of her love of playing the piano and that the more she learns about music "the better I shall love you, for I am fond of music."

William's declarations of endearment to his beloved Jane were always answered in kind, always addressed to "My Dearest Friend." Jane's letters were lengthy and filled with news from home, but included a great many expressions of affection and shared commitment. Whereas William signed his letters to her "W. C. Shipman," the practice of the times, she unbent by simply signing herself "Jane," preceded by an affectionate adverb or two. Typical of her letters is one written from her Waverly home in early 1853, a short while before they were united in marriage.

Never did life appear more dear to me than now. I feel as if I wanted to be able to live to [illegible] be permitted to work with you in the vineyard of Christ, carrying the bread of life to some heathen shore where we shall be the means of turning some from darkness to Jesus Christ. I hope and pray that your life will be spared, that you may someday stand upon the walls of Zion, and preach the Gospel and be successful in winning souls to Christ. I feel that I can cheerfully resign this world and its pleasures to spending my life with one thus devoted and self-denying.

With that response to her fiancé's query about her willingness to serve in foreign lands, Jane not only removed any doubts he might have had but also displayed the devotion and commitment vital to such an undertaking. Records of the Waverly Congregational Church show that the couple were married there on July 31, 1853.[3] The bride was attended by her sister Jenette, and the service was performed by her brother-in-law, James Weller. William was thirty years old and his wife twenty-seven. It was with this mutual bond of devotion, understanding, and commitment that the couple returned to New Haven, where William pursued his theological studies, as well as his case for ABCFM acceptance.

Jane's health was mentioned in writing for the first time by church personnel three months before the wedding.[4] Weller wrote to a Reverend Whipple of the American Mission Association:

The Waverly (Ill.) Congregational Church as it appeared when William and Jane Shipman were married there. It is still in use and retains its original character.

Bro. Shipman wishing me to give you information respecting his wife Jane, the Mrs. Shipman-to-be, as is necessary for the Ex. Comm. to act. . . . [She] has been for several months past a member of my family and is engaged in teaching in this place. I consider her well qualified for missionary service both in mind and in heart.—She has long desired to be a missionary and has pursued her education with that in mind.—She is even & consistent in her piety—gentle and kind in her disposition. . . . Her general health is pretty good tho not infrequently she has bilious attacks. Her [illegible] permanent is bilious nerves. . . . Mr. Shipman is a very [illegible] brother and I would suggest that if you want to secure the services of Bro. Shipman the Com. had better act and decide soon as he has other applications.

A week later, on March 20, 1854, William wrote Pomeroy that he would forward his wife's certificate of church membership, adding: "She is a native of Scotland but has spent most of her days in Quincy, Illinois. She is practically familiar with all departments of housekeeping. What

Mr. Weller has said I think is correct. She unites cordially in desiring to enter the foreign missionary field." In a subsequent letter to Pomeroy, Jane is only mentioned indirectly, and her health not at all. That subject, which seems to have been downplayed, or at least not considered a problem, surfaced a couple of weeks later. Jane's qualifications, including her health, were quite specifically spelled out by one G. Cowles in a letter to Pomeroy "reflecting on Mrs. Shipman."[5] The highlights of Cowles' seven itemized statements were:

> She is well educated, acquainted with German & French etc. She has been a teacher for five or six years in schools of a higher order than primary. Is understood to have been a thorough and successful teacher. . . . Her health is uniformly good—but may have been somewhat affected by her labors in teaching—but it is thought not seriously—Probably nothing to prevent her sailing at once. . . . No special tendency to disease—She has a decided, vigorous & independent mind—but controlled reason—A kind and benevolent disposition—I might have added that she is well acquainted with domestic matters etc.—she is now keeping house on a small scale & does her own work."

In a brief note to the ABCFM (May 1, 1854) William expressed his pleasure at being accepted and stated that they might sail for Micronesia in a month or so. He then revealed that "Mrs. Shipman has not been well for a week past and yesterday we called in the physician. She had a bilious attack, which is not uncommon for her, but we hope that she will recover in a few days."

Presumably she recovered enough for the couple to prepare for an early June sailing. One might speculate whether, if in those days a thorough physical examination had been required as is often the case today, Jane would have been given a clean bill of health. It was perhaps her determined commitment to follow her husband's career and the strong mutual understanding existent between them that eclipsed any physical problems that bedeviled the dedicated young wife.

The day for sailing was set and, according to the *Boston Evening Traveler*, "Early on Sunday, June 4th wind was N.E., but after 7 A.M. there was generally a strong, or rather brisk breeze from the S.W. The weather was foggy, but after 7 A.M. clear, warm and fine."[6] A Boston diarist of the time, who kept daily accounts of the weather, described June 4 as "clear, hot and dry. (Much rain needed)."[7] Another observer summed it up in one word, "Dusty."[8] In any event, it was an ideal day for the three-masted

## Daily Evening Traveller.

BOSTON.
MONDAY, JUNE 5, 1854.

PETITIONS FOR THE REPEAL OF THE FUGITIVE SLAVE LAW.—It has been suggested to us by more than one of our substantial and conservative citizens, that all the surrounding cities and towns of our Commonwealth be requested to get up petitions for the repeal of the Fugitive Slave Law of 1850.

This suggestion, we have no doubt, will meet with a ready response from every section of the State; and we would suggest that the example be followed by all the cities and towns of New England, and of the non-slave holding States. Let the floors of Congress be covered with the petitions of the friends of human liberty, for the repeal of a law which does violence to the best feelings of our nature, which is at variance with the moral and religious convictions of the entire population of the free states; and which has been heretofore endured only from the mistaken idea that by means of it peace might be purchased between the North and South.

OFFICIAL CORRESPONDENCE.—The Washington Union of Saturday publishes the correspondence between the President and Mr. Hallett, the U. S. Attorney in this city, in reference to the slave case. The Union takes occasion, in introducing this correspondence, to give President Pierce a first rate notice, as follows: "In the person of Franklin Pierce, the country has an Executive who will not shrink in fulfilling all his obligations to the constitution, no matter where the emergency exists, whether on the northern shores of the Atlantic or on the borders of the Mississippi in the far Southwest." The Union, indeed, never loses an opportunity, not to commend, but to puff the President—forgetting that "good wine needs no bush." The Union says further: "We cannot

## CITY MATTERS.

### Meteorological.

The Thermometer in this city stood as follows, viz:—On Saturday last, when highest, (11-2 P. M.) wind S. W., at 85; at 21-2 P. M., (wind N. E.) at 74; at 6 P. M., at 59; at 10 P. M., at 53; on Sunday at sunrise, at 51; 21-2 P. M., at 82 1-2; 10 P. M., at 65; this (Monday) morning at sunrise, at 61; at 11 o'clock, at 80.

Barometer on Saturday, when lowst, (2 1-2 P. M.) at at 30.06; Sunday at sunrise, at 30.13; Monday at do., at 29.98.

The Wind on Saturday was S. W. until about 2 P. M., when it suddenly changed to N. E. Early on Sunday, it was also N. E , but after 7 A. M., there was generally a strong, or rather brisk, breeze from S. W. This morning there has been a good breeze from S. W.

The Weather on Saturday was generally clear, and until the wind became easterly, very warm, afterwards much cooler, and in the evening and night very cool. Early on Sunday, the weather was very foggy, but after 7 A. M , clear, warm and fine. This morning it has also been clear and warm.

The Thermometer on Saturday rose to 85, or above 80 for the first time this season; with the change of the wind it fell rapidly, and on Sunday at sunrise, it was 34 degrees lower than on Saturday.

### The Case of the Cochituate Bank.

In the Supreme Court this morning, present Chief Justice Shaw, the case of the Bank Commissioners versus the Cochituate Bank came up. For the Commonwealth, Attorney General Clifford; for the defence, William Whiting and A. A. Ranney, Esqs.

William Dehon, for the Receivers (A. T. Hall, E. R. Colt, and Solomon Lincoln) read a report of the proceedings, of which the following is the substance:

| | | |
|---|---|---|
| Capital, | | $250 000 00 |
| Circulation , | | 250,514 00 |
| Deposits. | | 44,067 15 |
| Deposite Certificates, | | 3,578 21 |
| Dividends, | | 3 256 00 |
| Reserve, | | 20,700 00 |
| Gain, | | 1,572 55 |
| Specie balances, | | 44,000 00 |
| | | $617,687 91 |
| Over Drafts, | | 20,508 66 |
| Loan, | | 483,253 13 |
| Suffolk Bank, | | 5,000 00 |
| Bank of Republic, | | 30.038 41 |
| Nassau Bank, | | 145 92 |

When William and his bride sailed from Boston Harbor, the weather that weekend was mild and slightly windy, according to the meteorological report found in the 1854 *Daily Evening Traveller*. (Author's collection)

*Chasca* to depart Boston harbor, headed south.[9] The young couple, with their few belongings, had boarded early for the mid-morning departure. Their vessel was defined as a ship, as compared to anything smaller, such as a brig, barque, or frigate, as were many of the sailing vessels that had carried earlier missionaries from New England into the Pacific.

The only other recorded passengers were another missionary couple, the Reverend Edward Doane and his wife, also Micronesia-bound, 18,000 miles away. Whereas the Shipmans' destination in that archipel-

## ORDINATION OF MISSIONARIES.

Haven, Ct. May 14, Mr. W. C. Shipman; sermon by Rev. Mr. Gove, of Berlin, Ct. Mr. Shipman is expected to join Mr. Snow at Strong's Island.

At Farmington, Me. May 25, Mr. George A. Perkins; sermon by Prof. Shephard of Bangor Seminary. Mr. Perkins is under appointment to the Armenians.

## MARRIAGE OF MISSIONARIES.

In South Dennis, Mass. May 18, by Rev. I. C. Thatcher, Rev. Worcestor Willey, of the mission to the Cherokees and Miss Ann S. Chase of South Dennis.

## DEPARTURE OF MISSIONARIES.

From Boston, June 5, for Micronesia, Rev. Messrs. Edward T. Doane and William C. Shipman and their wives. Mr. and Mrs. Doane are to proceed to Ascension Island, and Mr. and Mrs. Shipman are to join Mr. and Mrs. Snow at Strong's Island.

Mr. Doane is a native of Tompkinsville, Staten Island, N. Y.; was hopefully converted in Niles, Mich., where he united with the Presbyterian church, Rev. John U. Parsons, pastor, in 1839; is a graduate of Illinois College, Jacksonville, and of Union Theological Seminary, and was ordained in New York city, February 26, 1854. Mrs. Doane (Sarah Wells Wilbur) is a native of Franklinville, Long Island, N. Y. where she hopefully became a Christian in the fall of 1852, and joined the Presbyterian church in that place, the spring following.

Mr. Shipman was born in Wethersfield, Conn.; was hopefully converted in Barry, Illinois, in the autumn of 1844, where he united with the Congregational church in 1846; is a graduate of the Mission Institute, Quincy, Ill., and of the New Haven Theological Seminary; and was ordained at New Haven, May 14, 1854. Mrs. Shipman (Jane Stobie) was born in Aberdour, Fifeshire, Scotland, became hopefully a Christian, January, 1840, at Quincy, Ill., where she joined the Congregational church in the following March.

From New York, April 17, Rev. C. W. Gaillard and wife for Canton, China, of the Southern Baptist Board.

From New Orleans, April 22, Rev. J. L. Shuck, of the Southern Baptist Board. Mr. Shuck is to labor among the Chinese, of whom it is supposed there are now 40,000 in California. He has been in China, as a missionary, where he arrived in 1835, and is said to have an unusual knowledge of the language. He will find in California members of his former church.

From Liverpool, England, February 24, Mr. Teal; March 24, Mrs. Dillon, for Sierra Leone, of the Wesleyan Missionary Society.

An unidentified periodical of mid-1854 cites not only the ordination of William Shipman but also the couple's background, along with that of other missionaries who were departing for service in Micronesia and elsewhere.

ago was Strong Island, that of the Doanes was Ascension Island (now Ponapei) four hundred miles from Strong. Ordinarily the *Chasca* would have carried more passengers going to Honolulu. However, there is no mention of other passengers, and despite a wide search through maritime libraries and museums, no log of the *Chasca* can be found.

The little that is known about the voyage is told in a letter to Pomeroy written three weeks after the Shipmans' arrival in Lahaina on October 19. Unlike many earlier travelers around the Horn, Shipman was able to report:

> We had an uncommonly pleasant voyage. Experienced but little unpleasant weather and not one severe storm. My ideas of a storm have by no means been realized. For the first two months we encountered much strong head-wind, but after once clearing the Cape, the winds were all favorable. Otherwise Mrs. S. and myself suffered from sea sickness for the first month. Bro. Doane suffered much from the Rheumatism: Otherwise, with the exception of Mrs. Shipman, the health of our company was good. She was as well as her circumstances would admit of, had she even been on land. I think that the

The good ship *Chasca* took only 137 days to make the 15,000-mile trip around Cape Horn to Lahaina. Some missionary vessels that encountered stormy seas took over six months. The above vessel is the *Ocean Pearl*, which resembled the *Chasca*. (Peabody-Essex Museum)

voyage has done her good, that her general health has improved—Everything with our company was pleasant and harmonious. Our captain was as kind to us as such men generally are. In some things he could have contributed more to our comfort. The first night out of Boston one of our crew fell overboard and was lost. Our cook died three days before our arrival.

Whether this last was from his own cooking or mal de mer Shipman does not say.

The Shipmans were fortunate that the length of their trip was only 137 days. Only two other missionary voyages had ever made better time: the barque *Mary Frazier* reached Hawai'i in 116 days, and the *Samoset* in 126. At the other extreme, the *Gloucester* took 188 days, more than half a year.[10] Like most missionaries who had preceded them, the Shipmans and Doanes had to endure close quarters, unappetizing fare, and a rolling ship—especially around the Horn—for 15,000 miles before sighting a Hawai'i landfall.

Jane Shipman was in her seventh month of pregnancy when their ship anchored off Lahaina. There, two physicians told her it would be unwise to proceed to what they called "a new field," apparently meaning that Micronesian midwives and medical care might not be all that she would expect. This professional advice was followed; the Shipmans debarked on Maui, their future station much in doubt.

# 5

## *Assignment to Paradise?*

William Shipman's first impressions of Lahaina and his feelings in general were buoyant. In a letter to Pomeroy November 10, 1854, written three weeks after his arrival, he reported: "We received a most hearty welcome. I never myself witnessed such unbounded cordiality from strangers, and hardly ever from intimate friends or relatives." The newlyweds were invited to make their temporary home with the Reverend and Mrs. John Pogue, a missionary couple who had been stationed at the Lahaina mission since 1850. Shipman related that, the first Sunday after their arrival, "we attended a native meeting and in the afternoon Pogue and myself addressed the congregation, through Mr. Alexander as interpreter." Shipman told Pomeroy that the church was well filled and that it had more of the aspect of a New England church and congregation than he had anticipated. "The female converts appeared zealous and full of love. We were received cordially by them as by the mission families."

He concluded by informing Pomeroy that, unlike the weekday noise and bustle on the streets, the Sabbath was quiet. "The vigilant police force arrests those who are intoxicated and one day this week the whaling fleet numbered 78 ships." While awaiting reassignment, Shipman busied himself over the next few months by assisting the mission in whatever tasks he could handle and struggling to learn the native language. In May 1855, the Hawaiian Evangelical Association, successor to the ABCFM, held its general meeting in Honolulu.[1] As many missionary representatives as possible from each of the scattered stations among the Islands attended these annual meetings, their purpose being to assess the past year and set objectives for the future. One order of business for this May meeting was to fill the vacancy left in the vast Ka'ū district on the southern half of the island of Hawai'i. The previous pastor had been Henry Kinney, also a Yale graduate and a native of LaGrange, New York, who had arrived with his wife in Hawai'i almost a decade earlier. Ka'ū was his first and only assignment, where he labored until his death from ill health at the age of thirty-eight in September 1854, a month before the Ship-mans arrived in the Islands.[2]

Minutes of the 1855 general meeting show that the Committee on Locations recommended two assignments: the Reverend William Bald-win and his wife were to be located at the remote station of Hāna, Maui. "Also, that Mr. and Mrs. Shipman be invited to take the station at Kau, on Hawaii."[3] They accepted the invitation, as indeed was expected, inas-much as no other vacancies existed. Four months later, in a letter to the ABCFM secretary, Rev. Selak Treat, Shipman unveiled his hitherto con-cealed disappointment at being unable to proceed to his preferred sta-tion, Micronesia. He began the lengthy letter by telling Treat, "It is both a privilege and a duty for me to speak for myself that you may know my sincere views and feelings." He explained that, had he anticipated the change from Micronesia to Ka'ū, he would have sought the direction of the ABCFM before the general meeting in Honolulu. He hoped the new assignment met with ABCFM approval, "Had I thought otherwise I should have been far from taking the step which I have."

Shipman's disappointment over being unable to continue on to Strong Island was balanced by his acceptance of God's will.[4]

It is just for me to say that the change is not one of my own seeking, neither one that I have desired except as it might be according to the will of God. My heart had been set for a long time on Micronesia; it had elicited my prayers and occupied my thoughts by night and by day: and to abandon it for a field of labor on Hawaii caused me more sorrow of heart than it did to leave home, friends and native land—I have *never* prayed for a favored spot, but ever prayed that God would send me where I could be the most useful. This case has been one of trial for me, for a long time I was in darkness, perhaps never more so in my entire life.

William told Treat that he remained conscious of desiring to be guided by his Sovereign's will, and then returned to the pragmatic reasons why Micronesia was not to be. He recalled that, when he had arrived in Lahaina, "the brethren were very much surprised that two new missionar-ies [he and Doane] had been appointed to Strong Island." When he learned that the island's population did not exceed a thousand, that its circumference was only thirty miles, "and no islands were closer than 3 or 4 hundred miles, I came to the same conclusion. I thought my labors were needed more in some other place . . . and abandoned the idea. . . ." Actu-ally, the ardent young missionary had not abandoned the idea of serving in another remote Micronesian mission and informed Treat: "my mind was now turned to Ascension Island, . . . or at least some other island in its vicinity; as the brethren there had asked for but one new missionary I had at that time no thought of remaining here but supposed there could be some other spot for me at Micronesia. After a time the brethren here began to talk to me of remaining and of occupying the place vacated by the death of Bro. Kinney."

William confessed to the ABCFM secretary that he had prayed and asked his Master for divine guidance. It came, first, by way of letters from Ascension that presented a negative picture of there being a need there. More direction came through a growing awareness that Ka'ū "was held to me as a destitute and needy field and one which should not be neglected for a new one, and one which would probably be without a teacher for some time should I not go there." He admitted to remaining doubts, still feeling that duty called him to Micronesia. But, he informed Treat, the doubts diminished when at the general meeting his colleagues "passed a unanimous vote, less one," to assign him to the Ka'ū station. After examining all aspects of the issue, he was satisfied "that for the present I was needed more at Kau." Shipman became even more convinced that Micronesia was not to be his mission in life when he learned that the only way he could sail there would be by the extremely expensive means of chartering a schooner. He also reminded himself, as he wrote Treat, of the two physicians who had advised against his wife's traveling to that far outpost. Yet he added, "She has been as desirous of going to Micronesia as myself, and counted it a great trial to stop short of there."

His letter concluded by observing: "Dark as it was at first, now it seems light. I feel more and more satisfied that I am in the path of duty. I think that God has heard and answered." The three Shipmans left Maui in the first week of July for an overnight sailing that would take them to the island of Hawai'i. Whether they debarked at the port town of Hilo or the isolated landing of Ka'alu'alu at the southern end of the island is unclear from Shipman's account. If the former, they would have enjoyed a layover and the hospitality of the Reverend Titus Coan, pastor of Hilo's prominent Congregational church. They then would have been faced with an overland trip, by foot and/or horseback, of sixty-five miles to Wai'ōhinu, at least a week away. If at the remote Ka'alu'alu, then they were just over six miles from their final destination.

In any event, Coan had been at one place or the other to welcome them, judging from a Shipman letter. In that they were fortunate, for in addition to being the respected and venerable pastor of the Hilo church,

Coan was something of an elder statesman among the missionaries on the island. He would not only have welcomed the newcomers but could have oriented Shipman to the task that awaited him in Kaʻū. It was Coan who would have provided him with information about the nature of the people of Kaʻū, what had been accomplished in the station's fourteen-year history, what remained ahead, and perhaps his own expectations of Shipman's pastorate.

The political and geographical district of Kaʻū comprises all the southern part of the island of Hawaiʻi, in itself larger than all the other combined districts on the island of Hawaiʻi. The district includes Kīlauea volcano and most of the massive Mauna Loa. It is by far the largest of all districts on the island. Its physical features consist in a sharp contrast between its hundreds of acres blackened by ancient and new lava flows, and miles of fertile relief offered by lush meadows and green forests. Its temperatures range from freezing atop Mauna Loa to the nineties on the coast.

The Reverend John Paris, the first missionary to be assigned to the Kaʻū area, described it as the most inaccessible station in the Islands.[5] This remoteness may explain its sparse population compared with other districts. At the time of the 1853 census, it was estimated that about 2,210 persons lived there, all Hawaiians except for perhaps a dozen foreigners. A great many of the Hawaiians lived along the seashore where a livelihood could be made by fishing. Those who lived in the uplands grew fruit and vegetables and raised goats; both groups would trade and thus maintain a balanced diet. An indication of the decline in the Kaʻū population at the time can be seen in the number of children attending such schools as existed. In 1857 there was a total of 235 students in Kaʻū's six Protestant and two Catholic schools.[6] This represented a decline of 530 from the count a decade earlier. There are two possible reasons for such a drastic drop. The native people throughout the Kingdom had suffered greatly for several years from imported diseases, to which they had no immunity. On top of the affliction from white men's diseases, Kaʻū suffered the loss of many adults, who with their children migrated to such communities as Hilo and Kailua—communities that had a market economy rather than the subsistence economy found in Kaʻū.[7] Many left the rural areas because the king's tax collectors demanded gold or silver, thus forcing the residents to earn hard coin instead of bartering with goods.

Kaʻū's remoteness also presented the problem of distance from markets for those who raised and sold produce. The farmers who chose to remain were at a distinct disadvantage. The nearest port, if it could be

The Shipmans were fortunate in finding that their first assignment included a comfortable two-story rectory in Waiʻōhinu. It had been built by Reverend John Paris, the district's first missionary, in 1843. It was probably superior to many rectories for other mission families. The building was completely destroyed in the great earthquake of 1868. (From a pencil sketch preserved by Jane Shipman, artist unknown)

thus designated, was Kaʻaluʻalu landing, six miles south of Waiʻōhinu, the area where most produce was grown. Vessels arrived at irregular, infrequent, and unannounced times. Land travel was either on foot or horseback. Farmers who had to go to Hilo faced a sixty-five-mile trip one way, for as long as a week, over such difficult terrain as barren lava flows, desert, and tropical rain forests.

The largest village of the twelve hamlets that comprised Kaʻū was Waiʻōhinu. It had a population of perhaps five hundred when Shipman arrived there in July 1855. Small though it was, it was Kaʻū's central community because of its favorable climate, ample water, and fertile soil, all conducive to comfortable living and a supply of food, barring periodic droughts. Waiʻōhinu, its very name—shining water—says it all. This well-deserved appellation derives from the freshwater springs that once flowed into the hamlet from the green-carpeted bluffs on its western flank. Blessed as it was by nature, Waiʻōhinu was indeed the oasis of Kaʻū.

Early travelers were inspired by what they found when they came over the rise and gazed down upon Waiʻōhinu. The English missionary

William Ellis and his party of three other missionaries and native guides traveled around the entire island of Hawaiʻi in 1823 to determine the potential for establishing missions. They were probably the first white men to visit Kaʻū; Ellis was the first to write about the district. In his journal he tells of traveling south along the leeward Kona coast and then heading inland. Under the chapter titled "The Beauties of Waiohinu," Ellis wrote:

> Our path running in a northerly direction, seemed leading us towards a ridge of high mountains, but it suddenly turned to the east, and presented to our view a most enchanting valley, clothed with verdure, and ornamented with clumps of kukui and kou trees. On the southeast it was open towards the sea, and on both sides adorned with gardens, and interspersed with cottages, even to the summits of the hills.
>
> A fine stream of fresh water, the first we had seen on the island, ran along the centre of the valley, while several smaller ones issued from the rocks on the opposite side, and watered the plantations below. We drank a most grateful draught from the principal stream, and then we continued along our way to its margin, through Kiolaakaa, traveling towards the sea, til we reached Waiohinu, about ten miles from the place where we slept last night. Here we found a very comfortable house belonging to Pai, the head man, who invited us in, and kindly entertained us.
>
> [When] we took leave of them . . . our road, for a considerable distance, lay through the cultivated parts of this beautiful valley: the mountain taro, bordered by sugar-cane and bananas, was planted in fields six or eight acres in extent, on the side of the hills, and seemed to thrive luxuriantly.[8]

Forty-three years later, in 1866, Mark Twain passed through the region and left his mark by planting a monkeypod tree; its offspring still shades Waiʻōhinu's main thoroughfare. Twain had arrived at Kaʻaluʻalu on the *Emmaline*. "We went ashore," he wrote, "and landed in the midst of a black, rough lava solitude, and got horses and started to Waiohinu, six miles distant. The road was good and the surroundings fast improved. We were soon among green groves and bowers and occasional plains of grass."[9]

Another visitor and traveler of the times was Sophia Cracroft, who was much impressed by the landscape: "After two miles of riding, we reached the very pretty village of Waiohinu, shady with fine trees, amongst which were conspicuous the *kukui* . . . there were palms, bananas, papayas, besides other tropical riches almost crowding the little valley and rising up the steep hills behind the houses which were not all of

Pictures of missionaries were usually taken prior to their departure. These of William and Jane were either taken in Boston or in Hawai'i after their arrival. (HMCS)

grass. Most conspicuous were the church of stone or lava blocks and the house of the Missionary, Mr. Shipman. . . ."[10]

Probably no more graphic and accurate description of the mission house and the region around it at the time has been written than that of an anonymous author whose article was published in *The Polynesian* in 1849.[11] Signing it only "Sailor," that individual indicated he had used all three modes of transportation—canoe, foot, and horse—in his Ka'ū travels. He began by saying that some of their party arrived at the Wai'ōhinu mission at midnight, the rest at breakfast, "and received a welcome from our friends there such as leaves a refreshing remembrance in the heart's recesses. . . . The house at Waiohinu is the most convenient one on Hawaii. . . . It is of two stories and has four large convenient, well arranged rooms on each floor, with abundant cupboard and pantry rooms. A clear stream of water runs through the premises. The garden is neatly terraced and produces a greater variety of fruit than we had seen elsewhere. We counted of fruits and flowers over fifty varieties. . . ."

The compound that "Sailor" visited during his short stay consisted of the residence, the church, and a small school. All occupied ten acres of good land at the base of the curving green bluff. He described the church, with its "Sabbath congregation of about six hundred," as a very neat edifice of stone," the best piece of native masonry I ever saw. The floor is made of large square blocks of stone laid in mortar, and the inside, so far as is finished, is very handsomely plastered and whitewashed." He observed that natives were still working on it and that, when completed, they would have a house of worship equal to any on the island for comfort and taste.

After expressing his delight with the mission house and garden, the unknown author was equally eloquent in describing the surrounding countryside, which constituted the major portion of what would become Shipman's station:

> [Later] we ascended the hills back of the mission, and when we had reached an elevation of about 5,000 feet were repaid with one of the richest scenes it was our privilege to look upon. Below us lay, fashioned by the hand of nature, within a range of ten miles, six lovely terraces, on which one thousand dwellings might be placed, each of which should have such a prospect of the sea, the rocky shore, the lava and verdant upland. . . . The grass, with which most of the land was covered, grows luxuriantly and attains a height of two or three feet. . . . Several crystal springs take their rise on the summit. . . . There is . . . everything desirable to make a rich farming country, and in a circuit of some fifteen miles might be grown the best products of the tropic zones. But alas, the farmers are wanting, the land lies in all the luxuriance of nature desolate, there are no passable roads except foot paths . . . and no harbor at which vessels could lie in safety is found within many miles.

The traveler and his party spent a few days at the mission, then reported, "and loth we were to leave it even then." Laden with goods, "we left this delightful place, . . . our route ran along the side hill. The path was good, and might with a little labor be turned into a carriage road for several miles. . . . On the way to the sea we had another fine view of the natural terraces, but in an opposite direction . . . they appeared if possible even more lovely and extensive than they did when we looked down on them."

It was in such a setting of mixed blessings—natural serenity and human unrest—that the young minister and his family found themselves in their commitment to Christ.

# 6

## *Man with a Mission*

The Wai'ōhinu station had been without a minister for more than a year when William Shipman arrived for duty. Never a large congregation, the mission in 1855 was suffering from the lack of a leader in the immediate Wai'ōhinu vicinity as well as the remote outstations in Ka'ū. Because of the Reverend Kinney's sudden demise more than a year earlier, Shipman was denied the advantage of a smooth transition of authority, with what-ever pastoral advice and inside information a departing pastor might convey.

If William and Jane were apprehensive about the mission's reaction to them as foreigners and newcomers, they could soon put their worries to rest. In his first annual station report to the Hawaiian Evangelical Association (HEA), successor to the ABCFM, Shipman related:

> A year has passed since we commenced our actual missionary life, in what was but a short time since a heathen land. . . . [We] entered immediately upon a new work—everything connected with it was new to us. New country, new people, new character and language. . . . On our arrival here the good people stood with open arms to receive us. They have stood by us with warm hearts and strong hands. . . . The worthy, the devoted, those who love Christ and his cause, have not failed to manifest their love toward us and their deep interest in our welfare.[1]

The couple's introduction to a mission so far removed from any other community was eased by a sturdy stone church and a comfortable two-story frame house. The former had been built by Rev. John Paris in 1843–1844 to replace a large grass house of worship built two years ear-lier. The new edifice had been constructed with the help of members of Paris' fledgling congregation. Many months were spent carrying stones, to be set in mortar, from the surrounding countryside. When completed it measured 85 feet long, 48 feet wide, and 15 feet high.[2] (It was completely destroyed, along with almost all other standing buildings in Ka'ū, during the devastating earthquake and eruptions of 1868, the worst ever in Hawai'i's recorded history.)[3]

The house presented a contrast to the more primitive dwellings that residents of Wai'ōhinu called home, which were made of thatch or rough planking with dirt floors and had only one or two rooms. Shipman could thank Rev. Paris for having constructed a very livable rectory during his pastorate. The bucolic setting described by "Sailor" was a pleasing environment for the two young Shipmans, who would long retain warm memories of the rural regions of their youth. Wai'ōhinu may have been a remote and isolated station, but it was not without a natural beauty not always found in other missions.

Although eager to launch into his first assignment, the newcomer was aware of his language limitations. Unlike Lahaina, where English was not uncommon, Ka'ū was very Hawaiian in tongue and traditions. William Shipman faced up to the need to converse with his people. A month after his arrival, in what would be the first of many letters to Coan, his Hilo friend and mentor, he wrote: "we felt lonely for a time . . . but on the whole we are getting along very well, find a plenty of business to engage all our powers. We are making some advancement in the language but slow it seems to me. I have not preached yet but am making preparations to talk to the people next Sabbath. I feel tongue-tied and constantly long for freedom." Five months later he told Coan, "We have been able to converse more in the native tongue, to conduct the meetings and preach with a stammering tongue, to listen to their difficulties with half-opened ears and partially understanding minds." While in Lahaina awaiting assignment, the young minister had developed a feel for the language, at least enough to build upon when the couple arrived at their new home.

Shortly after his arrival in Ka'ū, Shipman informed Coan that he had written and preached his first sermon in Hawaiian; also, that he was teaching three hours a day in the church school with its handful of "scholars." This he correctly saw as a step toward learning the native tongue. When he could spare the time from several other pastoral duties, he made home visits. He knew the value of such contacts with members of his church and those whom he would encourage to join. These individual contacts had the additional benefit of helping him gain facility in the language of his people. Shipman's early struggle with the Hawaiian language may have come to the attention of his superiors in the HEA. At its 1858 general meeting he was given the assignment of preparing a paper for the following year's convocation on "The Advantages and Disadvantages of Instructing Hawaiians in the English Language."[4] The result may have been a factor in Shipman's interest in promoting an indigenous Hawaiian ministry.

While Shipman was learning the language and otherwise gaining a foothold in the community, Pele, the goddess of Hawai'i's volcanoes, was rearranging the nearby landscape. Halfway between Wai'ōhinu and Hilo there was a fearsome eruption of Hawai'i's largest and most active volcano, Mauna Loa. Its wide and slow-moving lava flow was headed in the direction of Hilo, where the residents were waiting apprehensively for Pele to be appeased. The newcomer to this sort of volcanic action wrote Coan: "It seems you are threatened with destruction by old Pele. I think the Lord will stop its progress before it reaches Hilo. I am very anxious to have a sight of the new eruption, & I think of making a visit. Where is the best place for me to go to see it? Will you go with me if I go to Hilo?"

Three months later, in December 1855, he observed to Coan: "It seems the fire is drawing near you, we are anxious to hear of the progress and learn the result. I am tempted to make you a visit soon. I have a great desire to see that tremendous fire. I think that I shall regret it if I do not. I should have gone long before this had it not been that Mrs. S. does not like to be left alone so long." He closed by proudly announcing that "Little Willie has done with creeping & now *walks* like other folks."

A month later the crater's flow toward Hilo prompted Shipman to write Coan, "If you are in trouble with the fire come and stay with us." Coan might have sensed that this would not be wise inasmuch as Shipman informed him in the same letter of a "tremendous earthquake night before last." He expressed no more interest in the eruption in further correspondence to Coan; from then on all written matters were mission-related. Involvement in the church-sponsored school would command much of Shipman's time during his entire tenure. This is reflected in each of his annual station reports, which usually included such statistics as the number of children in school and of adults who had been admitted as church members. The latter was always a disappointment, as no doubt it was to any and all of the missionaries in the Islands or elsewhere, and at any given time.

Shipman's great concern for the progress and welfare of the young people surfaced again and again in his letters to Coan and in his annual reports. He worried not only that the children were less than faithful in attending school than he had hoped, but that their interests were not in anything that the church of Christ could offer, but were material, trivial, and even wayward. In deploring their preoccupation with things too worldly and their indifference to matters spiritual, he placed the blame on the parents, expressing concern that "Our youth have no wholesome family culture & but few restraints. They acknowledge no parental authority and but little respect to parents. A great many leave for Honolulu, Lahaina or go a'whaling. Our work must be to save the present generation. The question constantly arises as to how we can bring the Hawaiian youth under our care and educate them so as to secure their future influence in favor of their nation and for the cause of Christ."[5]

Like most other missionaries, Shipman was concerned not only that the young people were poorly represented in church membership but that older members, faithful to Christ, were dying off, and thus membership rolls were barely holding their own. To worsen the problem, there was the slow but ongoing out-migration from Ka'ū resulting from famine, tax problems, and better opportunities elsewhere.[6] Yet the pastor never lost hope, and one report tells of a communion class that was well attended by young people and states that God had blessed their mission with a strong, though small, core membership.

Any suspicions in the community that the young minister was of a retiring or complacent disposition were soon dispelled. Only seven months after his arrival he wrote Coan about his rebellion against what he considered excessive and unfair taxes and fines upon his impoverished people. It was the responsibility of the governor of each island to make assessments and set rates. And it was the duty of the konohiki, the king's land agent, to collect such taxes and fines. On the island of Hawai'i it was a governess, Princess Ruth Ke'elikōlani, who sent forth the konohiki on their appointed rounds. Though the princess resided largely on O'ahu, where she had two residences and visited frequently, the honor of being governess of the island of Hawai'i was conferred upon her by King Kamehameha IV. Ruth was no lithe Hawaiian lass. Her Polynesian body was well over a formidable four hundred pounds and she had a forbidding countenance. The writer Isabella Bird wrote, "her size and appearance are unfortunate, but she is said to be kind and good."[7] The princess' appearance might have tempered William Shipman's protest had he ever met her. To Coan he wrote: "You have perhaps not heard of any pilikia [troubles] at Waiohinu since the old governess came along this way. She gave orders to the konohiki to raise the taxes on the king's land, the care of which she pretends at least has fallen into her hands, the result of which is that many of the people have left."

Shipman cited examples of the taxes and fines he considered unfair. "For instance $6.00 a year for a flock of goats large or small, $1.50 per

Princess Ruth, governor of Hawai'i Island. Shipman defied her when she raised taxes on his impoverished people. (HSA)

head of cattle. For hitching a horse on the Sabbath on land near the church, 20 cents per month or $2.40 per year. If a horse or cow crosses or runs one day upon the land, a fine of 25 cts . . . and the *konohiki* had demanded the fine for even loose horses going along the road."

Enough was enough for the missionary advocate, who shared with his congregations much of the district's economic distress. He took a firm stand: "I have advised the people to leave the land if taxes are not made lighter. . . . I tell the people not to pay it . . . some one or two had paid before I told them publicly to withstand such oppression. I have written to her but have rec'd no reply."

Shipman may not have received a reply from "the old governess," but he seems to have won abiding and deserved respect from the people of the district, church members or not. They saw in this newly arrived shepherd one not only prepared to take their part but also willing to defy royalty—even the king—if justice was at issue. His letter to Coan relating his rebellion ended with the domestic observation that "Willie is cutting his teeth these days & is quite troublesome. I was never more busy. Mrs. S. is very tired tonight or would write."

The recipient of almost all of Shipman's existing letters was Titus Coan, his friendly and fatherly adviser. None of Coan's letters to Shipman have survived, though it is certain several were sent, for which Shipman frequently expressed his gratitude. He almost always closed his letters by apologizing for their brevity, because "I have so much to attend to at the moment," and signed them, "Yours in haste, W. C. Shipman."

It is a wonder that Coan himself ever found time to leave the pulpit and take up the pen. This Hilo minister was renowned not only as a spell-binding preacher but also as an evangelist without peer.[8] His fame was not confined to the Hawaiian Islands but extended to the United States and other corners of the world. He is credited with having converted over seven thousand Hawaiians to his Hilo district churches. His many revival meetings drew hundreds, so eloquent and persuasive were his messages of hope and salvation. Coan's reputation as being the greatest Christian evangelist of the nineteenth century and many years into the twentieth still stands. At one time his Hilo church could claim a membership larger than any other Protestant denomination in the world.

As is the case with a good many individuals who have found a new faith through the medium of a stimulating soul-seeker, there was a gap between those who subscribed to it in perpetuity and those who withdrew or fell by the wayside when emotions cooled and worldly attractions resurfaced. This is not to discredit Coan, for the dedicated and accomplished evangelist was no charlatan or fly-by-night. Besides being a convincing spokesman for Christ, he was regarded as a warm, understanding individual, truly the good shepherd for a hungry and growing flock. At the time of Shipman's acquaintance with Coan, the latter was on his second and highly successful revival mission. Shipman was Coan's junior by a quarter-century, and he considered himself privileged not only to enjoy Coan's friendship but also his continued guidance and counsel.

Another advantage Shipman had that he might not have appreciated fully was that as minister for the Ka'ū Christian flock he had the field pretty much to himself. The only competition for souls came from the Catholics, and they were a definite minority. The Catholic presence was usually played down, wherever it existed, by the Protestant clergy. The Catholics, generally referred to as "Papists," had been unwelcome intruders ever since the arrival of two French priests in 1827, seven years after the coming of the First Company of the ABCFM. Twenty-eight years later, when Shipman took his station, the welcome mat was not yet out, but the climate was much less hostile. When the first "Romish priests" arrived in the Sandwich Islands, prejudice burgeoned and lasted for a full decade.

The queen regent, Ka'ahumanu, had been on the throne since 1825, ruler in name and fact for the juvenile King Kamehameha III.[9] The dowager queen had been the favorite wife of Kamehameha the Great. She was a firm and resolute ruler, and her word was law. She had become an early convert to Protestantism, and a very zealous one at that. Greatly influenced by Hiram Bingham, she imposed rigid prohibitions on anyone practicing the Catholic faith, be it in private prayer or communal worship. Banishment was the fate of the first priests. Imprisonment, forced labor on road gangs, deprivation of food for prisoners, and general harassment were the punishments meted out to the growing and threatening Catholic population.[10]

This religious oppression continued even after Ka'ahumanu's death in 1832. Her successor as regent was Princess Kīna'u, a Ka'ahumanu clone insofar as persecution of the Papists was concerned.[11] Although Bingham condoned, if not instigated, such mistreatment—worse than any ever experienced in the United States—some of his colleagues felt that he had gone too far, especially when at least five imprisoned Catholics died from mistreatment. Matters came to a head in 1839 when the French naval frigate *L'Artemise* sailed into Honolulu harbor heavily armed. Its captain, C. P. T. Laplace, ordered *finis* to religious persecution on behalf of his government.[12] After three days of negotiations, the Act of Religious Tolerance was signed by the twenty-six-year-old king.[13]

Official oppression of Catholics ceased, but bitterness between factions lingered on for decades. The Papists, and the later-arriving Mormons (Latter-Day Saints), remained castigated minorities. But resentment of the Catholics diminished over time. Annual reports of the HEA show that, outwardly and officially, the Catholics were never openly taken seriously as a threat. But what some of the individual missionaries felt is another thing. At the general meeting of the HEA in 1854, the year the Shipmans arrived in Hawai'i, the former pastor of the Ka'ū mission reported: "The Papists are still numerous, but not very active. No priest resides permanently in the field."[14] At the 1857 meeting, which Shipman attended, the Hilo pastor reported that "Papacy and Mormonism are at discount with us."[15] Two years later the report read: "Popery about as usual. Not many disciples, but tenacious of life." In the North Kona area the pastor recorded that "Romanism makes no apparent advances. Secret influences are doubtless at work." The Lahaina pastor in 1855 told the general assembly: "There is a Papist church in Lahaina. Popery excites no attention, appears to be on the wane."[16] Another missionary reported in his district that Mormonism was nearly extinct and popery could be disregarded.

The port of Honolulu as it was in 1857 when Shipman went there to attend a general meeting of the Hawaii Evangelical Association. (HSA)

In his own general meeting reports and correspondence, Shipman always used the word *Catholics*, not *Papists*. And he stated the situation as he saw it, never with any hint of hostility or religious bias. There is no mention of his ever having had any personal contact with any priest who may have been stationed at Kaʻū. Had the opportunity presented itself, the Kaʻū minister would have come at least halfway. His first mention of the opposition was in reference to one of Coan's church members, Kahulipio, who moved to Waiʻōhinu. "He says," Shipman wrote Coan, "that he has been a member of your church but was cut off for going with Catholics. He wishes now to return & unite with the church here."

Shipman's only other written references to Catholics are in his annual reports. In 1860 he wrote: "There are now but two Catholic schools in the district, one of which is of a poor order, while the other is one of the best. The Catholics were very busy some months since the distribution of their tracts among our people; but from observations it was evidently labor spent in vain." The following year he reported: "The Catholics have been more than usually active . . . but I am unable to see any spiritual success. I know of none of our people turning to them, but quite a number of them have united with us. They do not as a church stand very high in the estimation of our people. . . . I have however fears that many of our young people, unless we are faithful & get an influence over them, may eventually be led to unite themselves with the Catholics."[17]

On the other side of the coin, had Shipman been granted his wish to be assigned a station in Micronesia he would have encountered, a decade later, strong opposition and even unholy hostility from the Catholics there, who were then in the ascendancy. This was epecially the case on Ascension Island, which had been Shipman's original preference for assignment.[18]

Missionary influence was felt throughout the kingdom long after the 1839 Act of Religious Tolerance. In 1860, King Kamehameha IV signed an "Act to Regulate Names."[19] One of the mandates required that "All children born after passage of this Act shall have Christian names suitable to their sex." No one seems to have asked for the precise definition of a Christian name. As it turned out, most were Old Testament names. Whether they were always Christian seemed unimportant. Shipman alludes to some of his church members whose given names were Paul, Job, and Lazarus. The Catholics, being fellow Christians, had no trouble with the new law. However, it must have been a bitter pill to swallow for the Hawaiians, bearers of such beautiful and meaningful names. Happily, there is no evidence that the law was strictly enforced, and whereas Hawaiians may have complied by giving a child a "Christian" name, there was no prohibition against using Polynesian names as well. (In 1961 this act, long ignored, buried, and forgotten, was officially rescinded by the Hawai'i state legislature.)

Life for the expatriate Shipmans was made more tolerable by correspondence with family members and some friends. Jane was the more dutiful writer of the two when her health permitted, but neither was her husband remiss in corresponding with his friends and relatives. In one letter to a minister friend in Illinois, "My Dear Brother Love," William expressed the need to be in touch with those he had left behind. He chided his friend, reminding him that it had been four years and one month since he had heard from him: "I will not however delay so long a time in answering and I most sincerely hope you will not in answer to this." William told Brother Love not only that he was anxious to hear from him and old friends but also that he was disappointed at not hearing from New Haven friends to whom he had written; that it was a pity they could not correspond more often, as this was the only way in which they could keep alive their old acquaintance and friendship. "I can assure you that your letter was truly as 'cold water to a thirsty soul.' You can scarcely realize what it is to be in a far country, almost solitary and alone. We felt it at first, we sometimes still feel it. There is no place like our mother country with all her imperfections and no persons like old home friends. I should not have said this, for we never had dearer friends than we have among our missionary brothers and sisters."

Jane was not without links to America, though both her parents had since died. Her three sisters—Jenette Weller in Illinois, Margaret Winters (also in "the West"), and Catherine Jones, who with her missionary husband lived in Jamaica—were all reasonably faithful correspondents, but no one kept Jane and William better informed than his mother, Clarissa Shipman. From her Pike County farm where she, her husband, Reuben, and their children continued to live, Clarissa's letters told "My Dear Children" of day-to-day events that affected the lives of family members, relatives, and friends. She also captured and passed along any events occurring in the wider world around them that she felt would be interesting and diverting in their isolation.

Despite Clarissa's advanced years, her letters were written in a beautiful script and worded in such a way as to identify her as a caring and rather well-educated woman. In one of her lengthy letters she told Jane and William: "I entered upon my seventieth year a month ago so you must not expect me to be very smart. I feel as if I had got almost through with this Earth, but it matters little when we go if we are ready to go."

Clarissa was generous in relating news of any kind about family members, neighbors, and relatives known to the two distant Shipmans. Their joys and sorrows, aches and pains, births and deaths, were religiously passed on to Ka'ū: "Poor Uncle Lourey has gone after a long and distressing illness. He was very loth to die, even after the doctor told him he could not live." (Apparently, Uncle Lourey was not a practicing Christian like most Shipman kin.) Clarissa commented: "I never saw a body cling to life with such tenacity. But during the latter part of his time he seemed to be more reconciled. We have hopes he may have made his peace with God, though I look upon deathbed repentances with distrust."

She presumed (correctly) that "you would like to know what is going on in our little Church affairs." It was not very encouraging: "We have had a number of ministers since you left. Somehow they do not seem the right sort to draw a congregation. We now have preaching every other Sabbath by a Mr. Williams. He is not a very smart man, but he is a good one." Other church news told them that Henry Shipman had converted from their Congregational denomination to the Freewill Baptists: "I was very much disappointed, but if he is a child of God, a mere creature of Christ Jesus, then I rejoice."

Clarissa mourned the plight of many farmers due to the poor market for their produce and spoke of neighbors who suffered for lack of bread: "We have enough for comfort but there are those who have been without bread for their families for many weeks." These sober, respectable, and industrious people were "fitted out in rags, patches and less than fashionable shoes. A sorry picture, is it not?"

The slavery issue came perilously close to the Pike County Shipmans. Although Illinois was a free state, Missouri, its neighbor across the Mississippi, was not. Consequently, western Illinois was a refuge sought by many Missouri slaves. Clarissa wrote of the "stirring times around here lately. Half a dozen of our neighbors caught four fugitive slaves from Missouri and carried them back to their masters, for which it is said, they got twelve hundred dollars. . . . There seems reason to believe that the fugitives are enticed to flee here. They came as far as Barry, as though they were among friends. There they were set upon and returned. I think we have fallen on evil times."

In a letter describing a trip to Quincy with her husband to have their "likenesses" taken, Clarissa wrote that they were "prepared to accept Jane's offer of an exchange for those of your children. O how I should love to see those dear little children! I do look forward to your telling us more and how you are getting along with the natives."

Jane and William kept his parents informed as best they could, and as time and circumstances allowed. They shared details of their lives, success stories mingled with those of failure and discouragement. No letter from Wai'ōhinu to Barry went unanswered, though weeks might pass before Clarissa felt she had enough news, with perhaps a pinch of gossip, to interest her distant children. When the "likenesses" of her three grandchildren arrived, along with pictures of their parents, she was elated. Commenting on her son's appearance, she observed: "I think you have altered some, but perhaps it is because of your beard. You look awfully like your brother Alfred. But Jane has not altered at all, she only looks a little older, and allow me to say a good deal better."

What some might consider as mere mundane matters were conveyed with the hope they would provide a touch of home. "Your cousin Solomon is very busy making molasses from Chinese sugar cane which he raised on thirteen acres of his land. He makes about a barrel a day which fetches sixteen dollars. It is excellent if made good. So you see we are getting quite independent of the South as to our sweetening."

The Civil War, with its ugly repercussions like the slavery issue, cast its shadow over the Reuben Shipman home. Not everyone in the area shared the belief that the Southern states had no right to secede. "There are secessionists in the neighborhood," wrote Clarissa. "One of them is C. Staats, who is a rabid one. It would go hard with us if he had his way. He has expressed his views fully, said he wanted to get a shot at a few of his Abolitionist neighbors. It is said he keeps three loaded guns by his bed. But Dr. Baker gave him to understand he was being watched and should any mischief occur he would fare hard. I think it frightened him." She added that some secessionist fights had broken out in Barry and Pittsfield, and that troops from Springfield had been activated around Quincy to quell disturbances.

Beyond reporting such major events, Clarissa was conscious of the need to supply the couple, so far from their homeland, with news of the circle in which they had grown up. She realized that the comings and goings of these people, however minor, would bring Illinois closer to Ka'ū. Whether she was reporting an item of broad significance or a church meeting or the condition of the crops or a family gathering, her letters would always abruptly conclude, "With love from your affectionate mother."

# 7

# God Writes Straight . . . with Crooked Lines

*My own health was never better.*

—REV. SHIPMAN, 1857 STATION REPORT

Shipman often commented to Coan that there were never enough hours in the day to accomplish all he considered necessary. Even in a wide and thinly populated district he still had the same responsibilities as his missionary colleagues. He wrote in his station reports that his days and weeks were consumed by teaching, preaching, visiting village church members and those he thought should be, trips to his faraway outstations, erecting new buildings while repairing old ones, and always writing, be it church records or correspondence. Even the details of small financial matters and finding messengers to carry mail eroded his hours.

Shipman's planned schedule and responsibilities were often interrupted by the specter of death that hovered over Jane, as it had when she lived in America. Her lack of stamina frequently prevented her from being active in church affairs such as teaching, something she yearned to do and for which she had been trained. When she was able, she coordinated various church meetings. And though her husband was able to attend some of the HEA general meetings, always held in Honolulu,[1] Jane's poor health prevented her from enjoying such welcome changes. Even William missed three of those meetings because of his reluctance to leave his wife with three small children. He wrote Coan, "Mrs S. is quite timid," and he mentioned again her reluctance to be alone at night. The young minister regarded his pastoral duties as paramount but still drew attention to the need for his presence at home. He also pointed out to Coan: "The want of suitable help for our school is a great drawback. We have other labors to perform and cannot do as much as we would. Our strength and time are divided."

A crisis occurred in 1858, when Jane fell ill and took a sudden turn for the worse. "Mrs. S. has been laid in her sick bed," he wrote Coan. "Dr.

Wetmore from Hilo came to our relief. It was thought her last moments had come and she bid us all adieu. But God, in his mercy, spared my dear one." Yet the household was not completely free of fear, for shortly after Jane's close call her husband related: "Our little Willie has been close to death. No physician was near. Our hopes sank. No sympathizing friends were near. During the illness of Mrs. S. Willie was sick with fever which threw him into convulsions. But he who afflicted us has also relieved."

As for his own condition, Shipman more than once commented on his good health. He was able to write: "My own health is good. Not one hour of sickness since we came to the islands." In 1858, in a letter to the ABCFM secretary in Boston, he wrote that he was blessed with good health and also a new baby boy, named Oliver. Another time he wrote that he was in robust health and had never felt better. His earlier life on the Illinois farm had apparently endowed him with great stamina and a strong body. He needed both, for when he was not traveling on foot, teaching school, or seeing to the upkeep, repair, and replacement of buildings, he worked his garden, which helped provide food for his family of five. On days when Jane was incapacitated, it was William who kept house and prepared and served the meals. Whether out of need or for relaxation or both, he exercised his skills as a woodcrafter by building handsome furniture for the house and toys for his children. At least one of these pieces, a graceful sofa, is still in the home of Shipman descendants.

William's New England energy served him well, as letters to Coan testify. Aside from physical output, the personal problems of church members required frequent time and attention. Some were cases of a member being suspended for nonattendance at services, or perhaps for adultery or drunkenness. He heard them out and endeavored to bring about a return to their church commitment. But as he wrote: "I find a large field here in much need of labor. Over 1,000 members in need of care and watchfulness." His early count of active church members was just over seven hundred. There were at least three hundred more whom he desired to see "in good standing." But this good shepherd was realistic and knew that increasing the flock would require much more labor in the field. It was with obvious disappointment that he reported the numbers of church members who were excommunicated or suspended. And he gave thanks to God that he was able to record satisfactory numbers of persons who had been "Restored."

Shipman cannot be cast as a gloomy person. The stereotype of the morose parson garbed in a black frock coat with a string tie of the same color did not fit him. His own New England values may explain his disappointment that many of his parishioners failed to attend "exercises" and to better observe Christian morality. In his eagerness to accomplish his mission, he told Coan he needed several sets of hands and feet. He confessed to finding the school a burden and was relieved when it was closed.

Although his disappointments are often reflected in his reports, which invariably note that he was being tried by the Lord, William Shipman accepted the trials and always called upon the Holy Spirit to "show his presence amongst us." Like Moses in the desert, he looked for the hand of God to strengthen him and his people. At the same time, he never failed to give thanks to God for progress made.

Feeling the need for more help, as there were no more hours in the day, it was with much hope and anticipation that Shipman wrote the secretary of the ABCFM about the possibility of his Scottish-born brother-in-law, Alexander Stobie, coming from Illinois as a colaborer: "My idea has been that he might aid us much by way of teaching and might also support his family. He has been engaged much in teaching and would be just the man for us. His heart is in his work. In fact he commenced a course in study with the ministry in view, but was compelled to abandon it on account of his health. Were he here with his family I think we could commence a small school for young girls and could accomplish a missionary spirit." (Jane's brother did eventually come to Hawai'i, but years later, and not in time to be of service to Shipman.)

Certain opportunities for relieving William's mind of spiritual discouragements did present themselves. One came like a gift from God. After about three years in the field, he reported that an agricultural society was being formed.[2] No other details were given, but since Shipman had been born and raised and worked on a farm, it is quite believable that he had a hand in its organization. It was with obvious joy that he reported: "Interest in this labor is increasing. It may be said that farming has actually commenced in the past year. The first plow has been brought in and the first ground plowed. Two years ago there was not even an ox cart in Kau. Now there are 3, and all in use."

The agriculturist in this minister soon blossomed. He saw farm activity as a boon for his otherwise unemployed and often indolent church members and neighbors. He had earlier observed that "Kau is not a place of money. Its capital is in goats and goat skins." Apparently with crop production in mind, Shipman took upon himself the ambitious task of acquiring government land—land that the plow could turn, land that could be used profitably for grazing large herds of goats, and, still better, for raising crops such as wheat. Heretofore the subsistence crops in the area had been mostly taro, bananas, and sweet potatoes. But a movement was afoot in the island chain to experiment on a larger scale with crops that might yield larger returns. Cotton, coffee, sugarcane, tobacco, and wheat were planted with great expectations. Shipman saw wheat as a salvation for both landowners and tenants; it was wheat that he had learned to grow on the Illinois farm. Wheat first found its way to Ka'ū shortly after Shipman's arrival,[3] but only with the formation of the agricultural society did he see its several possibilities for his people.

Shipman also knew that to be profitable wheat must be raised, not on small garden plots like those so many of his people maintained, but on large acreages. He set out to acquire such lands, and he knew just how to get them. Land grants from the government were not uncommon—that is, for those who could afford them. The price could be as low as ten cents per acre for poor land or as much as fifty cents or even a dollar for fertile soil. In 1858 Shipman applied for and received a grant for a ninety-acre tract of land at Pu'umaka'ā, a short distance from the village. Royal Grant No. 2523 soon became his for $22.75, only 25 cents an acre.[4] This grant was registered in the name of W. C. Shipman, paid for by Shipman, and was thus Shipman's own property, not that of the mission. He paid for it out of his modest salary of about $600 a year. The government required its payment up front.

Three years later Shipman applied for and received Grant No. 2787, a much larger tract of 1,557 acres, for $350.[5] Located southwest of Wai'ōhinu in an area known as Pūlena, the land was described as poor, stony, and of little value, at least for crops—but not for goats. It was the Pu'umaka'ā tract that Shipman chose for his people to sow their wheat upon. Whatever acreage he planted, it yielded five hundred bushels in 1858.[6] A year later he wrote Coan: "The wheat crop is very fine. The culture of wheat will prove one of the great temporal blessings to the natives. They have probably raised more than 2,000 bushels this year." This was a source of great personal satisfaction to the pastor, for he saw a twofold advantage. Such productivity not only supplied sustenance for the tillers of the soil, it provided the sort of industry that Shipman saw as a vital ingredient in the lives of people with few or no goods and no means of achieving more.

Judging from later correspondence with Coan, the farmer/minister took wheat growing seriously. Shipman told Coan he would send him some of the coarse flour he had milled. He had a small mill for his own purposes, whereas large amounts were sent to Hilo for grinding. "I think

my mill is too small to grind the quantity you speak of. It answers well for
family use. I will send some by mail so that you can sample Kau wheat. It
has thus far been but an experiment but I think it is evident that wheat
can be raised to advantage." It was a project to be proud of, there was satisfaction in seeing farming become a success in Ka'ū.

In 1859 Shipman's annual report noted that "wealth increases,
farms are fenced, lands and roads are improved. About 150 acres of wheat
is growing and promises well. The good effects of industry are being felt
throughout the district. The cultivation of wheat has given new impetus.
Corn and beans have also proved productive crops."[7]

But Shipman's exuberance was to turn sour. Hope was supplanted
by despair. Suddenly, brighter visions for the future, less laborious than
tilling fields and harvesting wheat, attracted his Ka'ū farmers and followers. It was with sadness that Shipman saw them leave the work in the
fields for what they considered less drudgery and quicker cash returns.
The new attraction was *pulu*, a wool-like fiber with a golden hue, soft and
glossy, that grew luxuriously at the base of the leaves of the prolific tree
fern. Unlike wheat, a once-a-year crop, *pulu* grew month in and month
out, year in and year out. Tree ferns grew in abundance in the highlands
above Wai'ōhinu, and the *pulu* was easy picking for the Hawaiians, whom
middlemen paid by the sack. Exporters bought all that could be provided.
*Pulu* had great value as a stuffing for pillows, cushions, and mattresses. A
ready market was found not only in the rapidly growing city of Honolulu
but even more so in San Francisco and as far away as Australia.

Three years after the successful commencement of wheat growing,
Shipman lamented to the HEA that

a new trade has put an end to all agricultural pursuits; even the cultivation of
taro, the staff of life to the Hawaiians, is greatly neglected. The effect of the
greater part of our people gathering *pulu* is not good. Not that *pulu* is not a
source from which they might secure comfort to themselves and families, but
the actual result is the reverse. They are offered goods to almost any amount,
to be paid for in *pulu*, . . . a strong temptation to go into debt. Almost all are
now in debt to some extent. The policy of the traders is to get them in debt
and keep [them] so as long as possible. They are induced to purchase many
things entirely useless . . . and much which might easily be dispensed with.
When . . . almost entirely under the control of their creditors, they are compelled to live in the *pulu* regions, at the peril of losing their houses and lots
and whatever other property they may possess. Their homes are almost
deserted, grounds uncultivated. Education of children neglected, meetings
unattended and to a great extent removed from the watch and care of the

missionary. The effect is deteriorating. Against the course pursued we lift up our voice hoping that it is not altogether in vain.[8]

Only the lessening demand for *pulu* prevented a bad situation from becoming worse. The market had become saturated as more suitable materials for stuffing were found. But the damage had been done. At one point Shipman felt that revenue from gathering *pulu* could be used to cover the costs of repairing the mission's schools and churches. But with the collapse of that market he had to seek support from his members and the HEA. "Our people are in poverty," he told the HEA board, "but they do their best in contributions." At one point their annual contribution to shingle the church amounted to $675, a sizable amount considering the regional economy. "The total cost will come to $1200 or $1500. Some have already given beyond their means. Others have doubtless fallen short. But they help to provide for the necessary 20,000 shingles by going many miles into the mountains for the wood and bringing it back by mule or on their own backs."[9]

Over the six-year period of 1855–1861, church membership rose from a low of about 700 to a high of 934 in good standing. Contributions by individuals and monthly concerts brought in about nine hundred dollars a year, or an average of a dollar per member. The money was stretched to cover the pastor's salary, and some was set aside for inevitable repairs and maintenance. There was even a fund to which the people contributed for the benefit of the mission in Micronesia. Shipman's appeal to the HEA stated that "Every effort is being made to fit our churches. One new one is to be built & three others to be shingled, floored and seated. . . . Our people in their poverty do well in contributions."[10] Money was set aside for a church, however small, to be built at the now nonexistent hamlet of Keaīwa, northeast of Waiʻōhinu.

In a special appeal to the HEA Advisory Committee, Shipman, now faced with feeding and accommodating a family of five, observed that

Scarcely one of the former Missionaries now in the field is without some personal resources. Often from land, herds or other property made over to them years ago. Consequently many of them have little expense and almost no outlay of money. I, being a new beginner have to purchase vegetables and often meat for our table. Labor, also. All these, and indeed all our expenses are and will likely be for some time, *cash expenses*. I find that it costs more in proportion, to live, than it does most of the older missionaries.

This glass-plate photo (1861) shows the entire missionary family. On Jane's right is Oliver, while the minister holds young Margaret Clarissa. Willie, the oldest, is at far right.

After nearly five years of service, Shipman felt the need to "ask for a grant from the board as salary of $400 and from the people $300. During the illness of Mrs. Shipman I have been to more than the usual expense. Our Physician's bill is $205. This with our other additional expenses I have not been able to meet. I am now in debt to Messers. Castle and Cooke to this amount. I would ask that this debt be removed by grant from the Board. The expenses of my family are gradually increasing and the salary granted scarcely meets our ordinary expenses."[11]

In 1861, in a similar appeal to the HEA Committee, Shipman requested a grant of $400 for house repairs, stating it was unfortunate that "this necessity should appear at this trying time, but wind and weather wait for no man. While my children were smaller they could be crowded into close quarters, but now they are older, they require more space. Hence the need for raising the main part of the house another story. . . . Although my roof leaks badly now I may be able by Saturday to repair it."[12]

It was typical of the man that Shipman kept meticulous records of his mission. These are reflected in his annual reports, in which he was not verbose but did provide considerable detail, sometimes repetitiously, perhaps for emphasis. The concluding page of each report carries figures that enumerate with consistency such items as the number of members admitted during the year by profession of faith or by letter, and the number suspended, restored, baptized, married, and deceased. Excommunications are also noted. Double-digit suspensions usually were balanced by the number restored. The year 1860 was an exception; he reported 33 suspended and 26 excommunicated, for a total of 59. New members were only six, five members were restored, and there were twenty baptisms. He still ended with 762 in good standing.[13]

Included in Shipman's statistics are the amounts of contributions received from church members and from their monthly concerts, and that which was set aside for the "support of pastor."

As pastor, William Shipman's greatest cross to bear during all his years of service seems to have been digressions from and disinterest in church affairs on the part of his members, those he considered his responsibility. In his discouragement over the issue of church-meeting attendance, he placed more blame on the adults than the young people. He had glowing praise for those who served the Lord as best they could and was grateful for the labors performed by members to keep the mission church and school alive. In the next breath, he wrote: "We need much more of God's presence. Truly we are in a lonely situation. Our greatest trial is the want of friends . . . to assist us in time of sickness and trouble." In one letter to Coan, William described the growing prosperity of the village, which now had five retail stores, one of which brought in over $1,000 a month. He told Coan that of the half-dozen or so foreigners now in the district none were church members, but one Gowen had given him much pain because of his evil influence over the Hawaiians: "I must confess I have lost many nights' sleep just over this one man." But he felt strongly that "we are in a place of the Lord's choice. Very dry weather these days. We also have a spiritual drought. I never felt so much the need of God's spirit among a people. I think preaching cannot move. . . . It must be God's spirit." He told of his own role in settling "little quarrels and difficulties among the people. They literally roll their burdens into our hands. It is then I must again call upon the Holy Spirit to give me wisdom as well as hope. I wonder sometimes if God is listening." Then he took time out to express gratitude for the progress that had been made, measurable one day, immeasurable the next. It was with just pride that, in one of his last annual reports, Shipman was able to claim over 932 church members, an increase of 200 in his five years on the job, and this in the face of a decreasing population. Despite this achievement, at one point the missionary was chided by his superiors for spending too much time on teaching agriculture and carpentry rather than leading his people to Christianity.

Day-to-day life at Shipman's post was a plodding schedule, relieved only by rare trips to Honolulu and an occasional jaunt to Hilo; also, once to Kona on horseback with young Willie, a trip the six-year-old would remember forever. William's only other respite from teaching, preaching, building, and circuit riding were infrequent arrivals of mail from America and even more infrequent visits from travelers passing through.

Perhaps the most eminent visitor, though not then so recognized in Ka'ū, was Richard Henry Dana, Jr. The American author had made his name twenty-four years earlier with his popular novel, *Two Years Before the Mast*. Now on a journey around the world, Dana was fulfilling his wish to visit the Sandwich Islands and perhaps make contact with Hawaiians he had met a quarter-century earlier in California, for whom he had much admiration and affection. Dana, adventurer and writer, kept notes regularly, often in abbreviated fashion. In October 1859 he and his small party

Richard Henry Dana, Jr., enjoyed the hospitality of William Shipman. His tour of Hawai'i Island was made twenty-four years after the publication of his famous novel, *Two Years Before the Mast*. (HMCS)

traveled south from Kailua, through Kona. Then "Within abt. 7 miles of Waiohinu comes vegetation . . . Waiohinu is very high land, some 1500 f. above the sea, but the sea is in sight. . . . Very rich and fertile here."[14]

Like many travelers of the time, Dana carried letters to be delivered when his route took him near the addressees. Happily for the Shipmans, there was mail from America. It was then that Dana noted: "Mrs. S. so ill that refused to stay there, and am introduced to a young man named Gowen, from Maine, with a young wife. Take my meals there & sleep at Mr. Shipman's. . . . Shipman's a nice house . . . neatly furnished. Is comfort to undress & sleep betw. sheets . . . first time in 11 days."[15]

The traveler noted that, in the 150 miles between Hilo and Wai'ōhinu (he had taken the northern route), Mr. Shipman and Gowen were the only white people. Dana had overlooked, or failed to include, the missionary and doctor located at Kailua. There were surely others, too, in the Kailua district. He did say that "the physician comes all the way fr. Kealakekua 80 miles to see Mrs. S. & spends a week there."

As for the Gowens, Dana recorded that this family with whom he took his three daily meals were "nice people of middle class, intelligent, interested in politics & literature, Republicans. Been here for over a year. Take the Weekly Tribune, Independent, & Atlantic Magazine. Have family prayers in the morning & evening, & are an acquisition to the mission."[16] This description is quite in contrast to Shipman's view of the man who, he said, gave him many sleepless nights. It is easy to understand Dana's appreciation of Gowen as a subscriber to good periodicals and a person interested in literature. Shipman, it would seem, would be the more accurate judge of the man, if only because of his close acquaintance with him as a neighbor.

On Sunday, the writer's second day in Wai'ōhinu, he wrote that it had rained the night before and all that day: "First rain since we came to the Islands." That morning he attended church services and found a "tolerably full & good choir. Mrs. Shipman so ill that Mr. S. did not preach. Service is conducted by a Kanaka, & becomingly. Singing good, to familiar old N. England tunes. . . ."[17] The following day he visited the "native school of about 70 scholars. [Shipman's] head teacher is a native, educated at Lahainaluna—an intelligent man. Object is to carry on all the teachings in the native tongue. . . . [I] Attended school and made an address." His last observation of the area was that he "Saw natives treading out wheat by horses,—men and women mounted, & rather furious riding. Have eaten fresh Waiohinu figs and like them."

Dana fell in love with Hawai'i; his diary records that "I am . . .

among Kanaka, Missionaries and Whites, the dream of my youth. . . . And I like the natives, the climate, the scenery, and all." His party moved on east and north "to visit the volcano of Mauna Loa. . . . and then set sail for China."[18] But not before he had visited Hilo, then boarded a Honolulu-bound vessel.

Over the years a number of missionaries assumed the mantle of public service. Usually it was an appointment by an agency of the Kingdom to serve as its postmaster (after 1851) or as supervisor of government roads. As for remuneration, wild horses could not drag from them the salary they received, if any. Post office records of 1859 for the island of Hawai'i list Rev. Wm. C. Shipman as postmaster for the Ka'ū area.[19] He did not serve past that year, quite likely because it interfered with his many ministerial duties and those closer to home. About this same time, however, he did allow himself to be appointed supervisor of government roads in his district.[20] The road, such as it was, which Shipman helped to lay out, ran from Wai'ōhinu to Honu'apo, then past Nīnole, along the coast to Punalu'u, a distance of perhaps twenty miles. It would be an exaggeration to define it as a carriage road or a thoroughfare. Four-wheeled carts would be a more accurate description of the vehicles used in the district. At that period, travel by horseback was quite common. Horse trails led out of Wai'ōhinu going west and north to Kona. It would be some years before government roads broke ground there.

As the road supervisor, it was not Shipman's job to carry stones or wield pick, shovel, and bar; such work was generally performed by prisoners or area residents who opted to pay off their taxes by the sweat of their brow. Here, too, the pastor found himself being robbed of time essential for tending his flock. In November 1860 he felt compelled to submit his resignation. Two weeks later, on December 13, he received a letter of regret from Chief Clerk Spencer of the Kingdom's Interior Office.

> . . . I am ordered by H.R.H. Prince Kamehameha to acknowledge your communication of the 29th Ulto informing him of your intention to resign the office of Road Supr at the close of this year.
>
> H.R. Highness directs me to express regret that you resign this office as it is doubtful whether any one can be appointed who will do the work as thoroughly as you have done since your appointment.
>
> H.R.H. also directs me to state that when he receives your resignation, he will either appoint Mr. Macomber or Mr. Reed who is leaving Hilo to remain permanently in Kau, to the vacancy.[21]

The missionary Shipman was wise enough to know that keeping busy was a tonic for converting despair into something positive. This may have been his motivation in pressing for a ministerial association. Whether it was to be for the entire island of Hawai'i, or only the part known as east Hawai'i, he was impatient for it to develop. It was to the ABCFM's credit that its original instructions to the First Company encouraged a Hawaiian ministry. The Lahainaluna Seminary was a step toward that objective. Years after its foundation, Shipman wrote in 1859:

"The subject of a native ministry is one worthy of consideration. I for one am anxious to have churches provided from our large fields and native ministers settled on them. Let us try the thing. Let us make a commencement and the thing will succeed. No doubt some will fall . . . but many efficient ones will be found." He was not discouraged by one of his assistants, "a graduate of Lahainaluna who was less than effective. I am not certain but had he the responsibility of a church he would prove himself." In his 1860 report Shipman supported a plan for indigenous ministers "as perhaps a good one. However let the change be made according to circumstances rather than by any fixed rule."[22]

In 1860 he wrote Coan: "I look forward with great interest to the time of our association. Hope there may be a good attendance." A few months later he inquired: "What about our association on Hawaii? Can we not get up one some time during the year? I will do all in my power. . . . I am most fully persuaded that it would be a great blessing to the cause of Christ. And I feel it is a duty for us to commence the operation." Shipman's high level of interest in forming an association produced results. The Reverend J. D. Paris reported that it was organized in 1860 in Hilo, and "Bro. Shipman [came] from Kau with a native delegate and a number of church *luna*."

The same drive to improve mission matters, the same sort of innovation, occurred when Shipman determined that it would be more effective to close some of the less frequently attended outstations and instead urge the people to attend services at Wai'ōhinu, the main station. "My plan is not to preach at the outposts at all . . . or very seldom," he explained to Coan. "Since the roads are good and the weather usually fine, and horses plentiful there is no good reason why the majority of members cannot attend preaching [at Wai'ōhinu]." He would expect the *luna* to encourage Sabbath attendance at the main station while at the same time conducting mid-week meetings and exercises at the outstations.

Church-related activities in the district had much improved by

A skilled carpenter, Shipman not only made toys for his children but many practical pieces of furniture. The sofa still adorns the Shipman manor on Reed's Island, Hilo. Sketches by Juliette May Fraser. (HMCS)

1861, but Jane's health had not. There were times when, William wrote Coan, ". . . once again we thought we would lose her. We waited anxiously for the doctor to return." She was bedridden for weeks at a time. Her undisclosed ailment hampered the pastor's progress, but he was unselfish in the care of his wife, often to the extent of foregoing visits to outlying stations.

A succinct summary of Shipman's first five years in Ka'ū is found in his letter of November 10, 1860, to Rev. Dr. Anderson of the Boston ABCFM board. Focusing on family matters, he told the official that six-year-old Willie was now a boarding student at Lahainaluna. He noted that this elder son was "not a very rugged child and rather inclined to delicacy of constitution." His younger son, Oliver Taylor, was four years old, and his daughter, Margaret Clarissa, named for his own mother, was just over a year.

Dominating this family report was the state of Jane's health, never good to begin with.

> Mrs. S. has been very sick a few times. Shortly after the birth of our daughter she was taken with a fever which laid her low for many days. There seemed to be no hope of her recovery. Brother Armstrong was previously with us [and] he objected to sending for a Physician on the grounds that she would not live for a messenger to reach the Doctor. He felt sure there was no hope for her. He at length sent for a Physician who reached here within 48 hours and through his skill and the blessing of God she recovered but is in a very feeble state. For months so debilitated as to cause many anxious fears. Her frail weakness of body affected her mind and we feared the result.

But they made a trip to Hilo, where Jane remained for six weeks to recuperate. Shipman again reminded Anderson that forty-eight hours was the minimal time in which it was possible to secure the services of a physician and stated that he, Shipman, had been compelled to be "something of a doctor myself in treating the natives in ordinary cases."

As to his mission work, Shipman told Anderson: "it has all been directed to one end, mainly the good of the people. We are sometimes inclined to feel discouraged because we do not see the work prosper as we would like. Yet we feel our stay here is not in vain. The work is arduous with many perplexities . . . yet it is evident to my mind that we are just where the Lord would have us. My former doubts on this point have all left." He shared with Anderson his conviction in the value of personal contact with his people when he wrote: "Of late I have done much by way of visiting among from house to house, in some cases from neighborhood to neighborhood, collecting in one hour 2 or 3 families and conversing and ministering them in spiritual things. It takes a great deal of strength both physically and mentally but it is a labor that pays well. I oftentimes grow tired in spirit and hope the Lord receives my work. I have no horses and can do nothing but only as an instrument in his hands."

Shipman's New England values surfaced when he conveyed to Anderson a concern that was frequently expressed in his earlier station reports and his letters to Coan—his disappointment with parents who seemed to show little concern about controlling their children.

> Another discouraging thing, aside from the fact that Hawaiians are not a reading people, is that there is no family governor; nothing like a well regulated family. The children are allowed to run like the young of lower animals. It is difficult to be able to get much permanent and lasting influence over the young. Many of them . . . who are 10, 12 or 14 years old leave, with the consent of their parents to go to Honolulu where they are subject to evil influences and are ruined so in body and soul.

It had always been important to Shipman to maintain close ties with his people, and this could best be accomplished by arranging his time so that he could make house visits. In the immediate area he traveled on foot; in the outstation neighborhoods, on horseback. When Jane's health permitted, the family would journey twelve miles to the pleasant Punaluʻu station, where the change of scenery and fresh ocean air were welcome tonics for her and a change of pace for her husband. There, too, William took the opportunity to make house visits in the small Hawaiian coastal community.

By November 1861, Jane's condition had improved to the extent that, judging from a letter to Coan, she was not only able to be up and around but also helpful. Her husband informed Coan that the vessel "The Live Yankee has just come to anchor & I hasten to send some wool. I have put it in a box with some oranges which you may divide with our brethren Lyman and Wetmore. Mrs. S. thinks there will be wool enough. . . ."

This was to be the last correspondence between Shipman and Coan. In mid-December the pastor, parent, and husband felt that, as his wife was now able to travel, a few days' visit to the Punaluʻu station would be good for the entire family and also give him the opportunity to conduct a service in addition to making house calls. A couple of days after their arrival, William felt ill and took to his bed. Jane soon followed with a fever, suffering from the same unknown ailment that had stricken her husband. It turned out that typhoid fever had infected the family. Help was called for. There were delays; and when help finally did arrive, it was too late to save William Shipman. He died on December 21, 1861.

# 8

# *Transition*

*The Providence of God in his dealings with us has been mysterious.*
— EXTRACT FROM REV. SHIPMAN'S LAST STATION REPORT

Dead at the young age of thirty-seven was the man who only a short time ago had written, "I have not experienced an hour of sickness since we came to the Islands." His healthy condition was attested to by the wife of Hilo physician Charles Wetmore, who wrote of Shipman: "He was the picture of health, strong, robust, cheerful. We felt he bid fair to labor long."[1] But, ironically, the life of the farm-bred man who could boast of such stamina came to an abrupt halt, whereas his wife, whose frail health and death-threatening illnesses he had so faithfully chronicled, would live into the next century.

The family had looked forward to the respite of Punaluʻu, particularly because both adults felt that the change would be as good as a rest for Jane, so often housebound at Waiʻōhinu. On the second day they had all felt unwell, yet William spent part of that day doing what he felt was highly important: preaching at his small seaside mission. Their condition worsened; seven-year-old Willie became so ill that his father sent sixty miles to Hilo for Dr. Wetmore, the missionary physician, asking that he come quickly. Wetmore was unable to oblige. Not only was his wife, Lucy, very ill and under his care, but also other Hilo residents were much in need of his services.[2] The messenger returned alone.

A second letter was written to Wetmore by Shipman, now on his sickbed. He related how ill Jane had become and how sick Willie remained. Though the letter began in Shipman's handwriting, its closing lines were in another's because the patient was too ill to continue. The letter went on to say that a messenger had been sent in the opposite direction, to Kona, to plead with Dr. J. Herrick to come speedily. That, too, was a sixty-mile trip one way.

Word of the appeal for help must have reached the Kona correspondent for the *Pacific Commercial Advertiser,* published in Honolulu. For, on Thursday, December 19, that paper carried the following news bulletin from its Kona columnist, which had been dispatched from North Kona one week earlier: "By letter from Kau, received yesterday. I learn that the Rev. Shipman, wife and one child were down with a fever. Dr. Herrick (the only physician in three Districts—North and South Kona and Kau) was required immediately. The messenger left Waiohinu the 9th instant, at which time it was said Mr. Shipman was delirious."[3]

Herrick had set out at once for Punaluʻu, but lost precious time because of distance. His arrival gave both bedridden parents hope, and for five days Herrick shared that hope. But on December 19 Shipman began to decline rapidly. Jane Shipman was far too ill to be near her husband as his time ran out. "Twelve hours before his death," she wrote in a letter several weeks later, "after he bid us farewell, we were removed to another room and we saw him no more."

Dr. Wetmore later informed Jane that her husband had come out of his coma sixteen hours before expiring and remained lucid to the end. The dying man talked with a few visitors, foreigners, and Islanders who had come to his bedside, except at intervals when he was praying. The doctor related that his patient had asked him and Jane to be administrators of his modest estate and to sell off such articles as were practical to do so. Wetmore said the missionary had died happily and without pain. Jane's letter continued: "Seventy-four hours after his death I was carried to look at his remains for the last time. I could not weep, he looked so calm, so peaceful in death. It seemed as if the angel's spirit had left its happy impression upon the clay tenant it had so lately occupied."

Funeral services were held at Waiʻōhinu on Christmas Day, at that time rarely celebrated by Protestants as a religious holiday. Shipman's friend and mentor, Titus Coan, made the arduous sixty-mile trip from Hilo to attend. Later the body was interred in the Hilo Homelani Cemetery.

Word of Shipman's passing traveled around the island community via "coconut wireless" in a matter of a few days. Those of the Kingdom's residents who were readers may have learned about it a week after the funeral. In its January 2, 1862 issue, the *Pacific Commercial Advertiser* reported:

DIED: Shipman—At Kau, Hawaii Dec. 21. Rev. W. C. Shipman, aged 37 years, Pastor of the Native Church and Missionary of the American Board. . . . The sudden death of this Missionary, in the prime of life and in the midst of his usefulness, we announce with unfeigned sorrow. During his missionary life of six years, he had established a reputation for great efficiency, eminent practical common sense, and a sincere devotion to the temporal and spiritual welfare of his people. . . . Mr. Shipman left the United States in 1854, with the design of laboring in Micronesia, but on his arrival in the Sandwich Islands, in 1855, he was transferred to the church in Kau which was originally organized by the Rev. Mr. Paris, now of Kealakekua. He leaves a widow and three children to mourn him.[4]

Others also mourned him, and letters of bereavement came to the widow from many sympathizers, particularly colleagues in Hawai'i's missionary community. Jane's close friend Fidelia Coan wrote, asking, "Will you ever be thankful enough that he had his reason in his last hours?"

Many friends from the secular community also sought to soften the sorrow and loneliness of the widow. Among tributes paid her husband was a resolution from the Hawaii Island Evangelical Association, of which Shipman had been a founder. Dated October 8, 1862, and written in Hawaiian, it translates: "This gathering recalls what Jehova, the High Lord of this church, has done in taking our friend and guardian W. C. Shipman on the 21st of December 1861. Therefore, we express our grief to the wife of the deceased and his children, praying to the Lord for them. Furthermore, we hear his voice urging and calling us to strive and be ever ready for we know not when the Lord, the owner of the house, shall come to us."[5]

Among the many other expressions of sympathy received by Jane Shipman in the following weeks was a resolution from the Department of Education in Honolulu, stating, "In the death of Rev. W. C. Shipman, our School Treasurer for the Dist. of Kau, Hawaii, the Board of Education has lost a most faithful and efficient co-worker in the course of education; and the people of Kau, a warm friend and self-sacrificing laborer in the cause of religion and civilization. . . . Resolved that the Board warmly sympathizes with his widow and children on account of their loss."[6]

Dr. Wetmore's wife, Lucy, wrote to her sister: "There was scarcely a missionary at the Islands who was so beloved and respected by foreigners and natives and whose prospects for usefulness seemed so great. We can only say in regard to it, 'Be still and know that I am God!' We feel that his life has been shortened by his zealous efforts for the spiritual and temporal good of his people."[7]

Lucy Wetmore's personal opinion that Shipman may have exhausted himself by expending so much energy on behalf of his mission cannot be discounted. Because he considered himself robust and claimed he had not had a sick day since coming to the Islands, he was selfless in carrying out what he regarded as his responsibilities. His care of old buildings, construction of new ones, his passion for visiting all homes in Kaʻū, his constant care of his family, his urge to see farming succeed, and above all his deep concern for the spiritual shortcomings of his people, as well as for their total welfare, could well have lowered Shipman's immunity when illness struck. His words "There are never enough hours in the day . . ." reflect his drive and aspirations.

The fruits of William Shipman's six and a half years of labor in Kaʻū are evident not only in his annual reports and letters but also in the station reports of his successor, the Reverend Orramel Gulick. Upon his arrival nine months after Shipman's death, Gulick chronicled: "From the people we received the most hearty welcome. Such as . . . ox carts sent at once to the dock landing . . . a distance of eight miles . . . and our baggage and furniture were all safely delivered at Waiohinu in fourteen hours after we landed. Though the quantity of furniture . . . was not small, these kind people would receive no compensation for their services."[8]

Gulick also reported that, despite severe famine in the district and the departure of many residents, the average Sabbath attendance was 150; at each of the three outstations the Sabbath saw forty to sixty members—all testimony to the fact that the spirituality of the community reached out to the new pastor and that those church members Shipman had struggled so hard to gain and hold fast had indeed kept the faith. It remains unknown whether Shipman was aware of the set of instructions given the Pioneer Company of 1819 by the ABCFM. In any event, the 1861 board would have recognized, forty-two years later, that their Kaʻū missionary had, perhaps unconsciously, carried out many of those early specific wishes. As for the directive to cover "these islands with fruitful fields . . . and schools and churches," Shipman certainly left his mark in high-yield wheat fields and the upkeep of old buildings and construction of new ones for the mission. Another ABCFM instruction to become reality in Kaʻū was his successful efforts to "obtain an adequate knowledge of the language; to make them acquainted with the letters; to give them the Bible with the skill to read it." Although the ABCFM had instructed its servants of God "to abstain from all interference with local and political interests of the people," Shipman would probably be forgiven for defying Princess Ruth by advising her Kaʻū people not to pay the oppressive taxes. Such an act could be balanced by the instruction that urged missionaries to do "all in your power to make men of every class good, wise and happy."

Shipman deserves much credit for having worked for the implementation of a ministerial association for the island of Hawai'i. This is alluded to not only in his earlier reports but also by Rev. John Paris, who wrote: "In 1860 we organized the first evangelical association in Hawaii . . . at Hilo. I held some meetings and spent a Sabbath with Brother Shipman at Waiohinu,—my first missionary station. A pleasant visit. We had a large gathering at Hilo from every district on the island. Bro. Bond came from Kohala, Bro. Shipman from Kau, with a native delegate and a number of church *lunas*."⁹ There is reasonable doubt that the association would ever have gotten off the ground had not "Bro. Shipman" pressed for its inception.

Nowhere in the ABCFM 1819 instructions was it spelled out that the development of an indigenous clergy should be an objective, though history shows this did occur. It may, however, have been implied in the instruction "of raising up the whole people to an elevated state of Christian civilization." Shipman was not the first to recognize that the long-term success of the missions would depend upon the use of Hawaiian clergy. It was at Lahainaluna that training was provided for potential ministerial candidates. Dana recorded that Shipman had just such a Hawaiian head teacher and preacher whose ability impressed him.

Only after his death did it become generally known that Shipman had just finished building a school for girls. This had come about as a result of a statement issued by the HEA and the missionary-dominated Board of Education for the Kingdom. A report from that committee stated: "The Educating and training of Hawaiian females is considered by this body as one of the most important branches of Education at these islands. . . . We recommend that each of the brethren do all in his power to carry forward the work, by establishing small schools for girls in his field. . . ."¹⁰

A few months before his death, this visionary man of God had consolidated plans for the construction and implementation of what would become the Kau Female Seminary. The school was scheduled to open in January and would have been directed by Jane, whose years at Mission Institute had prepared her for such an undertaking. When its doors did open some months later, it was under the direction of Rev. Gulick, Shipman's successor. Twelve girls from various parts of the island comprised the student body. The dream of William and Jane Shipman had become a reality. The school survived until 1865, when the Reverend and Mrs. Gulick were transferred to Waialua, O'ahu, and the Female Seminary went with them.

The conscientious pastor who had been struck down in midstride and so frequently felt despair over the human frailities he found among his people had actually made great progress. Had he been able to look back over his six and a half years of service analytically, he could have measured the gain. Prone as he was to pressing forward, he had deprived himself of a retrospective view of a pilgrim's progress, though progress perhaps at the expense of his own health.

Meanwhile, the young widow was left with three small children, no income, sparse savings, and a mission rectory that must soon be vacated to make way for a new missionary family. One bright spot in Jane's dark days and nights was an invitation from Fidelia Coan, who wrote on behalf of her husband as well as herself: "I am expecting you to come directly to our house, and stay till some arrangements for you can be made. We all want you to look upon our quiet town before anything is fixed upon. The sense of *utter desolation* which you now feel will pass away, my dear sister. I shall rejoice to do all I can for your comfort. May God bring you safely to us."

Fidelia Coan's wish was fulfilled, but first Jane replied:

Your precious and sympathizing letters were received yesterday. Many, many thanks for your kind words in our bereavement. No one knoweth the depth of our sadness and loneliness. While Mr. S. was alive I felt it a great trial to be left alone even one night with the little ones. Now we are entirely alone, only as Kauhane comes and sleeps here. I feel that the Lord has given me strength, if he had not I should have died with grief. He has wonderfully supported us in all our sickness and distress. . . . Oh how I miss my dear husband and head to look after things.

After describing the serious illness of daughter Clara and the fact that "the boys are very trying," Jane told the Coans that she accepted their "kind invitation to go to your house on our arrival in Hilo. I know not what we shall do. May the Lord direct."

Although the bereaved family arrived safely, as Fidelia had hoped, they did not go easily. In a letter to ABCFM secretary Rufus Anderson after her arrival, Jane related some of her experiences: "During our sickness and trials I did not see a white woman. There were none in the district. After I recovered a little my other two children were taken ill with the same fever. We had to hasten to Hilo to save the life of one of them." The price of that trip was almost more than the sick young woman could bear. But, urged by Dr. Herrick to make the move, she did so, and with little delay, for the sake of her own health and her childrens'.

One cannot describe what I suffered in mind and body on our overland journey with the sick little ones, and I was so feeble I had to be carried on a *manele* [sedan chair, litter] by natives . . . but in the end the journey proved a blessing to my sick child and broke his fever. But it proved to be too much for my strength and on our arrival in Hilo I was taken very sick, for a while my life was despaired of. But the Lord has brought me through it all. We are now enjoying good health with the exception of a feeling of weariness caused by hard work and care."[11]

The young mother was thirty-four years old when she was compelled to make that trying journey. At that time of year her party suffered under the heavy seasonal rains that often fall upon the Volcano area. In what was probably a week-long trip, the only shelter of any substance would have been the somewhat primitive Volcano rest house. It had been erected a few years earlier, possibly in 1846 when a map of that year showed "three houses" located at Kīlauea Crater.[12] Other references call it "an old shed." Perhaps a half-dozen rudimentary shelters, even more primitive, have been been reported as having been scattered along the forest trail. These were little more than lean-tos, but offered shelter from the elements and a place to recline, if only on rush mats. Not even a carriage road, the horse path was hardly a route travelers relished under normal conditions, much less those suffered by Jane and her children. Seventy-three years later, in 1938, Oliver Shipman recalled the trying experience. Even though he was only a three-year-old at the time, he remembered the trail being so narrow as barely to accommodate two people. Like his mother and two siblings, he was carried on a *manele*, sometimes so close to bushes that they would be soaked from the wet leaves.

Dr. Herrick's suggestion that the four Shipmans travel to Hilo when they did was considered quite out of order, and indeed premature, by Marie Pogue, wife of the Reverend John Pogue of Lahainaluna, who had hosted the Shipmans upon their arrival from Boston seven years earlier. In a letter to Jane, Mrs. Pogue remonstrated: "Oh what a journey for a sick woman and 3 children alone, with the natives. . . . It does seem to me, so far away, too bad Mr. H. should ever have allowed you to attempt it. . . . Of course I cannot understand all the circumstances, but it seems, to say the least, very inconsiderate on his part."[13]

Mrs. Pogue's blaming of Dr. Herrick may have been justified. Dana, while a lodger at the Shipman residence, noted that "The physician comes from Kealakekua 80 miles to see Mrs. S. & spends a week there . . . Dr. Herrick, a very homely old man, a *granny*, is a nurse & all, and gives emetic &c., in the true old style, to a poor feeble mother."[14]

Hilo's Front Street (now Kamehameha Avenue) shortly after Jane Shipman moved from Waiʻōhinu following her husband's early demise. (HSA)

("Homely" in Dana's time meant rather plain, unpretentious.) Otherwise Dana's comment, especially his description of the doctor as a "granny," suggests that Mrs. Shipman's health care, and even Herrick's diagnosis, may have been inadequate.

Seven months after William's death Jane considered returning to her Illinois homeland. In July 1862 she wrote Rev. Anderson, "I feel if possible we must return and be near my relatives. I am an orphan myself but I have many friends. If we should return could we receive any assistance from the Board, a certain amount each year?. . . . I wait to receive your instructions from the Board. Please write to me on the reception of this and give me such advice as you deem proper."[15]

Jane had to wait four months for the advice she had asked for "upon reception of this." Rev. Anderson informed the widow that "The Committee consents to your returning to this country and appropriates for the cost of passage of yourself and children in a sailing vessel around the Cape" the sum of $400. Somewhat ambiguously, Anderson stated that this sum, "allocated to you for the year 1863, so far as not needed at the Islands, and for your necessary outfit for the voyage, will go to the expense of your return. You may be assured of a fraternal reception."

Jane's wish to return to the United States may have been inspired

by an invitation from her mother-in-law, Clarissa Shipman. Shortly
before writing to Anderson, Jane had received a letter from Clarissa, who
still lived with Reuben on the farm in Barry, Illinois. It was a warm letter
of several pages, addressed to "Dear Daughter" and signed, as usual, "Your
affectionate mother." Clarissa Shipman expressed her own grief at the
loss of her oldest son, while consoling Jane in hers. Throughout her letter
ran a confidence in God's promises. She acknowledged that "we had
never expected to see him again in this world, yet it was a great consola-
tion to know that he was where he was needed and doing so much good.
We know that God does all things right and cannot err." She continued
with two pages of news about neighbors and relatives that she knew
would offer Jane a welcome distraction. She quite correctly surmised that
"the prospect before you looks harsh and gloomy—but trust in the Lord
and you will be sustained. You have told us nothing of your pecuniary
affairs. We would very much like to know what your prospects and calcu-
lations are. Will you write and tell us whether you intend to come back or
not. We do not know how to advise you because we do not know your
plans and prospects. Should you come you would find loving hearts to
welcome you and receive assistance should it be necessary."

The letter ended with a message to the "little children," admonish-
ing them to try to please their mother and that "Grandma, who thinks
she can tell a little by seeing your pictures, would like to see you all." It
was not the first, and it was far from the last, of letters to Jane from a loving mother by marriage.

But the intervening four months gave Jane time to have second
thoughts about returning to the mainland. The fact that the Civil War
was now raging may have been a deterrent. That sad situation had been
described to her by Clarissa, who exclaimed, "Oh how this unnatural war
is breaking up so many families and causing so much blood to flow. We
are feeling its effects here. Though I have no sons in the army I can feel
for those who do. . . . We shall be looking anxiously for your reply."

A few weeks after her husband's death, Jane's health had rallied to
the point where, thanks to shelter, love, and care from the Coans, she felt
able to strike out on her own. In 1862 she rented a house in back of Haili
Church. Encouraged by Coan, she supported herself by boarding and
teaching two Caucasian girls. What money she had at the time, aside
from what came from her two young boarders, was a meager $84.55 due
her husband for the balance of salary at the time he died. Jane proved a
good manager, for this sum, plus her boarders' payments, supported her
and her family temporarily. Her husband's modest estate had yet to be set-

# PROCLAMATION.

## KAMEHAMEHA IV., King of the Hawaiian Islands.

BE IT KNOWN, to all whom it may concern, that we, KAMEHAMEHA IV., King of the Hawaiian Islands, having been officially notified that hostilities are now unhappily pending between the Government of the United States, and certain States thereof styling themselves "The Confederate States of America," hereby proclaim our neutrality between said contending parties.

That Our neutrality is to be respected to the full extent of Our jurisdiction, and that all captures, and seizures made within the same are unlawful, and in violation of Our rights as a Sovereign.

And be it further known, that We hereby strictly prohibit all Our subjects, and all who reside or may be within Our jurisdiction, from engaging either directly or indirectly in privateering against the Shipping or Commerce of either of the contending parties, or of rendering any aid to such enterprises whatever; and all persons so offending will be liable to the penalties imposed by the laws of nations, as well as by the laws of said States, and they will in no wise obtain any protection from Us as against any penal consequences which they may incur.

Be it further known, that no adjudication of prizes will be entertained within Our jurisdiction, nor will the sale of goods or other property belonging to prizes be allowed.

Be it further known, that the rights of asylum are not extended to the Privateers or their prizes of either of the contending parties, excepting only in cases of distress or of compulsory delay by stress of weather or dangers of the sea, or in such cases as may be regulated by Treaty stipulation.

> Given at Our Marine Residence of Kailua, this 26th day of August, A. D. 1861, and the Seventh of Our Reign.
>
> KAMEHAMEHA.

By the King.

KAAHUMANU.

> By the King and Kuhina Nui.
> R. C. WYLLIE.

The fact that the Civil War was raging was a deterrent to the widow Jane's returning to America. On August 6, 1861, King Kamehameha IV issued a Proclamation of Neutrality. It was signed not only by the king but also by his Kuhina Nui (prime minister), Robert Wyllie. (HSA)

Haili Christian Church as it appeared in 1868. It was preceded by four other structures, each one outgrowing its predecessor. The 1824 building, Hilo's first church, was a grass building. The present edifice, dedicated in 1859, is still used and has been carefully preserved, its spacious lawn graced with verdant trees. "Mother" Shipman's home and school for "foreigners" can be seen behind the church. (Lyman House Memorial Museum)

tled. Like the slow-grinding wheels of justice, the probate courts could not be hurried. The widow may also have been influenced by the fact that her children considered Hawai'i their home and, like herself, spoke and understood the Hawaiian language. Further, she had a warm relationship not only with the Coans but with other missionary families on the island, and with some parents of her young boarders. The school had expanded to eight children, and she was finally in a vocation for which she had trained. Moreover, she had developed a self-confidence she had never before possessed and felt encouraged to count her present blessings. It is a matter of record that the HEA, at its June 1862 general meeting, noted: "Mrs. S. is now keeping house at Hilo. We have asked $400 for her family support."[16]

Jane Shipman had made a decision. She would make Hilo home for herself and her family.

# 9

# *Hilo, Crescent Moon*

*Hilo: Streets straight, houses neat,*
*fences neat, gardens all shaded so thick that just see the houses.*
*Prettiest town I have seen yet. Tho' small.*

—RICHARD HENRY DANA, JR.

The town that so charmed Dana in 1859, three years before Jane Shipman took up residence there, was indeed small. Honolulu, with its 14,300 people, surpassed Hilo by 10,000. Lahaina, then the second-largest community in the Kingdom, edged out Hilo by a couple of hundred but soon fell into third place.[1]

Long, long before Dana recorded his impressions, the name Hilo had appeared in ancient Hawaiian chants and stories. Centuries-old Polynesian legends told of a famed navigator named Hilo. He may have been a forebear of the Polynesian mariners who discovered and inhabited Hawai'i early in the thirteenth century.[2] In Hawai'i the name Hiro/Hilo is associated with Hilo Bay, perhaps in commemoration of this Polynesian ancestor. *Hilo* is also Hawaiian for the first night of the new moon, or crescent, a descriptive appellation for the prominent indentation that forms the bay upon which the growth and fortunes of the community rise and fall.

When Captain Cook arrived off the east coast of Hawai'i in late 1778, a month or two before his fatal encounter, he recorded the name as "Aheedo," as he understood it from the pronunciation of Hawaiians who came aboard. (Cook never landed in the area, judging the winter waters too rough.) Cook's chronicler, Lieutenant James King, provided the first written report on the vicinity. He noted that "Aheedo . . . has its beech [sic] of a moderate height, and rises very gradually . . . and extends far into the Island."[3]

It would be fifteen years, in January of 1794, before any other significant record would be chronicled, by Captain George Vancouver. Despite

This was the grand view from Hilo Bay to the summit of Mauna Kea around 1880. It was sketched by the famous artist Charles Furneaux, the United States consul and a Hilo resident. The original is in the Lyman Memorial Museum in Hilo.

his short stay of only three days in the bay, his journal quite amply describes bartering with the "very amicable" Hawaiians, who paddled out to the ship in canoes. More important and interesting is his account of visits from the thirty-six-year-old King Kamehameha the Great. Theirs was a friendly relationship. The monarch was, by conquest, now king of the entire island of Hawai'i and in fact master of all he surveyed. He had made Hilo his base off and on for about six years as he prepared war canoes for invasions of the northern islands. He had several shipboard discussions with Vancouver and was considered a willing and astute listener.[4]

Kamehameha I is also firmly and forever identified with Hilo by virtue of the legend linking him to the ponderous Naha stone then located at Pinao temple in what is now central Hilo. The story goes that any stalwart who could lift the rectangular stone would not only be royal but would also possess the power to conquer all the islands.[5] The legend was fulfilled when Kamehameha became ruler of all the islands in the chain.

Before Vancouver sailed on, he recorded the bay as "Whyatea," from a nearby substantial fishing village of the same name a mile or two south of the Hilo community. When the English missionary William Ellis arrived in 1823, he too referred to the bay as Waiatea. But he also knew of the neighboring village by the bay, which he wrote as "Hiro" in his journal.[6] Other visitors gave it the earlier pronunciation of "Hido." Ultimately, the mellifluous Polynesian *l* sound prevailed over the *r*, which the Hawaiians found difficult to manage. To them the crescent-shaped body of water was Hilo. Like Hilo village, the equally small settlements of Puʻuʻeo and Waiākea on either side of it owe their origins and their growth, even their elongated shape, to the wide, sweeping bay. Its three miles of shoreline, ornamented with sandy beaches and coconut groves, had no equal for hundreds of coastal miles. The general area took shape as a gathering place not only because of the ready supply of seafood and fresh river water but also the fertile slopes that swept seaward from the two massive volcanoes. White-capped Mauna Kea and long, lofty Mauna Loa, though many miles inland, dominated the lush landscape. Many early travelers, impressed by the setting, correctly assumed that these were by far the highest mountains in the Pacific.

William Ellis chronicled the region as

> the most fertile and interesting division on the Island. . . . Rain is frequent and is doubtless the source of the abundant fertility and herbage. . . . The climate is warm, always in the seventies. The inhabitants have better houses [than in Kona], plenty of vegetables, some dogs and a few hogs. Three streams of water empty themselves into the bay. . . . The face of the country is the most beautiful that we have yet seen, . . . probably occasioned by the humidity, the frequent rains and the long repose which the district has experienced from volcanic eruptions.[7]

The writer continued with a lavish description of fish ponds, luxuriant plantations of bananas, sugarcane, and melons, and concluded that, along with other fruits found in coconut groves and on breadfruit trees, there was ample sustenance.

Two years after the Ellis party, the bay was visited by HMS *Blonde*, commanded by Lord George Anson Byron, a cousin of the poet Lord George Gordon Byron. The Scottish naturalist James Macrae, who accompanied Lord Byron on his historic expedition, wrote: "The scenery around this bay is both beautiful and romantic; gently sloping lawns, interspersed with orchards of breadfruit and palms, belonging to the native huts, extend upwards for the space of about four miles, when thick woods succeed and clothe the mountain sides, til they are lost in the clouds, through which the head of Mouna Roah, and the peaks of Mouna

Keah every now and then arise."[8] The *Blonde's* chaplain, Rev. E. Bloxham, wrote to his uncle: "We entered this delightful bay, which will hereafter be known as Byron's Bay. . . . Nothing could exceed the beauty of
the panorama from the ship. On every side nature was covered with the
most lovely verdues. . . . Indeed so different was it in every respect . . .
that it is considered by our officers to be the Eden of these isles."[9] Macrae
went on to describe the bay and its neighborhood as very pleasant on
account of its woody appearance and plentiful supply of water. He
declared it far superior in scenery to anything seen "either at Mowee or
Woahoo." He observed that "at one end of the bay was a fair sized river
with several waterfalls, . . . convenient for watering ships. . . . Up a little
distance is a fresh water pond, tabooed for the use of the king and the
chiefs."

The bay was rechristened, this time by the *Blonde's* cartographer,
Lieutenant Charles Malden. The first to chart the bay, he labeled his map
"WAIAKEA or BYRON BAY." The latter designation received royal support
from Queen Kaʻahumanu. She held Byron in high regard as a friend and
navigator. Moreover, she was grateful to him for having returned for
burial the bodies of King Liholiho and his queen, Kamāmalu, who while
visiting London had died of measles within a week of one another. After
the funeral services, when the *Blonde* returned from Honolulu to Hilo,
the queen traveled on the vessel as Byron's guest. Her appreciation of this
was noted by Malden: "The name [Byron] was readily received by the
natives, and the powerful queen Kaahumanu issued positive directions
for it to be called by no other appellation."[10]

Aside from his pride in having the bay named after his captain,
Macrae predicted that because of the bay's natural advantages, "Byron
Bay will no doubt become the site of the capital of Hawaii." He was
wrong on both counts, for despite royal decree and cartographers imprint
none of these names took and the Hawaiian name of Hilo gradually
regained its popular usage, while Honolulu remained the distant capital.

Prior to Malden's charting of the bay many vessels avoided it, fearful
of what might be heavy seas. Malden showed it to be a basin, protected
by a wide, submerged finger of lava at one end. (It is still called Blonde
Reef, and the giant breakwater is built upon it.) Once its safety was reasonably determined, voyagers found the bay a convenient haven in
which to replenish their food and fresh water.

It was in the natural course of events that visiting ships made the
bay community attractive to other Hawaiians from less prosperous villages. Not only did these indigenous migrants contribute to Hilo's

growth, but ship-jumpers and drifters could be counted upon to call it their new home. One mid–twentieth-century historian, Milton George, suggests that escaped convicts from Botany Bay may have preceded Ellis. "So far as the record shows, . . . it must be remembered that there may have been sailors and escaped Botany Bay convicts in the islands who have left no accounts. . . ." George also refers to William Stephenson, "a Botany Bay convict escaped from New South Wales," as one who, with the king's counselor, John Young, may have introduced the method of distilling *ti* roots. In describing the pre-Ellis period, George comments, "But the dry rot of civilization had already set in."[11]

In any event, Ellis, in 1823, was convinced that the setting and time were ripe and right for the establishment of a mission station. From that time forth, in 1824, the community changed—however slowly—in character and population. By 1840, with its pathways, shops, trading posts, and a semblance of a harbor landing, Hilo became attractive to visiting sailors. Their presence brought a little prosperity and quite a bit of trouble. In that year a bunch of rowdy shipmen successfully defied lawful authorities to roister in and rule the town for three months. Only the intervention of a visiting American vessel calmed the community and subdued the would-be conquerors.[12] However, in general, Hilo, though becoming a busier commercial center, never came close to acquiring the rowdy-town reputation earned by Lahaina and Honolulu. More than one whaling captain favored the crescent-bay town because during that long period it had the rare distinction of being free of grog shops. In fact, because of its early missionary establishment, it was often referred to as a "church town."

By the time Jane Shipman made Hilo her home in 1862, meandering footpaths had become straight, though unpaved, streets. Boardwalks were commonplace necessities to cope with the frequent Hilo rains. Grass houses, whose average life span was four years, were being replaced with board buildings, some of which were handsome residences. Wooden stores became permanent fixtures. Merchants, carpenters, mechanics, and chandlers comprised much of the foreign—namely, white—population, often to meet the needs of whalers and a growing interest in sugar production. Four churches had now been established. One of the prominent thoroughfares was named Church Street. It is now Haili, named after the church. A public school of some size had been established, and the Haili Christian Church started its own boarding school, which would serve the community well into the twentieth century.

It was in November 1862 that Clarissa Shipman wrote Jane to com-

fort her in her loneliness and to send her news from Illinois, none of
which was bright. "I do not wonder you are lonely. It is doubly so when
one's companion is taken away and being without friends or relatives.
You must look to Him who has promised to be the widow's God and the
Father of the fatherless. His word is sure and will not fail if we do but trust
Him." She then went on to relate grim happenings in neighboring Minnesota, where Indian attacks had massacred five or six hundred settlers:
"Some say a thousand. House burnt, grain left in the field, cattle taken.
Lucretia [daughter] writes the excitement was fearful. One night over one
hundred sought safety in their house. Word came that Indians were at
New Ulm. She said Mr. Conrad [Lucretia's husband] had been sleeping
not only with his gun at his bed but also a pitchfork. May God in His
mercy save our beloved country."

Clarissa's letter detailed much of the suffering experienced by farmers sadly in need of help because so many male laborers had gone to war.
She said no gold or silver was in circulation but that merchants were issu-
ing small bills to pass among themselves. Prices of groceries she cited as
"outrageous and calicoes are from eighteen to twenty-five cents each. I
fear prices will be higher if the war does not come to an end soon."

This letter to her daughter-in-law was written before Clarissa
learned that Jane was seriously considering remaining in Hilo. She let her
know the welcome mat was still out. "I do not know what to say about
your coming home. But I should be very glad to see you. You will have to
exercise your own judgment. We feel very anxious about you. Solomon
saw your brother Alex in Quincy the other day. Alex felt that your children aught [sic] not to be there in Hawaii. And I think so myself. It must
be a poor place to bring up children. Should you come here you will be
provided for."

The year 1862 was one for Hilo to remember in a number of ways,
for it was then that Prince Lot Kamehameha paid a visit to the burgeon-
ing coastal village.[13] A year later, upon the death of his younger brother,
Alexander, then on the throne, Lot became King Kamehameha V. His
reign of a decade saw the continuing growth of what would soon become
Hawai'i's major industry, sugar. Hilo would grow and prosper proportionately, largely because of its bay being superior to any other harbor on
Hawai'i island for shipping raw sugar.

Perhaps most significant in 1862 was the planning for the construction of a landing wharf at the foot of Waiānuenue Street. The next year it
became a reality and a boon to commerce, located as it was near the central part of the community.[14] The sugar industry was getting a start in the

Islands, and Hilo had at least three mills, primitive though they were, which were forerunners of the plantations and related services that would put the city on the map.

The timing of Hilo's growth, however slow, and Jane's arrival was fortuitous for the widow with three children to support. The number of foreigners was increasing. Her school provided a service for those with children and a living for herself. From two students it had grown to eight, two of whom were six-year-old Ollie and eight-year-old Willie. The arrival of newcomers to the community increased not only the population but also the success and popularity of the school. A later Hilo historian, J. M. Lydgate, observed of Jane's school: "The original primitive foreign school had perhaps half of the children white, the rest being half white and Hawaiian. There may have been as many as thirty-five, a number of whom were boarders." Lydgate observed that the school became very popular and successful.[15]

One of the very young boarders was a part-Hawaiian girl named Mary Elizabeth Johnson, from Waimea. Many years later she would become Mrs. William H. Shipman. Still later, she would be fondly known as "Mother Shipman" and tell her own children that among those who had attended their grandmother's school were now Mrs. Wilfong, Mrs. Mobie, Mrs. Jules Richardson, Mrs. Paris, Mrs. Robinson and the Coney girls (daughters of Sheriff Coney), all of whom became well-established Hilo matrons.[16]

Jane's opening a boarding school was a practical move in light of the fact that, though her husband had left some property of modest value, he had died intestate, and it would be a long time before the so-called estate was settled. Even her having been named by her husband, with Dr. Wetmore, as one of the administrators could not hasten the final disposition.

In December 1862, one year after William Shipman's death, the circuit court judge, S. L. Austin, authorized "any and all [Shipman] real estate to be sold at Public Auction, or at private sale, as may be in the best interest of the heirs." The two administrators then petitioned that the real estate be sold at private sale, "good offers having been made for most of the real estate by private individuals." The petition was granted. Subsequently the 1,557 acres at Pūlena, for which Shipman, only a few months before he died, had paid $374.50, sold for about $500. The 94 acres at Pumaka'a on which Shipman grew wheat, purchased for $22.75 four years earlier, fetched $350. A four-acre parcel sold for $50; but a lot he owned at Punalu'u, estimated value $300, was unsold at the time of the final inventory.[17]

The record of all real estate and personal and household goods, plus monies owed the deceased, ran to three handwritten pages. The "goods and chattels" were sold at public auction as well as by private sales. Included were such items as family furniture, an ox-cart, a wagon, one beehive, a variety of tools, a safe, a melodeon, a desk, a library of unspecified size, and a wide assortment of other household goods. Livestock consisted of 1,500 goats "more or less," two mules, 150 sheep, three cows and one calf, and a carriage horse.[18] (There was no listing of the indispensable carriage.) Of note was the purchase of fifty head of cattle by the firm of Reed & Richardson of Hilo.

Money due Shipman from his savings account at Bishop & Co., plus back salary and repayment of several loans he had made, totaled $519. The inventory noted that, of loans due him, one of $90 was "doubtful." The final accounting of the estate, calculated down to the halfpenny, less probate fees and any debts incurred earlier by the deceased, amounted to $5,281.83 1/2. The probate was finalized with the 1864 petitioning of Dr. Wetmore and Jane to be discharged of their responsibility. Up to this point Jane Shipman had managed on the small income derived from her boarding school plus the sum given her by the Hawaii Evangelical Association.

Jane's school had been established for at least two years when Clarissa wrote how pleased she was to hear that the children and their mother were all doing well. "For once I rejoiced that you were not in Illinois," she wrote. "We have fallen on hard times and I fear a time of trouble is ahead of us. About two weeks ago Mr. Staats [the secessionist] was shot from his horse. Supposed to have been done by two soldiers home on furlough. The Copperheads were furious and threatened to kill a number of Union men in revenge. We do not know whose turn it will be next. Staats was said to have a colonel's commission from Jeff Davis."

Clarissa feared that her son-in-law, George Conrad, would soon be drafted, as President Lincoln had called for two hundred thousand more men. "Oh this horrid war. What trouble and distress it causes. . . . I have strong hopes it will soon be finished and might then begin to look for you to come home. How I do want to see you and those dear children. Sometimes I think I never shall. I begin to feel my age considerably. . . . Since I commenced this letter a month ago I have been quite sick with lung fever. I must cease now as my hand trembles too much and my head is worse than my hand. From your affectionate Mother."

When Clarissa wrote again it was early in 1865, the year the war would end; but she saw no signs of it. "We do not know when we are going to be through with this war. It lingers beyond my expectation. We have had rumors of peace but it all goes up in smoke. We are to have another draft in about two weeks. I can hardly expect my sons and sons-in-law will escape this time. If they must go I must be resigned. I do not feel that my children are any more precious than others, and this wicked war must be put down at all events."

Not only had the prolonged Civil War taken its toll of life among Illinois males but, reported Clarissa, an unidentified epidemic had decimated many young and old in Pike County and adjoining areas. "A great many have died. Mr. Cosgrove lost his wife and four children in one week. The complaint was the dysentary [sic]. For two weeks there was not a day but there was a funeral in Barry. Some days three and four, and one day as high as five. . . . Very few grown people died, though a great many were very sick. And it is very expensive being sick nowadays. $50 is the fee for setting a limb." She concluded, as she often did, with the hope that Jane and the children would "return home" when the war had ended: "I am anxious to hear from you what your calculations are about coming. I want very much to see you and the children. I presume you will write and let us know when you expect to come."

Correspondence from Clarissa to Jane grew sparser over the years, and in a 1867 it was clear why: "I have been sick off and on for nearly two years. Not a day but what I have had to lie abed part of the time. I have been almost confined to the house since the first of last May. I can't sit up but for a few minutes at a time . . . I think if anything I am gaining slowly. My mind has been kept at peace. I rejoice that I am in the hands of the Lord. He will do all things well." She again expressed her wish that she could see Jane once more, and unwittingly may have tried to entice her. "Teaching [here] is very profitable, a good teacher will command from thirty to forty, even fifty dollars a month. I have not urged you to come home for fear you would be discontented." She then informed Jane that Reuben, Jane's father-in-law, had set aside $1,000 for her. There were no strings attached, it was for her use should she decide to return to the area, or to be used as she saw fit in her present circumstances.

But by this time Jane had apparently resolved to stay where she was and make a living for herself by means of her school, now five years old. With sugar taking off and times becoming more prosperous, Hilo, thanks to its advantageous geographical location, grew proportionately. Its protected harbor attracted more commerce than any other coastal community on the island. For eighty miles to the north was a coast of spectacular cliffs with deep ravines, offering no anchorage for a vessel of size. Though

the coast to the south was free of escarpments, it was void of any appre-
ciable bays. Such few landings as existed saw cargo and passenger ships
accommodated by lighters. Although Hilo at that time also used lighters,
its harbor had many advantages over landings elsewhere on the island. In
1866 sugar was on the way to becoming king of Hawai'i, and Hilo, the
Crescent City as it became known, was its handmaiden. Coffee and sugar
often competed for the agricultural lands around Hilo.[19] The latter crop
survived, whereas coffee eventually expired. Despite a decline in population between 1860 and 1880, the town expanded, if only in terms of
improved dwellings, better commercial and public buildings, adequate
bridges, and street extensions. The white businessmen in the community
numbered less than twenty, and most of those were in retail and wholesale commerce. Such contractors and builders as may have made Hilo
their home are not in its annals of the 1860s.

One unlisted but enterprising individual who was to emerge and
meet the needs of a growing Hilo was an Irish immigrant, William H.
Reed. He would not only contribute to the city's geographical expansion;
he would, without ever knowing it, become the mother lode of William
H. Shipman, Ltd.

# 10

## *Enter William Reed*

William H. Reed, the man who, in the third quarter of his century, would expand the Hilo district by building bridges and a harbor landing and extending streets, was a native of Northern Ireland. Registers from St. Anne's Church of Ireland (Protestant) in the city of Belfast show that on December 4, 1814, in the district of Shankill, William Reid (often spelled thus) was born to William and Abigail Reid. As was common in those times, baptisms often took place as soon as possible after the birth. The same register shows that on the same day William, son of William and Abigail Reed *(sic)*, was baptized in St. Anne's Church.[1]

William was five years old when the Great Kamehameha, ruler of the distant Sandwich Islands, died in 1819. Why or when Reed came to the Kingdom of Hawai'i remains unknown. But by the time he was thirty-one he was a resident of Lahaina, a decade before William and Jane Shipman arrived at that same busy port town enroute to Micronesia. The first indication of Reed's presence in Hawai'i is a letter written in beautiful Spencerian penmanship addressed to His Excellency, G. P. Judd, Minister of the Interior, dated December 1845. Reed had learned of the Kingdom's interest in constructing a pier for the growing Lahaina shipping trade. In bidding for the job he wrote, "I beg leave to submit a Tender of Expenses," and that he would remove the earth for one dollar per yard and "the natives to be found by Government and I agree to pay them one rial a day for their services."[2] There is no record of who got the job. (A rial was approximately twelve cents.)

Reed did not resurface for another five years. The meticulously kept marriage records of the Reverend Titus Coan show that on Christmas Day of 1850 Reed was married in Hilo to a Hawaiian lady named Kanuimaka. She was listed as a resident of nearby Waiākea village.[3] Her later unrecorded death left Reed a childless widower.

By 1859 Reed was a business partner of Charles E. Richardson. The latter was engaged in such commercial enterprises as lumber, land leases and rentals, shipping, retailing, and ranching. In 1860, the year in which

William H. Reed, the widowed businessman whom
Jane Shipman married in July 1868 at the Haili
Christian Church.

Reed was a supervisor of roads for Hilo, the two entrepreneurs became
co-lessees of the expansive Kapāpala Ranch, fifty miles southwest of Hilo,
on the rolling grassy slopes of Mauna Loa. It was a partnership that lasted
for thirteen years. Back in 1862, when Shipman's Waiʻōhinu property was
auctioned, fifty head of cattle were purchased by the partners and put out
to pasture at Kapāpala. Hilo was a ready market for the beef and butter
the ranch produced for many years. Hides were a profitable by-product.

It was about this time that Reed purchased a large tract of land
known as Koloiki. A riparian island of twenty-six acres, it was split by the
Wailuku River on Hilo's northern boundary and was about one mile
inland from the coast. Earlier the property of King Kamehameha IV, on
January 1, 1856, it was leased by the king to Reed. Five years later the
property again changed hands. A document dated February 18, 1861,
commences: "Know all men by these presents, that I, Kamehameha IV,
king of the Hawaiian Islands, for and in consideration of the sum of

two hundred dollars paid to me in hand by Wm. H. Reed of Hilo, Hawaii. . . ."[4] That warranty deed made Reed sole owner of what would become Reed's Island. In the same document Queen Emma, the king's consort, waived all claims to the land in consideration of $1.00. Although it was then a relatively wooded area, Reed used some of the land for pasture. Later it became a rather extensive vegetable garden. Sheriff Hitchcock was also successful in growing pineapples on the island. Today it is a fashionable residential area, in which the William H. Shipman manse is located. It goes by the name of Reed's Island.

Although the firm of Reed & Richardson continued for several years, each also owned and operated his own individual business during the same period. Reed profited by commissions given him by the Kingdom for street extensions, district road improvements, and bridges in the Hilo area. Among the latter the most important was the bridge spanning the 150-foot-wide Wailuku River, which divided Hilo from the Pu'u'eo community on the opposite side. The river was often wild and raging when fed by heavy rains that poured down upon Mauna Kea's windward flank. The first bridge to cross it had been a cable suspension, built in 1859, which collapsed in the same year due to an excessive number of horses attempting to cross at one time.[5] Among those in the riding party who plummeted into the fast-flowing water was Richard Henry Dana, but he made light of it and continued his journey. A replacement bridge of the same type was constructed at once, with doubled chains and cables. This bridge survived for six or seven years. Then, in March 1866, Reed, the Hilo road supervisor, was informed that "His Excellency, [the Minister of the Interior] desires you to commence operations at once to build the [Wailuku] bridge." Reed estimated the cost at "about $4,000." His bridge, the third on this same site, lasted for seventeen years, a good record for bridge construction in that era.[6] It was seriously damaged by a storm in 1883, and the top portion rebuilt. (Present Keawe Street was formerly known as Bridge Street.)

Jane Shipman probably met William Reed several years before he became involved in his last major enterprise, coastal shipping. It is likely they met at one of the gatherings of the "foreign" community around 1867. Such gatherings, for one of the many minorities in Hilo, usually took place at a church or "social" at a private home. Jane had made it a point to keep herself busy running her school, taking part in church activities, and corresponding with her relatives in America and friends in the Islands. Mingling with mutual friends of their peers would inevitably have brought Jane and William Reed together. She was thirteen years Reed's junior.

On June 19, 1868, Sarah Joiner Lyman, a missionary wife in Hilo, wrote to her friend Mrs. Lorenzo Lyons: "You spoke of Mrs. Shipman and asked why we had not told you that she was going to change her name. I can only say for myself, I have not liked to report it abroad, or to speak of it here, except to my familiar friends. Mr. Reed is a kind hearted man and will, I hope, make her a kind husband. She will at any rate have the best name in town.[7] The carefully preserved Haili Church records show that the widow and widower were married on July 6, 1868, by the Reverend Titus Coan.[8]

Jane had already closed her boarding school and from then on devoted her time to being a homemaker for her new husband and Ollie and Clara, her two remaining children at home. The proud new husband and stepfather soon had a fashionable two-story frame house built for his family in a prime residential location on Waiānuenue Street, where the United Methodist Church now stands.

Less than a month after the marriage, Jane learned that her father-in-law, Reuben Shipman, had died suddenly on August 1, 1868, the day after his seventy-seventh birthday. Clarissa informed Jane that he had remembered her as well as her three small children, in his will. Appar-

By far the finest house in Hilo when Mr. Reed had it built for his new bride shortly after their marriage, it stood on the Waiānuenue Avenue site until it was replaced by the United Methodist Church about fifty years ago.

ently he had been a successful farmer, for after leaving token amounts to his own children and spouses, "The rest was all to go to charitable purposes, some fifteen thousand dollars or more."

This was the last letter Jane would receive from her caring mother-in-law. Clarissa reported that her own health was so bad that she had not been out of the yard in three years, being bedridden much of the time. She expressed her own grief when she reminded Jane: "You know something of the loneliness of being a widow. . . . Give my love to the dear children. I do hope to see you once more in this world. Your loving Mother." Clarissa died the following year.

Reuben's will, drawn up in in 1862, left everything to his widow, with few exceptions. The first was his singling out of William and Jane's children as the only grandchildren to be beneficiaries; he left one thousand dollars to be divided among them. Other bequests included his four remaining children and generous amounts to two mission societies and the Tract & Book Society of Cincinnati.

But one month after Reuben's death the court declared his will invalid on the grounds that the two witnesses had failed actually to see Reuben put his signature to the three-page document. Therefore his personal and worldly goods could not be distributed as he wished. Matters were further complicated by the fact that Clarissa left no will. Two years later the Pike County chancery court ordered that a public auction of Reuben's possessions be held. It took place at the farm residence, and family members bought most of the four hundred acres Reuben owned. The sum total of the revenue from the auction came to about $10, 000, a handsome sum in those post–Civil War days. This was divided among the sons and daughters, including the deceased William. His share was awarded to his three children, all minors.[9]

It would be another ten years before the last of the three Hawai'i heirs would be paid their share of Reuben's estate by the court-appointed administrators. Part of the delay was the forty-acre lot that had been deeded in 1839 in the name of William C. Shipman. At least three questions arose to complicate the disposition of the property. Could a minor, the fifteen-year-old William, have purchased the lot in his own name? Also, what about a record indicating that William had sold the lot to his father for a token $50 in 1850, the year he left Mission Institute to begin his theological studies in New Haven? When young William went to the Quincy land office in 1839, was his name, instead of his father's, mistakenly put on the deed?

The settling of the Reuben Shipman estate was, in the words of an

Illinois court researcher, "an absolute mess."[10] The upshot was that the troublesome forty-acre lot was divided into fifths, thus including each of the five children of Reuben and Clarissa. The long-dead missionary's share was just one of those fifths, entitling each of his children to one-fifteenth. Their inheritance also included a share of the revenues from the earlier auction. For reasons that remain murky, their share was doled out to them over a period of ten years. It is estimated, judging from the decree of the Pike County master of chancery, that each of the three Hawai'i heirs received $1,454.55, though not all at once. The signed receipts of Ollie and Clara, acknowledging payments of anywhere from $50 to $100, indicate that these funds were used to defray educational and personal expenses. Willie's Uncle Alex Stobie of Quincy signed for him, as the youth was then attending the nearby Knox Academy.

Jane and William Reed had a good marriage, and judging from the many surviving letters Reed wrote to "my beloved Jane" and his three stepchildren over the years, it remained a most satisfactory union. His tenderness is reflected in a letter he once wrote to little Clara while he was away at Kapāpala ranch. Addressed to "Miss Clara Shipman," the letter from her new father read, in part, "Dear Child, I received your last note and you cannot comprehend the pleasure it gave me. . . . I will be in Hilo three weeks from today and will be very glad to see you. I would like very much to have you come here if your mama will let you. . . . I got home in the rain last night [having] been on the mountain all week driving cattle. . . . Your true friend."

One of the first paternal acts of William Reed was to see to the education of his three stepchildren. Jane would never have been able to afford to send them to Honolulu's prestigious private school, Punahou, meaning "new spring." Established in 1841 for the children of missionary families, it later accepted a limited number of students from other families as well. When in 1867 it accepted Willie as a Regular Scholar, as opposed to a Preparatory Scholar, Punahou was already more than a quarter-century old. It had relaxed its policy to the extent that a small number of nonmissionary children, both male and female, were his classmates. But discipline was not relaxed; after all, it was a school founded by missionaries following Christian principles. (Its code of behavior, even by today's standards, cannot be considered unreasonable.) Printed regulations spelled out that "A moral discipline shall be maintained. The exercises of the Institution shall be opened daily by the reading of Scripture and prayer. There shall be a Biblical recitation once a week. . . . The

Clara Shipman when she was about ten years old. Her stepfather adored her and signed his letters to her "From your true friend."

pupils shall be kind and courteous to each other and shall render respectful obedience to the teachers, both in the school-room and out of it." Profanity, obscene language, lying, stealing, liquor, and tobacco were all taboo; violators would suffer dismissal. Punctuality at meals was mandated, "free and cheerful conversation being allowed at the discretion of the person who presides at the table." Attendance at Sabbath services was a must. Boarding students would attend at the Punahou chapel; local students could arrange it with their families. Damage done to any property by a student would be repaired by the author of the damage. Boarding students were to furnish their own rooms. They were forbidden to visit the rooms of those of the opposite sex, "except by special permission from the President or the Superintendent of the Boarding department in extraordinary cases." The regulations also ordained that "No Boarding Scholar shall be allowed to visit Honolulu, or any other place outside the College premises without permission from one of the Faculty."[11] Today Punahou has the distinction of being the oldest preparatory school west of the Rockies.

Punahou's roster shows that Willie Shipman was accepted a year before Reed and Jane were married. The fee was $36 for the full term. This was no small amount for the widow, and there was ship fare on top of the tuition. The school's accounts show that payments for the year 1867 were paid by "Jane S. Shipman." A year later, and for the balance of Willie's enrollment, the fees were paid under the name of Jane S. Reed. It is not unlikely that even the 1867 payments were made through the generosity of Jane's new friend, William Reed.

Young Ollie was enrolled in 1869, at twelve, and Clara (Margaret Clarissa) in 1873, when she was fourteen. Reed's fatherliness followed the children to their distant new setting. A letter to Willie beginning "My Dear Son" continued to fill him in on the many activities about the Hilo home and related matters. He explained why he had been unable to write for some time and expressed the hope that Willie had had a happy New Year. He said that Willie's mother had been ill with stomach trouble but was improving. He then related the misfortune of a Captain Babcock, who had lost his schooner and would be penniless: "We got up a subscription here of 640 dollars in one evening for him, although he is a stranger here. I do not think they will do as much for him in Honolulu. I think the people there have not too much the milk of human kindness as there is here. . . ." After reporting that they had had a series of earthquakes, he closed, "You must write me a long letter and let me know how you are doing."

Reed's suggestion that Willie write a long letter may have sparked a trait that Willie exhibited for the rest of his life, at least in letters to his mother, and to Reed while he lived. Willie continued to write long and affectionate letters to both of them, even during his student years in America. But as to whether Willie followed Reed's wish to "let me know how you are doing" there is a question. A page from Punahou's 1941 centennial commemorative publication[12] reveals that "William Shipman from Hawaii brought his horse when he came in 1867. For a while he and Sam Parker were the only boys boarding who had saddle horses. When they rode to church they took a short trail and arrived long before the bus." A diarist for the period noted in the Punahou history that "Willie and Arthur [Alexander] are the uncontrollable forces around the octagon drafting room."[13] Willie's grandson, Roy Shipman Blackshear, recalls hearing from family elders that when Willie arrived at Punahou he was very homesick, and just having his horse with him relieved the pain.[14] In his last couple of years he had the distinction of being asked to drive Mrs. Benjamin Dillingham, wife of Honolulu's leading businessman, to the market and to visit her friends. It was something he enjoyed and made him the envy of his schoolmates. In 1868, at the beginning of his second year, after sailing by schooner from Hilo, Willie reported that "We arrived in Honolulu Monday, after a passage of two days and two nights. I was sick most of the way. . . . John and I have been teaching a Japanese to write letters of the alphabet. . . . Governor Kekuanaoa was taken sick yesterday and they say he is desperately ill." As in most of his letters to his parents, he signed himself, in flowing Spencerian script, "Your loving son, W. H. Shipman."

In an October letter to his mother, Willie revealed a reoccurrence of his homesickness: "I wrote you last time that I wanted to go home. I hope you will say yes. . . . I always have a headache every day and it makes it worse to study." A couple of weeks later he complained that "I did not receive a letter from you this time and I did not like it very well. I hope you are not sick."

The boy's concern for family was frequently reflected in letters that ended "Give my love to the children." He seldom failed to ask Jane to "Give my love to all enquiring friends." He would ask her to "Tell Mr. Reed that I will write him soon," which he did. Sundry information imparted to his mother noted that he was working for a faculty member, Mr. Church, so he could earn some money of his own. Also that he was getting along well in his studies, and to "Please send me some jelly when you can." In late November he passed on the news that Governor Matteo Kekūanaō'a, the son-in-law of King Kamehameha the Great, "died last night. The man-of-war Ossope is firing cannons now."

Although he still longed for his Hilo home and friends, Willie was urged by his mother to persevere. At that point Sarah Lyman, the wife of a missionary and a friend of Jane Reed, wrote a lengthy letter to fourteen-year-old Willie. It was full of understanding, describing her own misery when she had first left home, a malady later experienced by her own children. She wrote of a young mutual friend whose homesickness had seemed incurable, but he had hung on and later related how happy he was to be enjoying life away from home. "As for your mother's plan to put you in a good school in the Eastern states . . . it is a good plan and I approve of it. It is what your father would have wished had he lived. You now have ample means for a liberal education. You will find it much easier to study when you have a definite plan in mind." Mrs. Lyman concluded with the suggestion to "give yourself to Jesus & unite with the people of God."

Despite Willie's homesickness, his grades during his first two years at Punahou were considered very good. By 1870, his final year, they had slipped somewhat. But his marks in deportment were always high, his octagon-drafting-room shenanigans notwithstanding.[15]

Reed's paternal interest in his stepsons was clearly revealed in a letter of January 20, 1870, in which he expressed pleasure that Willie had enjoyed his trip to Maui. He then pointed out that the school term would end in five weeks. "Soon you will be a man and the time to improve yourself is now. . . . I am grateful for your choosing me as your legal guardian. I will always look after and care for your welfare and interest as I would my own. I want you to look upon me as your best and truest friend outside of Mother. I promise you will always find me your sincere friend and I will do all for you that I could if I was your own father." The same letter alluded to property left to Willie by his Illinois grandfather, Reuben Shipman. "Your mother wants to be able to sign for you so as to settle the business." This matter would later enter into Willie's life, but he would be a married adult long before the Illinois property matter was settled.

First-time father though he was, William Reed showed no partiality among his children, as is evidenced by a letter written to Ollie at Punahou, also dated January 20, 1870. Addressing him too as "My dear boy," Reed commented on an improvement in his writing, hoped he had had a good time on his Maui vacation, told him that "your Mother will write you after Church," and signed off, "With best love, believe me, your sincere friend."

# 11

# *Notes from Knox Academy*

Sarah Lyman's friendly advice had such a positive effect that Willie not only persevered at Punahou but, in 1870, he and his brother Ollie were enrolled at Knox Academy in Galesburg, Illinois, seemingly half a world away. This opportunity for the boys to pursue a higher education in the United States was realizable, not only because of Jane's wish for it, but also because of Reed's own interest in their future welfare, demonstrated by his parental encouragement and munificent generosity. Knox Academy, a preparatory school, was chosen for its proximity to relatives of Jane's family and a good many Shipmans, all of whom were in an area sixty miles south of Galesberg. The knowledge that the boys would be near their kinfolk was a great comfort to their mother.

The transition to the United States, a region quite foreign to the two boys, was eased by the company of Jane, eleven-year-old Clara, and Mr. Reed. It was Clara's first trip away from Hawai'i. For Jane, it was the first visit in sixteen years to the region where she had grown up, attended school, and met and married William Shipman. Her parents, as well as Reuben and Clarissa Shipman, had died within recent years. Jane visited relatives of both families, including her brother, Alex Stobie, introducing her new husband and her three Shipman children. Once the boys found quarters in Galesburg, the Hawai'i trio retraced their steps after refreshing visits to relatives in St. Louis and sightseeing in California.

When they arrived home, a letter awaited them from Willie, the ever-faithful correspondent. He informed them that he had attended and enjoyed a concert at the Academy, that they were settled in, and that his courses included rhetorical exercises, algebra, grammar, geometry, and his nemesis—spelling. The schedule also included daily chapel services. He expressed a liking for his instructors and was particularly impressed with a Mr. Churchill, who was half-Indian: "no matter what, he is a good and smart man."

The Knox Preparatory Academy attended by the two Shipmans was operated by Knox College. The latter had been founded in 1837 by Congregationalists and Presbyterians from upper New York State. Because of denominational differences in the 1850s and 1860s, the College Board of Trustees removed Knox Academy from formal denominational affiliation in 1866.[1] Judging from Willie's comments over the next three years about chapel services and a Christian persuasion among students and faculty, a religious atmosphere lingered on.

Willie and Ollie would spend three years in this atmosphere before moving on to other and separate areas of interest. They would be particularly long years for Willie, whose letters frequently made it quite clear that he wished he were back home. He was faithful in carrying out the wish of his stepfather that he write, at least to his mother, once a month. Although it had been Willie's original intention to study medicine and then practice on Hawai'i island, where the need could not be disputed, he gradually lost that desire and was unsure of what his future would be.

The years from 1870 to 1873 were studded with Willie's reports on school, their health, his problems and activities, visiting relatives, Ollie's

When Willie and Oliver attended Knox Academy, they were meticulous in accounting for their living expenses, as these records show.

progress, and his own perennial desire to return home. His first letters made it crystal clear that he was unhappy in his western Illinois setting. "I don't like the States at all. I don't have friends and feel so homesick. I don't like the boys in Galesburg very well. They seem stuck up. I have been called a heathen once or twice. . . . It would seem more like home if we could see mountains and the sea. It is all prairie. One boy got so homesick he had to go home. I hope I won't be like him."

Before the end of the first semester he reported that Ollie, who was not much of a letter writer, was thinking of dropping Latin and was also growing out of his clothes. Willie showed an interest in music when he asked his mother if she would like to have him study it, and added that he was already trying to learn to sing. Jane, who had more than once despaired of his spelling in his years at Punahou, must have been heartened to read, "I hope I am improving in spelling."

While faithful in keeping his mother informed, Willie was not negligent in his attention to his stepfather, who was always referred to as "Mr. Reed." But correspondence to him always began "Dear Father" and usually concluded, as it did to his mother, "Your Loving Son, W. H. Shipman." This filial and formal farewell was also a sign of the Victorian times, and the signature, like his writing, was so consistently elegant that Mr. Spencer himself would have been delighted. In one letter to his mother he commented, "Your letter came but I did not receive one from Mr. Reed. I hope he is not sick." In an early letter to Reed he expressed regret at hearing that he had indeed been ill, wished him a happy recovery, and thanked him for the hometown newspapers he had thoughtfully sent his stepsons, hoping for more of the same. In the same breath he reminded Mr. Reed that he thought he had intended to "go East this year and stop and visit us. I sure would like to see someone from home." He concluded with mention of the great Chicago fire, in which "Cousin Maggie got burned out and lost a good many things."

As he prepared for exams at the end of his first year at the Academy, Willie found the June heat unbearable, quite unlike moderate Hilo temperatures. "It has been so hot these past few days that I cannot study, but the term will soon end." His fraternal concern for his younger brother is displayed in that same June letter.

Mother, I don't know what to do about Ollie. He don't get his lessons done at all and his teacher has been to me about it. He won't mind anything I say. I don't think this is a very good place for him at the present time. Maybe he should go some place where they would keep him in school to study lessons.

This school is made for one who is older than Ollie. The teacher is afraid he will not pass his exams. If so, he will have to repeat a whole year. I will try to get him to write. It is too bad he cannot write home once a month. . . . Please direct letters this summer to us at Barry where we will be on the farm.

Willie was not one to see time wasted, judging from a note to his mother a short time later. He had been in touch with his Uncle Alex and reported that "Cousin Willie Stobie has stopped going to school & is doing nothing but playing ball and loafing." It became characteristic of Willie in later years that he would be a guardian of time. It was even demonstrated while in his first year at Knox, when he asked his mother about Harry Rogers, a hometown friend. "Do you know how he is getting along on Maui? He ought to stick to one trade. A jack of all trades is good at none."

Before the year was out, Willie wrote his mother: "you will be glad to know I am studying Latin & Greek. I have made up my mind that I will go through college. I never took so much interest in my studies as I have this term. I just enjoy it. Ollie is getting along in his studies first rate. He is one of the best in his Latin class."

At the end of the Christmas season Willie reported on their holidays at the farm, where the pond had frozen and they did their first skating. Then he asked Jane, "Did you have a nice Christmas tree this year?" and wished he could get some kind of present for his sister, Clara. He also informed his mother that, as Clara would be studying Latin at Punahou, he had some brotherly advice. Instead of getting her the Harkness grammar and reader, as Jane had planned, Willie made it quite clear that Clara "should get the introductory book first."

His own reading, as he started his new term, consisted of the life of Abraham Lincoln, which he found to be interesting. "I am also studying Roman history, but in English, not Latin." One subject that Willie found fascinating, he admitted, was German. "I like it first rate, even though it crowds me for the weekly music lessons I am taking." In subsequent correspondence home he told of studying trigonometry, which he also liked "first rate," and French, which he admitted he did not care for half as much as he did for German.

At the beginning of the second semester, Willie wrote home that he had "passed exams OK," then gave a rundown on relatives he and Ollie had visited over the Christmas holidays. The Mississippi had frozen over and he was more than elated with his first river skating experience. Part of their holiday, like many more to follow, was spent with Uncle Alex

Stobie, a merchant in nearby Quincy. It was Uncle Alex who gave him *Pilgrim's Progress*, "which I find very interesting—as far as I have read." He then informed his mother that he didn't think her brother was getting along in business very well. "Folks don't pay their bills. He is talking about going on a farm. I wish he would go into some business in the Islands. I think he would but for his family." Then in despair he concluded, "When will I ever learn to spell right? Remember, I am 16 now."

The boys spent most of their first summer on the Pike County farm of Uncle George Conrad, whose wife, Lucretia Shipman, was sister to the Reverend Shipman. Willie informed Jane that all the relatives of both families were well, and that "cousin Ruth is as talkative as she was last year. It has been terribly hot here, but I suppose you are having splendid weather at home. . . . I have been working these days and have plenty to do. Yesterday I plowed all forenoon and in the afternoon stacked hay. I am going to stay here all summer. I would like to go East but cannot go very far on fifty dollars. I will wait until I get enough."

On another farm vacation he related that he and Ollie had "been helping Uncle Fred to plow but I can hardly bare [*sic*] the hot weather. And I cannot help dreading going back to Galesburg. I never will like the place. The sooner I leave it the better." Quincy was more to his liking, perhaps because it was not associated with Knox. The Mississippi held a certain fascination for him, and he would describe when the boats were running or when the ice was too thick for boats but ideal for skating, which he enjoyed despite the cold. He was thrilled to write home from Quincy that "they have built a bridge across the river to Hannibal and it is going to open today."

As for other relatives in the area, mostly Pike County Shipmans, he was fond of many, but of others he asked why "our relatives don't agree more? They are always jawing about each other." He cited an instance in which one set of cousins "would tell lots of stuff about other cousins, and they would do the same thing. Only it would be just the other way."

Willie's aches and pains, real or imagined, were surely intertwined with his longing for home. Early in 1871 he told his mother, "I have been in bed with bilous [*sic*] fever. It don't agree with me to go to school much. Oh, I will be glad when school days are over for me. I should not say it, but I cannot help it, I am so miserable." But, determined to carry on, he wrote, "I am going to study hard and get to the Senior class, but I will have to go some to do it."

If Ollie suffered any pangs of homesickness it was not made known in any letters home. In a letter to Father Reed Willie reported that "Ollie

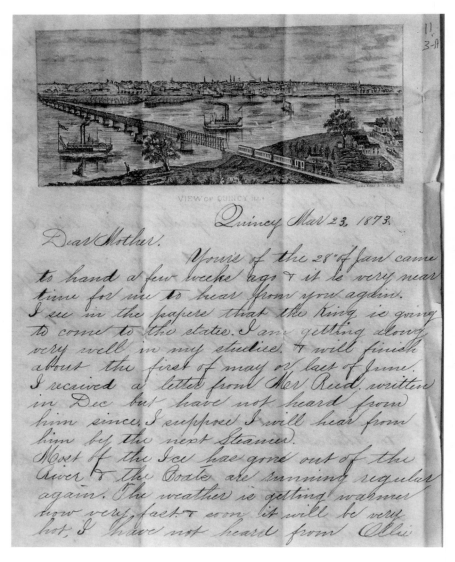

VIEW OF QUINCY ILL⁵

Quincy Mar 23, 1873.

Dear Mother.

Yours of the 28ᵗʰ of Jan came
to hand a few weeks ago & it is very near
time for me to hear from you again.
I see in the papers that the King is going
to come to the states. I am getting along
very well in my studies. & will finish
about the first of may or last of June.
I received a letter from Mr Reid written
in Dec but have not heard from
him since, I suppose I will hear from
him by the next Steamer.
Most of the Ice has gone out of the
River & the Boats are running regular
again. The weather is getting warmer
now very fast & soon it will be very
hot, I have not heard from Ollie

Facsimile of a letter from Willie to Jane shows an engraved view of Quincy from
across the Mississippi. Willie wrote his mother with enthusiasm about the opening of the bridge. The engraved letterhead portrays Quincy as seen from the Missouri shore. The railroad bridge, the second built across the Mississippi, went up
in 1873, the year Willie and Oliver were students in Galesburg. They often visited their uncle Alex Stobie in Quincy.

is now going to writing school every afternoon." But it may have had little effect, for he concluded that "I have been trying to get Ollie to write you but he says he hasn't any time." He included a note to his mother, saying, "Don't forget to send a box of things for us. Poi anyway, whether you send anything else or not."

Though Knox Academy had earlier divorced itself from sectarian ties, it had not, judging from what appeared to be compulsory chapel services, abandoned religious training.[2] Willie more than once referred to twice-daily quarter-hour chapel services. Whether he was influenced by that association or one not identified, early in his second term Willie wrote Jane: "I suppose it will be news to you that on Feb. 1st I gave my heart to God. I am trying now to live the life of a Christian, along with ten other boys here at Mrs. Curtis. I haven't said much about it to Ollie. Five of us have been converted this term. We have prayer meetings among ourselves twice a week, and each of us is expected to take part." Then followed a long paragraph telling of the expectations of the college president that all of the boys in each class become Christians. His own concern was expressed when he asked, "Do you think, Mother, that I had better join the church here? I don't know what to do about that." As for his landlady, Mrs. Curtis, "She is just like a mother to us. She is always anxious if any of the boys stay out late, as if they were her own sons." He finished his confession of faith by asking that Clara write him, then asked, "Has Mr. Reed joined the church yet & is he a Christian? I must stop now and write to Mr. Reed."

It was at the beginning of the second year that Uncle Alex suggested that both boys owed it to their stepfather to keep an account of their expenses, that Mr. Reed was entitled to know how his money was being spent. At the end of the first 1872 quarter, each boy meticulously accounted for every penny spent, itemizing by the date the expense was incurred, the item, and its cost. A month's board was $40 plus $4.65 for a cord of wood and 25 cents for a gallon of oil.

Samples of other spending: a German grammar $1.15, buttons for coat 25 cents, corn 10 cents, trip to Quincy $2.00, cravat 85 cents, box collars 25 cents, trip to Galesburg 75 cents, post-office box 10 cents, going to tableaux 25 cents, music bill $8.50, stamps 25 cents, watch repair 50 cents, lecture 25 cents, skating ticket 20 cents, Society bill $1.50, German lexicon $4.60, picture taken $1.00, washing $3.00, New Testament 85 cents, fix boots 90 cents. A total of eighty items, some as small as a ten-cent key ring, were faithfully recorded. The four pages of twenty items each totaled $207.45 for the full three months. There is no record of Reed's ever having required such an accounting, nor is there any record that his stepsons ever provided another.

How long Willie's Christian commitment endured is unknown, but some months after he had made that declaration, he wrote his parents, "We had a little prayer meeting tonight. All took part in it. Ollie too. It was very interesting & will do us all good. . . . A letter from Uncle Alex said he is glad we have given ourselves up to Christ." Future letters make no mention of any religious activity or affiliation. But that is not to say Willie dropped out of social intercourse. He was proud to inform both parents: "Was chair of the Society the other evening. The first time for me. The boys got to cutting up so I fined them ten cents. I got along better in the chair than I thought I would. Next term I am going up for debate. I don't know how I will do but I will try. Please tell all the news from home next time."

It was in this quarter of 1872 that he wrote his mother he had been "unwell most of this term. Prof. Churchill said I'd better stop school for a month or so. I think I had better stop school altogether. I don't think I can ever go through college. I want you and Mr. Reed to talk it over and let me know as soon as you can. This may make you feel bad but I think it is the best thing for me to do." He then reported that Ollie was getting along fine in his lessons "& I hope he will do better than I ever will." He went on to relate that a young friend attending Yale College suggested that both brothers go there the following year "as the colleges back East are older & better. Amherst then, if not Yale."

Willie did follow the advice of Professor Churchill and went to the farm for at least a month to convalesce. While there he wrote to Clara, asking her if she remembered, from her first and only visit, the black horse that Uncle George used to have. "Most everything else on the farm is the same as when you were here. I do not feel well now and must stop writing. All your cousins are well." While still recuperating at the Pike County farm, he wrote Jane to tell her that two of her long-lost letters had finally showed up at the same time, but he was bothered by not hearing from Mr. Reed. "Perhaps his letter got lost too. . . . I felt pretty bad last week but am better now. . . . Uncle George has been trying to fix up the Estate and Uncle Henry and Alfred did not pay him and he has got to pay it himself, but since he cannot raise money enough he will have to sell the farm. He feels pretty blue about it. I am sorry for him. If the farm is sold he will probably go to Minnesota. . . ." Signed, as usual, "your loving son, W. H. Shipman," with a postscript that read, "I cannot write such long & interesting letters as you, and so you must excuse this badly written letter." A few weeks later he wrote that he had come back to school a week before and was doing all right in class, and that the farm had done him good; he now felt more like studying.

In Jane's letters to her sons she commented from time to time upon visitors who had come to Hilo and stayed at the Reed residence. Wrote Willie, "It seems to me from your letters that everyone that ever goes to Hilo stops at your house. You ought to make a hotel of it. Most every time you write some stranger is staying there." That brought on another mild attack of homesickness, for he followed up with "Spring is coming and everything is commencing to look green. It is now nearly two years since we arrived in the States. Tempus Fugit. How I wish I could get back to the Islands & make you a visit."

Although Willie remained the constant correspondent, Ollie did write home occasionally. In a letter midway into his second term he wrote his mother telling her she must be becoming fashionable, because "you are learning how to make flowers for your bonnet." He told her that Willie had returned from his convalescence at the farm, "but if I was him I would have gone out East because I don't think he is going to take a classical course & this term won't do him much good." Ollie then spoke of his reluctance to spend their money on his education, and that, "while Aunt Ann wants us to spend part of our coming vacation in St. Louis I want some work to do. I wish it would not cost so much to go to school, but I will do my best. The only news I have is that I have passed my exams."

Although Willie's letters were for the most part written to his parents, some went to St. Louis relatives and others in the area—cousins, aunts, and uncles—especially in regard to forthcoming holidays and vacations. Nor did he neglect his sister, Clara, by this time a Punahou student. Her future plans concerned him. "Do you know what school back East Mother is going to send you to? . . . Ollie and I got a present for you and sent it by Dr. Wetmore [the medical missionary who had treated the Reverend Shipman before he died]. It is a breast pin and a pair of earrings. And for Mother a silver butter knife. We got a silver watch chain for Mr. Reed. . . . Give my aloha to all enquiring friends. From your brother, W. H. Shipman."

Days within writing Clara, Willie wrote asking his mother: "Do you know where you will be sending Clara to school and do you expect to come with her? How often do the steamers run, once or twice a week? Is the volcano active now? I hope you do not have such hard earthquakes as you did in 1868. . . . Ollie received the draft for a hundred dollars from

Mr. Reed but has not cashed it yet. He will wait until he goes to Quincy." Then, for the first time, he told Jane that he had been having severe toothaches, and that he had been having tooth trouble for quite some time. On one occasion he had "stayed home from school until the swelling went down." There was no mention of having visited a dentist in Galesburg.

When the summer vacation of 1872 loomed, he told Jane that there were only a few more weeks of school left, and "Ollie & I are doing well with our lessons. . . . My vacation plans are not formed yet. I may go down to the farm, Aunt Ann wants us to come to St. Louis. Cousin Samuel Jones [living in Jamaica with his Stobie missionary parents] wrote & said he cannot find much to do there, so may come to the States." He then told his mother that he didn't get homesick as often as he had, but in the next breath asked: "Do you think you will come to the States when you send Clara off to school? I hope you will. I may be able to go home with you then."

His next letter went to "Dear Father," and was from St. Louis; he and Ollie had taken up Aunt Ann on her invitation. "Ollie received your letter of the 23rd, but none came for me. I suppose you were very busy and could not write to both of us. The last few days I came to St. Louis I had to stay away from school because of toothache. . . . We are not sure what we will do this summer. Ollie will probably go onto the farm. I am going to get something to do in Quincy. If I can't I will go to the farm too." After casually reporting that Uncle Alex "had bought a store with a german and is doing a nice business," he asked his stepfather a question that showed his hand and would shape his future in Illinois, and even more so back in Hawai'i. "Does Akana's brother still keep books for you?" He let it go then, but would pick up the thread over the next few months. He closed by telling Reed that "All the talk now days is about who is going to be President of the United States."

A month later, in the summer of 1872, Willie wrote his stepfather that they had skipped commencement exercises because they would be too dull, that he enjoyed himself "first rate" on the Fourth of July, and that he thanked him warmly for his part of the money draft, which had enabled him to buy a watch. He made reference to discord within the Knox establishment, that the president had resigned and, furthermore, that "I had heard that some years ago they had some trouble with the college & I would not be surprised but what they will have more." Then he quietly moved on to the subject of helping out at home. "I should think you have your hands full if you have to tend the shop lumber yard & you ought to have me there to help you. I hope to some day. You wanted me to make up my mind what to do. I think I will be able to by the next time I write. How is business now? Here it is very dull. . . . The thermometer has stood at nearly 100, so I just stay in the house and read. I feel as if I ought to be at some better business than that but it can't be helpt (sic)."

Willie's next monthly letter home, also to Dear Father, thanked him for a recent letter and told him that Uncle George had a fine crop of oats but had lost all his wheat. Then he launched into the subject of what had been on his mind for many months:

> I wrote you that I would make up my mind and let you know what I want to do. First I intend to go to a Business College & then get a place in a store as a bookkeeper. Uncle Alex thinks I ought to learn a trade but I don't care about one. I would very much like to be at home, but I know myself I am not ready. . . . Who have you got in Henry Gandle's place? Are your sheep doing well now? . . . I am glad that Mother is getting to be a good rider. I wish you could make us a visit sometime. I thought I would succeed in writing a long & interesting letter, but I have failed. I cannot think of anything more to write now, so you must excuse me. I remain your loving son. . . .

Shortly after that, in a brief letter to his mother, he commented upon her statement that she did not think she could write a decent letter: "But I thought it was a nice letter." He then told her of the resignation of the Knox president and that "four teachers have also left so we now have no president, though the trustees are trying hard to find one. I don't think they will get another as good. Some years ago Knox had trouble with each of two denominations trying to claim it. They settled it, but now I think they are going to have more trouble." He then told her that, as far as certain relatives went, "I think it is more pleasant to be here with Aunt Ann than with Aunt Emmaline. There is considerable difference between the two." Also that Uncle James "is still doing nothing."

"Back at Old Knox again," as Willie put it in a September 1872 letter, he gave Jane a rundown on family relatives he had seen during the summer, making special mention of his "bushels of cousins." He gave her encouraging word about Ollie, first, that "he seems to be studying better and that if he doesn't Uncle Alex had threatened to take him out of the Academy." Willie told Jane that Ollie had grown so that he didn't think his own mother would recognize him. "I think it was a good thing you sent him away from home. But I think, Mother, you ought to send him East & prepare him for one of the Colleges there. It is not so good here as it was last year, as I have already told you." He then trailed to a close, informing her of preelection excitement and the probability that General Grant would be elected.

In late November 1872, he rejoiced that "we only have three weeks left in our term and Ollie and I are getting along first rate in our studies. I hope Clara is doing the same. Isn't she old enough to come to the States by now? By the time she gets here I will be ready to go home. . . . Do you think I am improving in my spelling? You know I never was a very good speller." He ended by asking if Mr. Reed had been ill, it had been so long since he had heard from him. As a final note he told his mother that "there hasn't been much news now, [but] Grant is elected president."

Reed had never pressed Willie to pursue a course in medicine; nor had he discouraged him. But he had suggested that he take a course in accounting, pointing out that such background would prove valuable in almost any career. Thus Willie finished out his term at the Academy and

Willie Shipman was a student at Galesburg, Illinois, when this studio picture was taken ca. 1873.

then made the move he had earlier told Mr. Reed was his plan. At the beginning of 1873, with parental blessings, he enrolled in a commercial school in Quincy. He also had a home away from home, boarding with his Uncle Alex, who had chosen a school for Willie suited to his new plans. Bookkeeping and general business were the courses he took, the skills he knew were necessary to be of genuine assistance to his stepfather and, of course, to fulfill his dream of returning to his beloved Hawai'i Island.

A month after enrolling in the business school he wrote Jane, mildly complaining as he always did when more than a month passed without a letter from home: "I believe the steamer must have had some sort of accident. . . . My work in Book Keeping requires much writing. I am not sure what I will do when I finish this school but I would like very much to come home. I am in very good health but do not like this below zero weather." He had had word from Ollie, he told her, and the news from Knox was not good. While his brother was doing well in his studies, "I heard on pretty good authority that Knox is running down and I think you aught to send Ollie East to school." He felt it important to tell Jane that her brother, his Uncle Alex, "has not much business now and is talking about going on to a farm. I wish he could go into some business in the Islands." (This wish would be fulfilled years later.) In closing, he let her know that Hawai'i was making the Illinois newspapers. "There is a good deal of talk here about the Islands since the king [Kamehameha V] died. I have also heard that Brigham Young is going to move to the Islands, but I suppose that is all talk."

As was so often his custom, that same day Willie wrote to "Dear Father," imparting much of the same information. He expressed satisfaction with the school and his courses. "It would have been better for me had I gone to such a school when I first came to America." Then again he expressed his unrepressed desire to return to Hilo. "Don't you want me to come home & help keep books for you next fall? I would like to very much." He shared with Reed the fact that annexation of the island kingdom was being discussed "pretty freely these days. I guess folks would like to see them connected."

Before closing, he again reminded his potential employer that "one of my cousins [Charles Stobie] would like to go to the islands if he can find something to do there. He is now working in a Bank. If you could find him a place at a good salarie [sic] let me know. . . . It doesn't seem like three years since we left home."

A month later, in response to Willie's wish to return home soon,

Reed made no objection. He expressed satisfaction that he had gone to "Commercial School" and that his stepson had seemingly found his scholastic niche. He then dropped a bombshell that would eventually change the course of many lives. He said that he had bought out the shares of his partner, C. E. Richardson, of Kapāpala Ranch "for you. I gave him $17,000 for it. . . . I have made a will giving you one half interest in the business. Now I want you to give your mind to your studies and to make yourself perfect in bookkeeping so that you will understand it perfectly. I want you to stay there until about November, and then come home." He went on to tell his now junior business partner that he would be pretty busy with three ranches to manage, plus the lumber business. After informing Willie that he, Reed, would meanwhile find someone to manage one of the ranches, he got down to other equally serious business. "Before you leave there I want you to look out for some young lady for a wife, unless you left your heart behind when you went away. I got your mother to write you about this. I know the country well and it is no place for a young man without a wife, it will be best for you in every way."

Shortly afterward, in late March 1873, Willie wrote his mother that he saw by the papers that the new king, Lunalilo, was going to visit the States.[3] It never happened. He told her his own school work was progressing and he would finish in June. And he proudly let her know that he had received a prize in spelling, out of a class of twenty-five. The next evening he was planning to attend a lecture on temperance by a Mr. Gough. "I do not know whether you have heard him or not. I did two years ago and thought he was a splendid speaker."

He asked if Mr. Reed was going to bring Clara to school, adding that he was looking for a letter from Mr. Reed and that "if he is going to buy out Mr. Richardson he would want me to come home to help him. I am so near through school now that I can. You do not know how I have wished to come home ever since I came to the States." He then made an oblique reference to a gubernatorial choice on Hawai'i Island. "I always thought that the natives like Rufus Lyman for Governor. Mr. Reed must be pretty well liked by the natives." (Reed may have been considered for governor of the island, but there is no evidence he sought the office, or that he ever held any office other than Hilo road supervisor).

Willie then got down to the business of presenting his plans to travel East for a few weeks before severing his Illinois ties upon completion of school. "I will first want to take a trip to Niagara Falls, Boston, New York, Washington, Philadelphia & other places of importance." As usual, a similar letter went to Reed letting him know that he was doing well in school, would be out in May or June, and would then be ready to come home, "if you want me to." He expanded on his winning a spelling prize by saying that it had an unspecified dollar value.

Three months later, in June, Willie heard from his stepfather that he was "glad you want to come back to the Islands. . . . I have bought the Lyman Ranch for $15,000 and sold my interest in the Kahuku Ranch. I have got plenty to do and you will be home soon to help me. We have now got the best place in the Islands."

He then responded to Willie's proposal to bring home with him his cousin, Charles Stobie, who was itching for greener pastures. Reed agreed, suggesting, however, that Charles first come and see the country for himself before burning his Illinois bridges. He warned that business was not too good. "But if Hawaii gets the Reciprocity Treaty with the United States [primarily eliminating a tariff on sugar] things will be alright." He concluded by naming some of his projects, and added, "I want you to manage the whole of them, that is with my assistance, matters we can talk about when you get here." He once more reminded his stepson and heir that "I want to see you married to a nice wife and then I think we might all be as happy as clams. With best love, I am your loving father."

In a touching letter, Willie replied: "Dear Father: your kind letter received. You do not know how thankfull [*sic*] I am to you for giving me such a good start in business. It is better than what most boys would get. I am trying very hard to learn all I can." As for acquiring a wife before his return home, he said it was something he had not thought much about. "I think I am to [*sic*] young, and then I have not seen any I like well enough. You may be disappointed about my not bringing a frau home." He reiterated his desire to help in the business, such as keeping the books. "And I think I will be able to come home sooner than November, but don't tell Mother, I want to surprise her."

In a letter to his mother at about the same time, he shared much of the same information, particularly his gratitude toward his stepfather. As for news from America, he assumed she had heard of "the Indian Wars they are having in Northern California. The Medocs will probably be all killed off."

To Reed, in mid-May, he wrote: "I cannot rid my mind about coming home." He shared with Reed his enthusiasm for some of his bookkeeping and accounting assignments, particularly "playing Actuary . . . we buy and sell merchandise. I think when I get through I will have a pretty good knowledge of business." In a subsequent letter to his parents in late June, he showed not only his enthusiasm over completing his business course the following week, but again moved his return home forward by a month: "I think I will be able to come in September. There is hardly a day but what I think of going home. I am so sick of weather so hot & so cold. . . . I suppose the people in Hilo will celebrate the Fourth of July in a big way." (Although annexation was still twenty-five years away, members of the American community celebrated many of its own holidays.)

Willie's last letter, written from Quincy, informed his mother that he was leaving soon for Washington: "Right now the wether [*sic*] is 103 degrees in the shade. When I am traveling I will be unable to write you. Ollie will do the writing. I got a letter from Fannie Wetmore and she does not expect to be in Buffalo when I am in the area. So that let's me out."

"Soon" was the last week in July. The day after his arrival in Washington he wrote, "It was a fine trip. The scenery between Cincinnati and here was splendid—the country so mountainous I thought of the mountains at home. . . . Today I go to see the White House & Treasury Department. In a couple days I will get to Philadelphia. I must close now to get some breakfast and commence my Washington rounds."

A lengthy letter to his mother was then sent from Glastonbury, Connecticut, near the birthplace of his father and other Shipman forebears. If Willie's visit to New York impressed him, he failed to record it. Nor did his New England visit please him much, for "the relatives here don't seem to care much whether I came or not." What Willie had lost sight of was that whereas his many Illinois relatives were either his peers or only a generation removed, his Connecticut kin for the most part had never heard of this William Shipman, much less of the Reverend William Shipman who had moved away when he was a lad of about eight. Nonetheless, he described his several visits, some with more "bushels of cousins." He did not overlook a call on Col. William Buckley (thought to be a brother of Margaret Clarissa Bulkley Shipman, Willie's grandmother and wife of Reuben, though the spelling differs). "After that I leave for Boston, then to Niagara Falls, then to Chicago, then to Quincy, St Louis and home! It has been lonely traveling alone. Had I known it before I might have backed out. . . . I am hurrying up with this trip so I can get home as soon as possible."

The stops Willie made after leaving Chicago were only to bid farewell to his Shipman and Stobie relatives, both young and old. He would of course make it a point to see Ollie before leaving and be able to tell his parents how his brother was doing. Ollie was doing quite well, for he entered Amherst College, as Willie had suggested, in 1873.

His farewells completed, Willie lost no time in heading for California, there to board the S.S. *Murray*, the first available steamer headed for the Kingdom of Hawai'i, where he would debark in Honolulu on October 27 and search for the first interisland vessel whose destination was Hilo.

# 12

## *Lunalilo*

The year in which Willie Shipman returned to Hilo—1873—was one of significant change in global, national, and island affairs. In Europe the first Spanish Republic was proclaimed, and in France German occupation forces withdrew following the death of the exiled emperor, Napoleon III. English physician William Budd proved the contagious nature of typhoid fever, the disease that had struck down the Reverend William Shipman sixteen years earlier.[1]

In North America the Northwest Mounted Police were established in Canada and Prince Edward Island was admitted as a province to the six-year-old confederation. The United States, not yet a century old, saw the gold standard replace silver. The new monetary medium also affected the Kingdom of Hawai'i, although William Reed had long since changed his proposed payments to Lahaina laborers from rials to the American dollar. On the West Coast the first cable-car system in the world was put into service in San Francisco, providing a thrill for visitors from Hawai'i and elsewhere. A financial panic left the United States with widespread bank closures and the failure of some five thousand businesses. The Great Depression, which lasted five years, brought hard times to the many Hawaiian businesses that had ties with the mainland.[2]

The Hawaiian Kingdom, invaded by a devastating epidemic of leprosy, took little, if any, note of a young Belgian priest, Father Damien DeVeuster, who volunteered for what was to become a lifetime commitment to Kalaupapa, the Kingdom's area of isolation on Moloka'i for hundreds of afflicted Hawaiians.[3] The renowned Scottish world traveler Isabella Bird arrived and immediately began her adventures, which she would later publish as *Six Months in the Sandwich Islands*.

More momentous, perhaps, than any other event in the Hawaiian

Islands was the ascent of Prince William Lunalilo to the throne. A decade later the disposition of his properties, particularly in Kea'au, would affect the life of Willie Shipman and become the keystone of William H. Shipman, Ltd.

Prince Billy, as he was often called before becoming king, was born on January 31, 1835, near what is now the Hawaii State Archives on the present Iolani Palace grounds. He was a chief of royal lineage. His grandfather had been a half-brother of Kamehameha the Great, and his grandmother a sister of the powerful regent, Ka'ahumanu. His mother, Miriam Kekāuluohi, was a high chiefess in her own right, and Charles Kana'ina, his father, was a high chief.[4] The boy was named William in honor of the English monarch William IV, who had earlier befriended Hawaiian royalty. When he was about to be given a Hawaiian name, his mother rose and proclaimed in a loud voice, "I luna, I luna, I lunalilo-loa." That is, "The highest, the highest, the highest of all."[5]

Like some other young chiefs and chiefesses before him, at an early age Lunalilo was educated at the Royal School in preparation for the possibility, which became a reality, that he would someday be a monarch. It is debatable whether the schooling was as effective as hoped, for years later William, who had grown into a somewhat uncontrollable youth, was seen as incompetent in matters of diplomacy and government. His days of "living it up" and subsequent alcohol addiction earned him from his detractors the sobriquet "Whiskey Bill." Charles DeVarigny, a French-born statesman who had once been Hawai'i's minister of foreign affairs, described Lunalilo as "markedly ungovernable and wild during his youth," but also "energetic, intelligent and ambitious."[6]

Another well-known observer of his contemporaries, Mark Twain, who visited Hawai'i in 1866, had this to say about Lunalilo: "Prince William is a man of fine, large build, is thirty one years of age, is affable, gentlemanly, open, frank, manly; is as independent as a lord, and has the spirit and will of the old Conqueror himself. He is intelligent, shrewd, sensible; is a man of first rate abilities. In fact, I like the man. I like his bold independence and his friendship for and appreciation of American residents."[7]

The prince's intelligence, his interest in Shakespeare, and his own poetic nature were attested to by others inside and outside the royal circle. Who knows but that he was moved to compose some of his better compositions when in the arms of Bacchus?

Back in 1860 King Kamehameha IV had felt it was high time that the Island Kingdom, now recognized by several nations, had its own national anthem. To this end he offered an award to any composer who could come up with an appropriate song to the tune of *God Save the King*—naturally, in Hawaiian. Lunalilo, then twenty-five, was encouraged to compete, and was convinced he had the skill to win. Indeed, out of many entrants Lunalilo was chosen as winner and came away with a prize of ten dollars.[8] That would have been a munificent sum to a young man whose spending habits, in accordance with his father's wishes, had been limited by an allowance of twelve dollars a month.

It is said that Lunalilo spoke English as well as or better than his native tongue. Although gifted with poetic talent, he was even better known for his genuine love of his fellow Hawaiians. Twain may have been somewhat off the mark in characterizing him as appreciating Americans; let it be said that he tolerated them.

When, in December 1872, King Kamehameha V died a bachelor and without naming a successor, it became the legislature's job to elect a king. A month later, on January 8, 1873, at the age of thirty-nine, the popular prince won hands down against the only other main contender, David Kalākaua.

One of King Lunalilo's first acts was to visit his subjects on the neighboring Islands. The royal tour was made on the USS *Benecia*. In Hilo on February 21, the king was welcomed by throngs in song, dance, speeches, and feasts. Schools were closed, houses were decorated with Hawaiian flags, and the majestic (for Hilo) courthouse was festooned with colorful bunting and a plethora of Hilo floral decorations. It was from the courthouse lanai that the king greeted the crowd of well-wishers. Eighty boys from the Hilo Boarding School, adorned in their white uniforms, sang for their ruler the same Hawaiian national anthem that he had composed many years earlier. Then came the *ho'okupu*, the age-old Hawaiian custom of gift giving. People came from as far as eighty miles away bearing homage and gifts for their new king. The procession, consisting of nearly twenty-five hundred admirers, presented their gifts of huge piles of bananas, taro, breadfruit, oranges, and other fruits. They came with pigs, scores of fowl, eggs, rainbow-colored flowers, and treasured feather leis. Even the Chinese plantation community gave gifts of money to their new ruler. This outpouring of love for the first sovereign most of the populace had ever seen in person could not have been more munificent.[9]

The following evening the royal party entertained on shipboard the government officials from the island of Hawai'i, leaders from both the Hawaiian and foreign communities, members of royalty, and others impor-

King William Lunalilo. He reigned for only thirteen
months, from 1873 until his early death in 1874. In
the first three months of his rule he visited Hilo,
where he was given a royal Hawaiian welcome.
(HSA)

tant to the welfare and progress of the Kingdom's second-largest city.
Among the guests were Mr. and Mrs. William H. Reed.[10]

Although alcohol and eventually tuberculosis shortened his reign to
just one month over one year, Lunalilo proved to be a popular and democratic sovereign. This "people's ruler" lost no time in his endeavor to
amend the 1864 constitution to provide a more open government for his
people.[11] He pressed for two bodies in the legislature, a House of Nobles
and a House of Representatives, and for a constitution that gave more
power to the people and less to the king. Moreover, he objected strongly
to the present constitution's requirement that to be able to vote a man
must be a property owner—a decided advantage for foreigners whose gold

and persuasiveness had purchased land from the Hawaiians at bargain-basement prices.

The legislature accepted Lunalilo's proposals but did not enact them before his death in February 1874. As a proponent of democracy, the monarch, also a bachelor like his predecessor, did not name a successor. He preferred that his people should choose, as he had been chosen. (Sadly, his successor, Kalākaua, under pressure from American business interests, voted down every one of Lunalilo's proposed amendments.) Sugar barons had long been pressing for reciprocity with the United States, which would enable the commodity to enter duty-free; in return, certain American products would be allowed into the Kingdom free of tax.

Although Lunalilo had been a firm advocate of reciprocity with the United States, he opposed the ceding of Pearl Harbor as a sweetener for a signed treaty.[12] For this he fell out favor with the Kingdom's American business leaders. Later those same interests forced the hand of Kalākaua when the Reciprocity Treaty was signed, with the condition that the United States be given a portion of Pearl Harbor as a maritime coaling station. The camel's nose was in the tent.

The last few months of 1873 saw the king declining beyond the help of his physicians. A trip to the island of Hawai'i's sunny Kailua failed in its therapeutic purpose. He returned to his Waikīkī residence, where he died on February 3, 1874. An election for his successor took place within a few days. The winner was David Kalākaua, but only after a bitter contest with the dowager Queen Emma. Rather than be buried in the Royal Mausoleum in Nu'uanu Valley, with others of his lineage, Lunalilo had preferred to be laid to rest near his people, in central Honolulu. On the green grounds of Kawaiaha'o Church, where he had been invested a year earlier, he was buried in a tomb two hundred yards from his birthplace across King Street.

Lunalilo's legacy to his people was expressed in his will of June 7, 1871. There he named as his executor his future foreign minister, the Honorable Charles R. Bishop, the husband of Princess Bernice Pauahi. The welfare of the Hawaiian people, especially the less privileged, had always been close to the ruler's heart. In clear, concise, and legal language, his will spelled out how the income from the many lands he had owned would be used for the construction and maintenance of what is today known as Lunalilo Home. (The Lunalilo Trust still cares for, in the comfortable and spacious Lunalilo Home, those elderly Hawaiians the king felt were most in need.) His last will and testament read "and in case I shall die without issue lawfully begotten I give and devise all of the real estate . . . to three persons to be nominated and appointed by . . . the Supreme Court or the Court of highest jurisdiction in these Hawaiian Islands, to be held by them in Trust . . . to sell and dispose of . . . to the best advantage at public or private sale, and invest the proceeds . . . in the erection of a building or buildings . . . for the use and accommodation of poor, destitute and infirm people of Hawaiian (aboriginal) blood or extraction, giving preference to the older people."[13]

Lunalilo was the first of the numerous high-ranking chiefs to leave his people a generous charitable trust.[14] (One of the few other monarchs to do so was Queen Lili'uokalani.) The real estate that belonged to Lunalilo, either through the Great Mahele or family inheritance, comprised many lands. They totaled several thousand acres on the five major islands, largely made up of 33 *ahupua'a*. One of these, about 65,000 acres, was the Kea'au Tract.

At the time of the king's death in 1874, Willie Shipman was being tutored by his stepfather in the ways and means of ranch and other property management. Reed was happy to have someone to whom he could turn over the bookkeeping chores and other duties that kept him from more pressing responsibilities. And Willie was free at last from the confinement of classrooms at Knox Academy, the grimness of Galesburg, and the extreme temperatures which, in his loneliness, had constantly reminded him of Hawai'i through odious comparison. Still, a year after Lunalilo's royal funeral, William H. Reed decided it was time to give the young William H. Shipman a taste of roughing it, combined with ranch management. Kapāpala Ranch was to be Willie's home away from home for the next two years.

# 13

# *Kapāpala Ranch*

At Kapapala is a tract of land bounded by the ocean and the sky, or as
high on Mauna Loa as grass can grow, and has an extent of pasturage
like a pampas in Brazil. At the shore the cattle are tame and form a rich
herd; but in the upper forest region they are wild, and are hunted only
for their hides. The proprietor counts cattle, sheep, goats and acres by
the tens of thousands. Here the stranger is sure of a cordial reception,
and at this point preparations may be made for the ascent of the 14,000
feet elevation to the summit crater of Mokuaweoweo.

— HENRY N. WHITNEY, 1875

The "proprietor" Whitney mentions here was William Reed. But several
decades before the author penned this description for *The Hawaiian
Guide Book*[1] Kapāpala was well known to travelers, both native and foreign. The name comes from *pāpala*, a native shrub or small tree with
light, flammable wood. It was found in abundance on the slopes of
Mauna Loa and in Hawaiian forests elsewhere.

Kamehameha the Great, by virtue of being ruler, was king of all he
surveyed—and that was all the Hawaiian Islands. Upon his death in
1819, all lands became the property of his son, Liholiho (Kamehameha
II). Following Liholiho's brief reign, Kauikeaouli, the second son of
Kamehameha I, ruled as Kamehameha III, and without so much as the
stroke of a pen all islands became his domain.

But not for long. Western ways were infiltrating Hawaiian culture
and land ownership became a growing concern, especially to foreigners
who had been granted parcels of land by kings or chiefs but had no guar-
antee they would not be withdrawn. It was Kamehameha III who
accepted the proposal, known as the Great Mahele, to divide the lands
among king, chiefs, Crown, and commoners, though not equally.[2]

Rank, then as now, had its privileges. In 1848, after records showing
who had occupied what land when and where had been gathered and sur-

veyed for months, the *ahupua'a* of sprawling Kapāpala officially became the property of Kamehameha III. Upon his death in 1854, the title automatically passed to his heir, Kamehameha IV.

In a 1860 document, Kamehameha IV leased "unto said W. H. Reed & C. Richardson . . . all that tract of land known as the *ahupua'a* of Kapāpala situate in the District of Kau" for a period of thirty years for the sum of $300 per year.[3] In a separate transaction with F. S. Lyman and others, Richardson acquired several large parcels of ranch land in neighboring Keaīwa, which became part of Reed and Richardson's Kapāpala Ranch.[4] The *Hawaiian Gazette* later described the vast area as "including two extensive lands known as Kapapala and Keaiwa extending along the shore perhaps ten miles from Punaluu eastward, thence up towards the summit of Mauna Loa, embracing an area of 200,000 acres, more or less. . . . There are supposed to be ten thousand head of cattle on it, with many thousand sheep and goats. . . . There are no streams of water on the land though numerous springs abound and the pastures are always fresh and green from frequent showers."[5]

Charles Richardson, like Reed, was a successful businessman in Hilo. Fourteen years younger than Reed, he had a background in mining,

Kapāpala Ranch nestles in a bosky dell on several thousand acres of pasture land on Mauna Loa's slope. Much of the charming ranch residence, built in Reed's time, still serves as the main dwelling. (Courtesy Gordon Cran)

carpentry, and construction. His arrival in Hilo in 1855 followed Reed's by five years. Like Reed, he married a Hawaiian and later lived in a comfortable Western-style house in Hilo. Also like Reed, he was somewhat reserved, took no part in politics, and sought no public office. It was natural that these men, who had such similar tastes and ideals, would meet and combine their interests and efforts. Their leasing of Kapāpala, and their entrance into ranching, particularly cattle, was the first of a number of joint endeavors.

Cattle ranching has never been an industry that a great many people, especially visitors, associate with these islands in the middle of the Pacific. Yet it has been a major business in Hawai'i for well over a century, being eclipsed in later years only by sugar and pineapples. It was Captain George Vancouver who, on his second voyage to Hawai'i in 1793, brought the first cattle as gifts to King Kamehameha the Great.[6] First were a bull and five cows; then, a few months later, the gift was supplemented by another bull, two cows, and two bull calves. These were landed at Kealakekua Bay, along with some sheep and swine. At Vancouver's suggestion, the king put a prohibition on the killing of any cattle for a period of ten years; some say thirty. An exception would be made if the bulls became too numerous.

These first cattle were longhorns and increased rapidly as they grazed on the vast slopes of Mount Hualālai, Mauna Loa, and Mauna Kea above Waimea. They multiplied to such an extent that by the time Reed and Richardson acquired Kapāpala Ranch there were over twenty thousand cattle on the island of Hawai'i. Of these, only eight thousand were domestic; the rest were considered wild cattle.

The importance of cattle grazing in the Kingdom was stressed by The Honorable William L. Lee, an American lawyer who served with distinction in the development of Hawai'i's judicial system. Judge Lee had a genuine interest in agriculture, and his optimism earned him a seat in the Royal Agricultural Society. In an address to the society in 1851, he stressed the importance of tapping Hawai'i's lands for grazing.

One of the most important interests under the care of the Society is grazing. Our highlands are particularly adapted to pasturage; and I doubt if the graziers in any part of the world have been more successful than in these islands. With no winter to contend against, their labors are comparatively light, the increase of their flocks certain and rapid, and the owner of a small herd is sure, with a reasonable degree of care and attention, to become wealthy in a few years. Beyond question the raising of cattle, has thus far been the most successful pursuit connected with the soil yet undertaken in the islands.[7]

Reed and Richardson acquired their first cattle from Harry (a.k.a. Jack) Purdy, a cattleman at Waimea. They already had the fifty head of cattle bought at the 1862 Shipman auction. The next few years saw their enterprise prosper, as Kapāpala Ranch found a ready market in Hilo and Honolulu for butter, cream, meat, hides, and wool from herds of cattle, goats, and flocks of sheep.

The two ranch owners divided their time alternately between Hilo and Kapāpala, where ranch management not only meant fiscal scrutiny but also long cattle drives from used pastures to fresh ones. Fattened cattle were herded down the side of the mountain to the Punaluʻu Landing, where they were shipped by interisland steamer to their destinations. Ranch hands, many with families, lived in quarters at cool Kapāpala. These cowboys, like other Hawaiians who had become expert with horse and lariat on island ranches, had miles of open range on which to practice their skills.

On April 2, 1868, at about four o'clock in the afternoon, a violent earthquake shook the entire Kaʻū district. The force of the quake was largely on the southern rift of Mauna Loa, but all of Kaʻū district and miles beyond were affected. Even Honolulu was shaken. It is still regarded as the most severe earthquake and volcanic eruption in Hawaiʻi's recorded history.[8] One who described it quite graphically was the Reverend Titus Coan, forceful preacher, traveler, and faithful recorder of Hawaiian events. Coming from a volcano watcher of many years, Coan's accounts are today regarded as quite accurate and reliable considering the lack of measuring instruments in that era. Of the 1868 eruption and quakes Coan wrote:

Kau was startled by heavy explosions and roarings. . . . The Mountain was rent . . . from near the summit crater, Mokuaweoweo, half way down its southern slope, and jets of steam and smoke went up from many points, while four distinct streams of lava flowed down the mountain. One of these streams flowed nearly due south halfway down the mountain towards Kahuku. At the same time a terrible earthquake shook down the large stone church at Kahuku, and also all the stone dwelling houses in that place, including the houses at the foot of the mountain. . . . On the day of our awful crash in Hilo, the earth rent between Reed and Richardson's ranch, at Kapapala. . . . At this moment the houses of Reed and Co., of Mr. Lyman, of the native pastor, Kauhane, and of others were shaken down, or so racked as to be uninhabitable.[9]

Among the stone buildings that were leveled was the sizable stone church in Wai'ōhinu. The pastor's residence, that fine building erected by the Reverend Paris in 1843 at the foot of the bluff, was demolished. Likewise, most other dwellings in the vicinity, wood or stone, were flattened. One exception was the small but sturdy stone Catholic chapel on Kamā'oa Road, below Wai'ōhinu. It had been built in 1866.[10] Homes that stood in the path of the flow were completely wiped out by mud or lava, and many lives were lost.

Another chronicler of the event was Frederick Lyman. He was a surveyor, the son of the first Hilo missionaries, David and Sarah Lyman.

> Soon after four o'clock P.M. on Thursday we experienced a most fearful earthquake. First the earth swayed to and fro from north to south, then from east to west, then round and round, up and down, and finally in every imaginable direction, for several minutes, everything was crashing around, and the trees thrashing as if torn by a hurricane, and there was a sound of a mighty rushing wind. It was impossible to stand; we had to sit on the ground, bracing our hands and feet to keep from being rolled over. We saw what we supposed to be an immense torrent of molten lava, which rushed across the plain below . . . swallowing everything in its way;—trees, houses, cattle, horses, goats, and men, all overwhelmed in an instant. This devouring current passed over a distance of about three miles in as many minutes."[11]

This was known as the "Great Mud Flow of 1868," but it was more of an avalanche.

As is often the case, this awesome earthquake caused a sizable tsunami. According to Coan, the ocean rose six feet above the watermark in some areas and twenty feet along the southern shore. Over one hundred homes were swept away, forty-six people with them. Among the villages that were washed away was the coastal community of Punalu'u, where Shipman had visited his outstation every month or so. Its stone church and houses, wharf, and other buildings were simply swallowed up by the sea. Even portions of the government road that Shipman had once supervised and that followed the shoreline, sank into the disturbed ocean floor.[12]

Kapāpala, being on the more easterly side of Mauna Loa, was spared the sort of damage wreaked on the south and western flanks of the mountain. But whether it was at Kapāpala or elsewhere among Reed's holdings, he suffered sufficient damage to prompt Jane's sister Catherine to write from Jamaica, "That was a very great loss he [Mr. Reed] suffered in the earthquake." Numerous aftershocks were felt at the ranch and for many miles around and lasted for months. So fearful of further terror and damage were a great many residents of Ka'ū that they evacuated to Hilo or Kona, never to return. Ka'ū's present sparse population may be attributed in part to the 1868 disaster.

It was in 1875, seven years after the devastation wrought by nature's volcanic energy, that Willie left Hilo to share with Reed the management of Kapāpala. Because he had been given an interest in the property at the time Reed bought out Richardson two years earlier, he was expected to carry his share of the load. And the load, judging from Willie's many letters to his mother over the next two years, did not consist of management from a ranch office. With advice and direction from his stepfather, Willie was to spend many months between the ranch house he called home, and distant ranges where, along with the cowboys, he would be responsible for frequent cattle drives. Reed divided his time between Hilo and the ranch, well aware that his new ranch hand and partner would need morale building and guidance. He realized that although Willie was eager and ambitious, he was still quite young and would be faced with long, lonely days in remote Kapāpala.

Willie and his stepfather proved to be Jane's faithful correspondents when either or both were at the ranch. Once-a-week letters to the mother or wife were not unusual. Quite often only three days elapsed before another letter went to Hilo by courier, always referred to as the "butterboy," as it was the task of that individual to take to a waiting market in Hilo several of kegs of fresh butter from the ranch. Pack mules were the means of transport, and the butterboy, whose name was never used in the letters, usually made his trips about twice a week. Along with the butter, he could be expected to carry letters to the Reed residence, on his return trip, often the next day, bringing letters from Jane to Willie or Reed. On days when both were at the ranch, Jane had something for each of them.

Those letters from Kapāpala were often written after the writer had had a strenuous day driving cattle, or had come up to the mountainside ranch house on horseback from the steamer landing at Punalu'u. Both writers were faithful in reporting weather conditions in the area, often describing serious droughts, despite the *Hawaiian Gazette's* painting a picture of eternally green pastures. When it rained—well, that was always good news to share. Domestic matters were revealed when Willie would ask his mother to send back with the butterboy some bluing, denim cloth, or something to read. His next letter would thank her for those items, as well as the surprises, goodies from the kitchen, that came back with the butterboy. News of visitors coming to or from the volcano, staying over, and then moving on, frequently filled letters. Sometimes these interruptions caused a strain on ranch operations, but travelers were always made to feel the warmth of a Hawaiian welcome.

"Willie gets along with the boys pretty well," Reed observed, "because Willie spoke Hawaiian very well." His work was almost entirely with the ranch hands, 95 percent of whom were Hawaiians. Their native tongue was the lingua franca of Kapāpala, and it would have been essential for Willie to be fluent in it. This posed no problem, for his early years had been spent in the thoroughly Hawaiian community of Wai'ōhinu, and his playmates had been Hawaiians. It was easily his second language.

A story has come down from Willie's mother of one time when he was returning on horseback to Kapāpala after being in Hilo. Darkness fell, and before long he saw another horseback rider ahead of him on the trail. He spurred his horse until he came abreast of the stranger and they were soon engaged in Hawaiian conversation. When Willie learned that his traveling companion had a great distance still to go, he invited him to spend the night at the ranch house, an invitation the man accepted gladly. The house was dark, and the first thing Willie did was to strike a light for the lantern in the room. No sooner had he done so than the stranger looked at his host with amazement and then uttered, "E' ka haole!!"—loosely translated, "Hey, you're a white man!!"

Extracts from letters reveal success and failure, joy and depression, questions and answers—all providing a loving link. Willie almost always signed his "your loving son, W. H. Shipman." Reed never failed to sign every letter to his wife of seven years, "I am, Your Loving Husband, W. H. Reed."

The following letters are all addressed to Jane, unless otherwise indicated.

Reed, Apr. 9, 1875: "My cough is still bad and I have had no sleep for three days. The sky above Kilauea [Volcano] was very bright last night. I will be home Tuesday for sure but first must look to the sheep shearing."

Reed, May 18: "Willie is at Waiohinu, will be back tonight. Things are so-so. Not what they ought to be. Three of the boys, Kaiue, Kalii and Wailehua are sick, but my cold is better. Other boys are shearing sheep."

At some point early in 1875, Jane seems to have complained to Reed about a matter relating to her children. In a letter to "Dear Jane" while she was visiting at Kapāpala and he remained in Hilo, he wrote, "I think you have little reason to feel bad about your children as I think they are better than average." He then commented that Willie might have overestimated his fitness in being prepared for college in the United States. "I have no doubts it will all be for the best." Reed then shared with Jane the news that an English warship was in the harbor on its mission to observe the transit of Venus. Also that "I have tried hard to collect some money due, but without success. . . . Do not go to work again and make yourself sick. That the Lord may watch over you and guard you from all harm is the sincere prayer of Your Loving Husband."

Willie, June 6, 1875: "I am late with this letter because I was out driving cattle with Noah and Sam. As for Sam, I am sick of him, but don't like to send him away. Noah stopped all night. He was some company for me." Six days later he wrote, "Some strangers stopped by with Akana. They seemed to be pretty good people . . . I suppose Clara will be up next week."

Willie, July 4: "Mr. Reed [Willie, in verbally addressing his stepfather, always used 'Father.' Elsewhere it was always 'Mr. Reed,' the style of the time] leaves here for Hilo tomorrow. Kipi and the Minister of Interior were here last Friday night. Came with a big party, but I did not see them. Was driving cattle. Mr. Reed will tell you all about it. The weather is very dry and the cattle need water very bad . . . I don't see much of Sam now. I believe he is up to Waiohinu . . . trying to start a school. I hope he will stay there and not show himself around here."

Willie, July 11: "Two gentlemen came along Saturday night from the Volcano, enroute to Waiohinu where one of them was going to preach Sunday. Mr. Richardson came along Sunday, bound for Hilo. He stayed for lunch."

Reed, July 15: "Got to the Volcano at 11 pm, stayed over and got to the ranch 4 pm next day. I think Willie gets along with the boys pretty well. They all seem willing to work. Willie has got a nice horse to send in for Clara the next time the butter goes in. . . . My dear Jane, I hope you will forget and forgive the past and look to the future with confidence in the Lord helping me. You need have no fears of the future. You little know how I appreciate the kindness and affection you have shown me. I know you will pray for me."

Reed, July 19: "I was glad to hear from you by the butterboy and to know you were well and not lonesome. I have been driving cattle, all in the rain which we needed badly. . . . Another cattle drive starts up to Kauainapo today and tomorrow. . . . I wish we had news of the reciprocity treaty."

Reed, July 24: "I have been away all day looking after cattle at

Ninole and at the lava. . . . I will not look for Willie before Friday, he need not be in any hurry."

Willie, Aug. 1: "Mr. Richardson and his family came Thursday, stayed all night. There was quite a crowd of them but we managed to stow them away. Mr. Peebles starts for the top of the mountain tomorrow, and Mr. Reed goes to Hilo. So I will be alone again, except for the hands. . . . I hope Clara will have a chance to come over before she goes to Honolulu. . . . I don't think my trip to Hilo did me much good. I wish I had taken a long trip and gone to see Sam Parker [Parker Ranch scion]. Mr. Reed will tell you what is going on. Good night."

Willie, Aug. 9: "Your letter was received. Also one from Mr. Reed. Mr. Hitchcock is here tonight, and also Mr. Berger from Honolulu. . . . I was out to the Lyman place today with one of the boys and planted 90 coffee trees. . . . I am well and hope you are the same."

Reed, Sept. 2: "The steamer got to Punaluu at 1 am. Clara was quite sick. Willie was not down to meet us because he was out driving cattle. It is now four o'clock, and since I had no sleep last night or the morning because of getting freight in the storehouse I am all used up. . . . I hope you will get a little rest and feel better."

Reed, Sept. 5: "The butterboy got here this evening with your letter. I was much disappointed that he did not arrive a day earlier for I wanted to hear from you. I will not be able to leave here before next week. There is so much work to be done. I must be carpenter and mason both. Willie, now that he is through driving cattle for a while, has been helping me with the masonry. . . . I am sorry you are not getting better. You must take it easy, you know you are not too strong. . . . I am not aware that your children are worse than other children, and it is only God who knows who is numbered among his children. I hope you will not get looking at the darker side of things, but the state of your health makes you despondent. I would write more but I am very tired."

Willie, Sept. 13: "We have been having some trouble with the boys but it is all right now. Mr. Reed will tell you all about it. He and George Castle start for Hilo tomorrow. . . . I have been up on the mountainside this past week seeing about the sheep and goats. . . . If you write Ollie tell him I will write as soon as I can."

To Willie from Jane in Hilo, Oct. 11: "My Dear Son; I don't write because I haven't anything new and strange to communicate for there is a perfect dearth of news. . . . I worked so much in the flower garden that I am very stiff and can hardly stoop today. . . . I wish when you go up to Waiohinu you would get me a slip from that rosebush Mrs. Spencer took from father's grave.[13] . . . Clara is playing the organ, it sounds so nice, she plays very well. Don't you feel tired on the go so much? I feel tired for you."

Reed, Oct. 13: "Willie will go to Waiohinu for cattle on Monday and not return until Friday. He will have 8 of the boys with him. . . . I counted 654 goats below the ridge, so the herd has increased 244 in two months. I see Willie's coffee trees are all dead. I think they were not planted well. . . . Take things easy like your old man and you will feel better for it."

Willie, Oct. 17: "Mr. Reed got here Saturday. I had been up on the mountain for two weeks. Tomorrow I have to go to Waiohinu to get some cattle. If it was not so near the end of the year I would like to take a vacation. I did not enjoy myself when I was last in Hilo. Sam Van Cleve wants me to go down to Honolulu. But I don't think Mr. Reed would like me to leave the ranch now."

Reed, Oct. 20: "I was rather disappointed last night in not getting a letter from you. I was up to the sheep ranch and got home at 8 pm. but no letter. I hope you are well. As for myself I felt tired after my trip to the mountain. The butterboy will not be back til Saturday as he went to Keaau to visit his dying mother. Which makes about ten mothers of his that have died before."

Subsequent letters from Reed filled Jane in on ranch developments and weather reports, such as being rained in on the mountain and being shaken up by earthquakes—nothing new, as Kapāpala rests on Mauna Loa's flank.

Willie, Nov. 1: "I am going back up on the mountain again. When Mr. Reed comes back again I will go into Hilo and then make Sam Van-Cleve a visit in Honolulu. But don't tell Clara, I want to surprise her. I received a letter from Ollie last week and will send it to you. . . . If Emma is in Hilo please give her my aloha."

In mid-November, Reed told Jane that things were not going as well at the ranch as might be. It was the first real sign of any friction between stepson and stepfather: "Willie will not attend to the place but instead goes on to the mountain after bullocks, which he must not do in the future. His place is here at the ranch, at least be here every night. . . . I think Willie had no business being in Puna, that it was his business to stop in Hilo and pay a little attention to you and the business at the beach. I think it is better that the schooner did not get away as one week is plenty for Willie in Honolulu. I wish he would meet with some young lady he would like better than himself."

In an ensuing letter Reed indicated that the dissension between him and Willie had become an issue with Jane, and he sought to end it. "What you say about Willie, I will not say anything. The Lord who will judge me at the last day will be better able to decide. I have no other object in view but his own interests. I leave [him] alone not from choice but necessity, and had no particular business for him to attend to. But his presence there while in Hilo I thought might be a benefit, as he has or ought to have as great an interest in the business as I have and he should get acquainted with the people, which is quite important to our business. This I asked him to do and look after you. What I wrote you I do not know at this time as I have enough to take all my mind and I am not as retentive in memory as I have been, but hope to get over it by and by. . . . We had a very heavy earthquake here. The ground rose and fell so that my horse went from side to side on the road. . . . Give my love to Emma, Noah and Cora and with lots to yourself."

Willie, Dec. 17: "Your letter came by steamer Thursday. I thank you and Emma very much for the birthday presents [his twenty-first]. I don't feel any older than a year ago. I have been very busy since I came back driving cattle. I also have plenty of other work to keep me busy. There is so much to do here I need some one to help me. Bishop is not worth a fig."

Willie, Jan. 16, 1876: "I suppose the lumber vessel has got in by now and you will soon be over here. I have got Kauila at work cleaning house but I don't know what kind of a job he will make of it. He does not wash my clothes clean at all, in fact he does nothing well unless I am around. . . . Mr. Lancaster, an Englishman, was here last Sunday. Joe Crediford was along this week with a sister of his from Cal. and her daughter. They went to the volcano. I have somebody here most all the time. I wish they would not come so often."

In March of 1876, Jane, looking for a change of scenery and pace, spent some time at the ranch. Reed wrote to her from Hilo, sending regards from friends such as the Allens and Austins, and mentioned that he and Claus Spreckles, the financier and sugar baron from California, had gone to church together. He told her that with his letter he was sending supplies such as blankets, cartridges, honey, and one hundred stamps. He wrote that they were selling much of the beef in Hilo and only one keg of butter remained. He concluded by saying he would start for the ranch one week later and would be there by Tuesday.

Reed to Willie at Keaīwa, Mar. 3: I have not been very well since I got in [to Hilo] but am feeling better. I will be over one week from tomorrow. Aloha nui loa from your Father."

Willie, Mar. 18: "Your letter came last week but I was up to Ainapo lassoing. We did not get back until after dark Saturday. Mrs. Richardson came along this afternoon on her way to Hilo. I will send this by her. . . . The woman who keeps house does not do it very well, not half as well as Mrs. Halau and she was not much. We need a housekeeper very bad. . . . Is Clara going to come over here before she goes back to the States? . . . We are all well and hope this finds you and Clara the same."

Willie, Apr. 4: "Mr. Reed and I have just come up from the landing. I guess the steamer got in early. Also he looks as if he had been drawn through a not [sic] hole, he is poor and pale. I wish you and Clara would make us some denim britches. They last better than anything I have had yet. If you are too busy please buy 10 yards and send by the butterboy and I will have them made here. . . . Ching Sai [the cook] is very anxious to get back to Hilo. I can cook a great deal better than before. . . . We are all well. Your son, Will." (This is the first time he signed himself other than Wm. H. Shipman. In subsequent letters he went back and forth.)

Willie, May 23: "I have been limping around with a bad heal [sic] for the past week. I skinned it going after sheep. It is very painful nights. . . . I suppose Clara will come over with Mr. Reed next time. I close now with love to Clara and a good share for yourself."

Willie, June 18: "Since Mr. Reed went into Hilo I have been thinking of his selling the ranch and what I would do if he does. . . . If I could borrow the money I would like to buy out his part. I think I could make the ranch pay. I do not think there is any business I like better than this. I think Luther Wilcox would buy one third, and I could take the other if Mr. Reed did not ask more than $45,000 for his part. . . . I do not like the idea of Rufus Lyman getting the place."

Willie to Reed, June 26: "Dear Father: The butterboy got back all right. I am sending in 33 head of cattle this time. Rufus started in on Saturday. I went as far as the Volcano by way of Ainapo. There have been a good many sheep lost. We are still having very dry weather, everything is dried up. . . . I will ship by steamer this week about 70 or 80 hides. I will not write Mother this time."

In the second week of July 1876, Willie and Charley Richardson went to Waiʻōhinu, where they visited briefly with the missionary, Rev. Pogue. The following day they visited friends, the Browns, near Kahuku. He wrote his mother that, in the afternoon, "We went up to a cave in the woods and there were about seventeen or twenty men's skulls. We went in as far as we could and built a fire so we could go in further. We went in and saw three grave sites. Then we went back to Waiohinu and started out the next morning for Kapapala."

Friction between Willie and Reed surfaced again, possibly because Reed still felt that Willie was not keeping his nose to the grindstone. Word that Ollie was not doing too well at Amherst may also have contributed to Reed's dissatisfaction. He seems to have shared this sentiment with Jane, who may have felt that she had done too much for her children, even spoiled them. Willie wrote his mother on the subject.

Willie, Aug. 16, 1876: "You spoke of helping your children too much. I do not think [you have]. I wish now I had never gone in with Mr. Reed. He thinks I am depending upon him for a living. I wish he would take my one-third and keep it and pay me wages for the time I have been here. I think I can earn my own living. If I ever get out of this I am going . . . to the States. I think I was foolish to ever go in with Mr. Reed. He can talk very good with me, but talks against me to other people. I do not like that. I must go to work now and must stop."

The disaccord must have been resolved, for Willie made no further reference to it, nor did Reed. Willie also put to rest any desire to strike out on his own.

Reed, Aug. 23: "Richardson was here Monday to assess taxes. The ranch, stock, buildings and all is assessed at $67,200. . . . I hear that the reciprocity treaty is laid over til next year. That will close up the firm of Hitchcock & Co. and perhaps some others. . . . The home here is looking nice, all papered up. I am putting on an addition to the house by the gate as three of the boys have got married. Road workers have been working on the road today from here to beyond the mud flow. . . . I am anxious to hear from Clara."

Willie, Sept. 12: "Old Tiger is dead. He was hooked by a big bull when we were up to Ainapo and he died a few days later. . . . I expect Mr. Reed today so will not write to him now."

Willie, Oct. 17: "I got a letter from Ollie last week and will send it to you. I suppose Mr. Reed will be back here next week on the steamer. I hope he will not sell the ranch to Rufus. . . . We had quite a feast here at the church on Saturday night last. It was to raise money for Mr. Kauhane's salary. They got, I believe, $60.00."

This was the second indication that Reed was thinking of selling the ranch, although his letter regarding its assessed value was also a clue. Apparently, he felt that the returns from the ranch were not commensurate with the amount of energy being pumped into it. His health was in decline, and at sixty-two he found cattle driving tiring. At the end of October 1876, he concluded a sale of the ranch to businessman and banker Charles R. Bishop. Bishop paid the ranch owners (Reed and Willie) the sum of $75,000 for the ranch lease, livestock, buildings, "and all appurtenances."[14] Two months later Bishop sold the same property in its entirety to the Hawaiian Agriculture Company for $120,000.[15]

Willie, Dec. 7: "We had quite a houseful tonight. Mr. Reed is here and has the small room. Rufus has the *makai* room. Henry & wife at the end & Eddie the centre room. Another man is upstairs and I have the sofa. . . . Mr. Reed will tell you how I am getting along. Good night."

Two days before Christmas, Reed wrote Jane, "I never hated to leave home as much as I did this time. . . . I hope you will have a good time at Christmas."

Reed owned a much smaller tract at neighboring Keaīwa, where he continued with scaled-down ranching. But he had also shown an interest in growing sugarcane. Like many others in Hawai'i at the time, he saw the possibility of good profits in several business prospects now that the long-drawn-out Reciprocity Treaty was signed and the tax on sugar exported to the United States removed.

Willie's next letter to his mother was from Keaīwa on December 21: "Your letter received. I expected one from Mr. Reed but did not get any. I suppose he is very busy. I am getting along quite well in cane planting. I like this kind of work first rate. We have got quite a number of acres in now, and will have ten or more by January. . . . I get the Honolulu paper here but it does not come regular. I wish you would send me something to read.—magazines or Cal. papers when you and Mr. Reed are done with them. . . . I cannot write Mr. Reed this time. I enclose a transfer of Honokoa's lease for Mr. Reed."

Willie, Jan. 7, 1877: "I am getting along very well with the cane. I hope to get done sometime next month. I had quite a long letter from Clara. She said she had heard I was engaged to Cora, and congratulated me, and thanks me for giving her such a nice sister. I wonder where she heard this report from because I have never had much to do with Cora and don't know who would start such a report."

Willie, Feb. 2, 1877: "I will try to get a slip of that rose you wanted from Mr. Spencer before I go back to Hilo. . . . Mr. Brewer [Charles] is picking out a place to put the mill.[16] Today they were looking about bringing water down. . . . Mr. Reed says you will leave Hilo on the 21st of next month. I must try to get over a week or two before that if we do not finish by that time. [Willie was alluding to plans for Reed and Jane to visit the mainland.] Rufus has bothered us a good deal in this work or we would have been done by now. He is a regular granny. I don't think he knows much."

The letters cease at this point. Kapāpala was no longer a Reed operation. He had enough work in his other properties and Hilo construction jobs to warrant his presence, and Willie's assistance, closer to Hilo. Furthermore, he had plans to take Jane on an ocean trip to the United States.

# 14

## *Expansion*

MARRIED: SHIPMAN—JOHNSON.
*In Honolulu, April 29,*
*by the Rev. S. C. Damon. W. H. Shipman, Esq. of Hilo. Hawaii,*
*to Miss M. E. Johnson of Honolulu.*
— The Friend, MAY 1, 1879

At the very time Reed was midway into the coastal shipping business, Willie Shipman was involved in the business of getting married. This was a milestone that surely gratified his stepfather, who at least three times had expressed in writing his wish that Willie should wed. Surely Reed had verbally expressed this desire to Willie more than three times. Willie's tendency toward shyness had been mentioned earlier by Clara. In one of her letters she was quite direct in expressing her personal concern: "Are you just as quiet as you used to be?—and hardly talked at all with any one? If you are, you must try and break yourself of that habit. I know it will be hard, for I have to do that myself. At times I feel as though I did not want to talk with my room mate at all, and I know it makes it unpleasant for her. I suppose it is selfishness on my part, for I ought to do all I can for others. I wish I had a more social disposition."

The above news item gladdened the heart of William Reed and brought to Jane memories of a young female student she once had in her private school. The officiating minister, the Reverend Samuel Chenery Damon, was the editor of *The Friend* as well as pastor of the Bethel Union Church, where the ceremony was performed. (This was originally known as the First Foreign Church, and for many years was Honolulu's only church for English-speaking residents. Most of the city's haole couples were married there.)

A dozen or so years before, Jane Shipman had had among her hand-ful of "scholars" a fourteen-year-old part-Hawaiian girl named Mary Eliza-

This is to Certify that _W. A. Shipman, Esq,_ of _Hilo, Hawaii,_ was legally married to _Miss M. E. Johnson_ of _Honolulu,_ in accordance with the Laws of the Hawaiian Kingdom, on _the 29, th, of April,_ A.D. _1879_ in Honolulu,

by _Sam'l C. Damon_

Pastor Bethel Union Church.

" What therefore God hath joined together, let not man put asunder."—JESUS CHRIST.

The marriage certificate for William Shipman and Mary Elizabeth Johnson was signed by Samuel Damon, who officiated. Damon was one of Hawai'i's early missionaries, having arrived in Honolulu in 1842. His family is still represented in Hawai'i.

William and Mary Shipman were married in Honolulu's Bethel Union Church, once known as the First Foreign Church. It was destroyed in 1900 by a fire that consumed much of the city. (HMCS)

beth Johnson. Jane's three children were among the students: one of them, William, was ten years old in 1865.

Mary Johnson's Caucasian lineage can be traced back to the middle of the eighteenth century in Great Britain.[1] Her paternal grandfather was John Davis, who departed from Wales around 1810 to search for his Welsh uncle, Isaac Davis, who had left England as a sailor.[2] Isaac had the misfortune to be in Hawai'i on the vessel *Fair American* when, in 1790, it was attacked by Hawaiians seeking vengeance for an earlier attack on a Hawaiian chief by Captain Simon Metcalf of the brig *Eleanora*. Isaac Davis was the sole survivor of the attack, but just barely: he was found tied to a canoe, half-blind, and more dead than alive.[3] After his rescue by Hawaiians, he later became an adviser to King Kamehameha I, and in this capacity was made a chief by his sovereign. At this time Kamehameha was engaged in war with other chiefs on his own Hawai'i island and was planning to conquer the remaining islands in the chain. Davis, along with a John Young, boatswain of the ship *Eleanora*, was "detained" by King Kamehameha I and, like Davis, became a trusted adviser. Both men served their king well in both diplomatic affairs and such military matters as training in the use of cannons and other European weaponry. Their contributions gave Kamehameha the upper hand in the eventual conquest of the archipelago.[4]

Isaac Davis died suddenly and mysteriously in 1810, probably the victim of poisoning by jealous court followers of the king.[5] The young John Davis arrived in the Sandwich Islands from Wales that same year, but too late to find his long-sought-after uncle. John learned that Isaac had left two daughters and one son, George Heulu Davis, who lived on Hawai'i island. John made his way there and presented letters of introduction from Wales. His half-Hawaiian cousin, George Davis, invited him to remain on the island and make his home there. He did so, settling on a piece of land in Waimea given him by George; nor was it long before he was accepted as a nephew of the deceased but well-known Isaac Davis.

On one of his trips on what was now his home island, John met and was attracted to a young woman named Kauwe. He asked his friend Kuakini, then governor of the island, for her hand in marriage. They were married in Kona by Kuakini and later moved to Waimea to live.[6]

Kauwe was the daughter of a couple named Kaukamoa and Nahulanui. The latter's parents, Kaimakuawela and Oheleluiaikamoku, had come from the Lahaina district of Maui, probably around 1770.[7] Kauwe must have had the blood of *ali'i* (chiefs) in her veins. Her great-grandson, Herbert Shipman, recalled meeting her when he was a small boy, around 1896. "She was pure Hawaiian," said Shipman, "and I don't know what her rank was, but the regular Hawaiians only approached her on their knees."

In 1821 John Davis and Kauwe had a daughter whom they named Eliza. She would become the wife of a William Johnson, an Englishman who had emigrated to California, where he later had land interests in the Feather River valley. Later he found his way to Kona, where he met and married Eliza Davis.[8] Even though Eliza only had half-Hawaiian blood in her, apparently it was blue enough to warrant that "the regular Hawaiians" depart from her walking backward. William and Eliza Johnson had five children, all born on the Johnson ranch at Kainaliu in south Kona. The first child was a daughter born in 1852. They named her Mary Kahiwaaialii. The name means "the sacred vine only the chief eats." She was christened by the renowned "Father" Lorenzo Lyons in Waimea's Imiola Church. The name Elizabeth, for Eliza, was added to Mary (the Miss M. E. Johnson of the Shipman wedding notice.)

Whatever the amount of blood from Hawaiian nobility that flowed in the Davis–Johnson veins, it was enough to make a connection with

Kauwe, the grandmother of Mary Johnson Shipman, was born about 1780 and may have seen King Kamehameha I when both lived in Kona. She lived to be about a hundred and four. Her full name was: Kauwe-a-Kanoa-akaka-wale-no-Haleakala-ka-uwe-kekini-o-Koolau. *Kauwe* means "the cry." The full name comes from the story of a much-loved queen who died on Maui. Many who loved her mourned her death, and their cries were so loud that they were heard all the way from Mount Haleakala on Maui to the Koolau range on the island of Oahu. (Kona Historical Society)

Princess Ruth Ke'elikōlani, the hefty, hot-tempered former governess of Hawai'i island whom the Reverend Shipman had once confronted in a letter. The Davis relationship would have brought little Mary Elizabeth Johnson into a friendship with Princess Likelike, who was about the same age. (Miriam Likelike was the sister of King Kalākaua and Queen Lili'uokalani, and became the mother of Princess Ka'iulani of Robert Louis Stev-

Eliza Davis Johnson, the daughter of Kauwe, was half Hawaiian and the mother of Mary Johnson Shipman. (Kona Historical Society)

enson fame.)[9] As children, Mary and Likelike sometimes met in Kona when the young princess visited there from Honolulu. Ruth, who was looked upon by the young girls as their "aunty," enjoyed their company, and they hers. She would insist that the two girls sleep with her, one on each side. At Ka'awaloa, on a steep place above where Captain Cook's monument now stands, Ruth enjoyed jumping down into the water below with one of the two little girls under each arm. Ruth's four hundred pounds would make a majestic splash, recounted Mary Johnson Shipman many years later.[10]

The years between Mary's attending Jane Shipman's school and her later residence in Honolulu, where she was married, are obscure. It is known that for a while she resided with the well-known Ward sisters, who lived with their family at the Old Plantation, then at the edge of the city. How she and Willie met as young adults after a space of several years is not revealed in any of their letters. But meet again they did, when she was twenty-seven, and he, when he went to Honolulu to marry her, was twenty-four.

After the marriage the couple moved to Hilo and for some time lived in the Reed residence. In November of 1879 a life was taken from

Mary Shipman's father was William Johnson, an
English-born entrepreneur who came to Hawai'i after
leaving his mining interests in Feather River, California. He became a successful rancher and landowner
in the Kona district, where he married Eliza Davis.

that house, and on the very same day another was born into it. William
Reed died on the evening of the eleventh, only a few hours after the birth
of a boy to Mary and Willie Shipman. They named him William Reed
Shipman.

One of Willie's first entrepreneurial enterprises was getting into
what was considered the lucrative sugar business. He was already experienced in the planting of cane and had been pleased with the results on
several acres at Keaīwa a couple of years earlier. Thanks to the Reciprocity Treaty, it seemed that many businesses were becoming prosperous:
shippers, service agencies, planters, retailers, wholesalers, and sugar-mill
operators. But not everyone fared well, for a variety of reasons. Some
were novices at the complicated business of growing, harvesting, milling,

and manufacturing of cane syrup into raw sugar. Others were completely inexperienced in management and finance matters. Laborers in great numbers were necessary but often wanting, as were accommodations for them. Transportation raised a serious obstacle on at least two fronts: first, to the mill from the fields, where oxen and carts frequently became mired deep in mud from the rains so necessary to growing cane but otherwise a plague; then there was the need to transport the unrefined sugar, often from remote mills, to a suitable harbor for shipping. Trial and error soon thinned out the ranks of sugar manufacturers; the only survivors were the strong, stubborn, and well financed.[11]

When Willie gingerly entered the sugar business in 1878, he had the good sense not to go it alone. He chose to form a partnership with retired German sea captain Johannes Emil Elderts, long a Hawai'i resident and known to be an energetic and capable entrepreneur.

Elderts had been born in Germany in 1818.[12] He was six years older than Willie's own father. After going to sea and eventually earning his captain's papers, in 1854 he decided to make Hawai'i his home. This was the year before Willie was born on Maui. Elderts first became engaged in the lumber business in Hilo, then ventured into cattle, for which there was a substantial market in hides. When Reed and Richardson acquired Kapāpala, he worked for them, ranching and hunting wild cattle in the high forests. He also gathered and marketed *pulu*, for which there was then a ready market. It is likely that Elderts and Willie first met at Kapāpala. Two years after Willie left Kapāpala and Keīwa, the partnership of Shipman & Elderts was formalized.[13]

Early documents reveal that as early as 1878 the partners established what would become the Waiākea Plantation, but not before laying out their prospects for the operation to the Commissioner of Crown Lands. From him they sought written consent to lease the necessary Waiākea acreage to commence the business. Consent was granted, as witnesses a receipt for $400 paid the commissioner by Shipman & Elderts for lease of future sugarcane lands.[14]

A year later Elderts' name no longer appeared as a partner of Waiākea Plantation, the name of Charles Richardson replacing it. The start-up date of the plantation under the management of Shipman and Richardson is recorded as 1879. However, this arrangement lasted only about a year, possibly two. There was nothing wrong with the locale; the fields were fertile and lay close to Hilo Bay, a convenience for shipping the raw sugar. But the partners appeared to have had a vision of troubles ahead. Although Richardson may have remained for a short period with the new owners, by 1881 Willie had disposed of his own Waiākea interests.

Willie never went back into sugar. The fact that there were about 125 plantations and mills already operating in the Islands may have been a storm warning to Willie, Elderts, and, later, Richardson. The rest of Willie's life would be devoted to what he knew best, cattle ranching. Archival records show that, beginning as early as 1879, even while still involved with Waiākea, Shipman & Elderts rented numerous large parcels of government land for ranching, most of it located in lower Puna between Makuʻu and Kapoho. Included in such tracts were Hālona, Kaʻohe, Pōpōki, Pualoala, Pūʻālaʻa, Pohoiki, and Keonepoko Nui.[15]

The partners were enterprising enough to become their own retailers of beef. In July 1879 they were granted, for twenty dollars, a butcher's license, a requirement of the ever-involved minister of the interior. In acknowledging their payment and enclosing the license and bond, the office of the ministry reminded the partners that they "still owe[d] $2 for postage."[16]

The above early land leases were granted while Willie and Mary were still living in Hilo, which then had a population approaching eight thousand. This was one–tenth of the total population for all the Islands. A measure of growth in the area was the launching, in 1882, of the Hilo and Hawaii Telephone & Telegraph Company. It provided services not only to Hilo and its neighbor to the north, ʻOʻokala, but also to ʻŌlaʻa and Puna, which more and more was to become Shipman country.[17]

Although sugar was the mainstay of Hilo and an impetus toward its future growth, the community was also becoming attractive to visitors, some of whom stayed on to become residents. The charm of the area was captured by a chronicler of the era, E. S. Baker, in "A Trip to the Sandwich Islands." He wrote:

Hilo is an attractive and tropical looking village, with an aura of thrift and prosperity everywhere noticeable in the taste surrounding its comfortable residences. The courthouse occupies the center of a square, attractive for its beautiful lawn and exotic trees, and adds much to the beauty of Hilo. Here under one roof are the Post-office, Governor Kipi's and Sheriff Severances offices, with the police courts etc. Its location is central and convenient for the public business. . . . A more beautiful panorama than that seen from the deck of a steamer approaching Hilo would be hard to find."[18]

One of those comfortable residences was occupied by William and Jane
Reed and, for a while, by the next generation of William and Mary Shipman after their marriage. It was the same balconied residence that Reed
had constructed on Waiānuenue Street in 1868, the year he and Jane
were married.

Shortly after the birth of their first child, Willie and Mary wanted
to make their home at Kapoho ranch, at least temporarily. It was about
twenty-five miles southeast of Hilo, part of the Reed estate, and Jane
Reed was its legal owner. Originally the property had come into the
hands of Reed and Richardson in 1869 by a lease from Judge L. Kaina, its
owner. Three years later the two lessees added to that acreage through a
thirteen-year lease from Charles Kana'ina (father of Lunalilo) for two
hundred dollars a year. Kapoho was in a sparsely settled portion of the
lower Puna district, but was blessed with some fairly fertile soil. The carpet of green vegetation was excellent for raising beef cattle. Later a dairy
would be added to Kapoho Ranch.

In 1881, when Ollie returned from college in America (his first trip
home since he left for Punahou), it was Jane's intention to have him
manage Kapoho in place of a man named Wood. For unknown reasons,
Jane wished to dismiss Wood and replace him with her second son. It was
then up to Jane to seek legal assistance. This she did by writing Judge
Lyman that "Ollie served notice that Mr. Wood must leave at the end of
the month, that Ollie was to take his place & I have given him power of
attorney to attend to anything of the kind. My nerves are not [illegible]

Kapoho Ranch, where the newlyweds lived for a while after their marriage. Pencil sketch by the artist Charles Furneaux. (Lyman Memorial Museum)

... it makes me darn sick ... I must have help. .... If I am wrong I want to know it. For I wish to be honest & just & true."

Judge Lyman responded at once, informing Jane that notice to Mr. Wood of his dismissal could not take place without the knowledge or consent of Mr. Coan (who, with Jane, had been an executor of Reed's estate). Lyman added, "If your son [Ollie] wishes to learn the business and he is to carry on he assuredly can do so with Mr. Coan's consent, and as soon as he has been in the business long enough to take Mr. Wood's place, then the latter could be dismissed by the mutual action of the disputants."[19] The upshot of all this was that Willie took over the management of Kapoho Ranch. As for Mr. Wood, he and Ollie must have resolved their differences, for later the two joined in business ventures of their own.

The partnership of Shipman & Elderts continued to run cattle on lands apart from Kapoho but in the same area. During 1880 and 1881, Willie, Mary, and the small Shipmans spent much of their time at the Kapoho home. But frequent horseback trips were made to Hilo, there to look after other matters of interest to Willie as well as to visit family. Their own little family had expanded beyond their first child.

Another boy, Robert, died in infancy due to a freakish accident. Mary was breast-feeding him when she was bitten on her breast by a centipede. Scarcely feeling it, she brushed it off and resumed nursing. But its poison was transmitted from mother to infant. Death occurred within hours. The young parents were devastated, but some months later rejoiced in the birth of their first girl. She was given her mother's name, Mary Elizabeth.

The trips that Willie and Mary made to and from Kapoho took them along what was fancifully called by some "the king's highway," though it was at best a horse trail along the coast or over higher ground where cliffs intervened. Midway between Kapoho and Hilo was the small Hawaiian fishing village of Hā'ena. About a half-mile inland was another small community called Kea'au (not to be confused with the present village of Kea'au, built farther inland and formerly known as 'Ōla'a). The Hā'ena portion was endowed with one of the few attractive beaches for many miles around. A beautiful lagoon, fed by fresh mountain-spring waters, bordered the beach and was itself enhanced by an abundant grove of coconut trees and other colorful native flora. On one of the many trips when they passed through Hā'ena, Mary Shipman told her young husband, "I would very much like to have a home here someday."

# 15

# *Business at Large*

One of the first letters Willie received after moving to Hilo from Kapāpala and Keaīwa was from his sister, Clara, in her second semester at
Abbot Academy in Andover, Massachusetts. "Now that the ranch has
been sold what do you expect to do? I want you to write me and let me
know all about what you are doing." She related that she had spent
Thanksgiving with Ollie and met some interesting young men. She especially expressed the hope that "nothing will happen to prevent Mother
and Father from coming here next summer." She shared with Willie his
strong aversion to mainland weather. "I don't blame you for not liking
winters while you were here, for I dislike them *very much*."

Once Reed had sold Kapāpala, he turned his attention to pleasing
his wife by fulfilling her long-held desire to visit friends and relatives in
the United States whom she had not seen for nearly a quarter-century.
Included would be a trip to Jamaica to see her only surviving sister,
Catherine, wife of missionary Rev. Samuel Jones. This would also be a
vacation for Reed, a long overdue respite from years of ranching and construction work, among other businesses. Jane thought it might improve
his health.

They made reservations on the SS *City of New York* for departure
from Honolulu to San Francisco on March 29, 1877.[1] Prior to sailing the
Reeds had a week to themselves in Honolulu. The day before leaving,
they attended the funeral of Charles Kana'ina, father of the late King
Lunalilo and one of Hawai'i's royal chiefs. Jane observed: "There were a
great many out but very little display. The coffin was beautiful. At first
the king [Kalākaua] forbade *kahili* [royal standards] but he must have
given his consent to three, as they carried that number. The Prince
[Leleiohoku] has been very sick, . . . was able to sit up yesterday. It won't
be long before all the chiefs are dead." (Leleiohoku, also known as William Pitt, was the brother of Kalākaua and Princess Lili'uokalani. He was
next in line for the throne, but died ten days after Jane Reed made these
observations.)

When Jane reached the Illinois she had left in 1854, she found changes everywhere. What she had remembered as small villages or hamlets were now budding towns and small cities. Growth could be measured by the iron bridge that crossed the Mississippi River joining Illinois with Hannibal, Missouri. Railroads now criss-crossed Illinois, some over Shipman farmland. They had carried many individuals and families she once knew farther west, especially to the promised land called California. Among those who had sought brighter horizons were some of the Stobies and Shipmans. The latter were the second generation in Illinois, Jane's contemporaries, the siblings and cousins of her first husband. (Her own parents had died even before she was first married.) Reuben and Clarissa Shipman, whose warmth and loving concern had comforted her for many long years, had been gone nearly a decade. Reacquainting herself with family and former friends in the Pike County area and introducing her husband of nine years was, for Jane, a long-delayed happiness.

Moving on to New England, the couple traveled to Amherst to visit their long-absent Ollie. After that they went to see Clara at Andover. Clara wrote Willie of her excitement and delight at having her mother and Mr. Reed pay her a visit of two days and one night. Brief as it was, it was a source of joy to all three. The couple's next stop was New York City, where they were delayed for a week before boarding their ship for the West Indies. Intervening days were occupied by visiting some of Reed's acquaintances in the area.

The ship took them not directly to Jamaica, "but to Hayti." Jane described their brief stay at Port-au-Prince as "very hot as we lay at anchor." By transferring to the Royal Mail packet *Maselle*, they arrived at Kingston the following day. After a couple of days' rest, a two horse carriage took them on a five-hour journey to the village of Beverley, where the Jones family lived. Jane had earlier suggested that Catherine and her family might meet them at Kingston upon their ship's arrival. In her reply to Jane, who obviously knew nothing about the geography of Jamaica, Catherine pointed out that it would be quite impractical for a family of five to travel there and back on horseback, a round trip of sixty miles.

Jane was quite shocked to see the change in her sister, whom she had not seen since 1847, when Catherine and Samuel accepted the ministerial assignment in Jamaica. "I should not have known her," she wrote. "She looks so pale and thin. No color in her face but deathly pallor." Catherine was the one sibling with whom Jane had kept up a reasonable correspondence over the intervening thirty years. Their sister Jenette, wife of the Reverend Weller, had died some years earlier, as had sister

Margaret. Both Jane and Catherine complained that their brothers were poor correspondents. They also had reason to complain about the mails, which took months to travel between Hawai'i and Jamaica. Catherine once wrote Jane about a letter that had taken fourteen months to reach her "from the Sandwich Islands." Not only letters, but valued newspapers were delayed, and often completely lost.

The surviving letters reveal that over the years the two sisters and the Reverend Samuel Jones had shared their experiences and family concerns. They compared customs, food, climate, clothing, and education. Samuel Jones once wrote: "There is a great deal of similarity between your people in the Islands and our people here in Jamaica. They are capable of much improvement for this world and the world to come, but to get them to improve much for either is a very difficult thing."

Earlier letters from Jamaica disclosed that the Jones family lived a very frugal life. Once, when asked by Jane to send some "likenesses" of her children, Catherine had to refuse, "being poor of purse at present." And whereas Jane and William Shipman had received support from their church affiliation, the Joneses were dependent on the members of their small, and poor, congregation. Also, the Jones family included more children. Three of the six died, one whose name had been Sarah Shipman Jones, "named after your dear departed husband." Another girl, Lydia, died at thirteen and was mourned by her frail mother as "my helpmate, my joy, my delight."

The Reeds' month-long visit was a welcome tonic to the somewhat isolated and deprived Jones family. Jane sensed that the previous misfortunes of the family lay heavily upon them, and before Jane and William departed they brought cheer to Catherine. It is more than likely that William Reed tried to lighten their burden with a monetary gift.

In the weeks the two couples and the Jones children spent together there was, thanks to rainy weather, more than enough time for conversation. In catching up on years past and exchanging the highlights of those years, Catherine remarked that "it was indeed a very great loss that Mr. Reed sustained by the [1868] earthquake." Jane wrote home that "it rained almost constantly the time we were there. I was not able to go out but once and then we got a good soaking." She also found the Jamaica climate hot and uncomfortable. "We were glad to get away without getting the fever," the illness which had carried off the three Jones children. But Jane was not one to be discouraged by oppressive heat and a rainfall that far exceeded Hilo's. She reported: "Jamaica is the most hilly and romantic place a person can possibly conceive of. It is all hills and valleys."

In late June, back in New York, Jane wrote Willie from the Grand Hotel of their plan to visit New Haven friends, then go on to Boston to meet Ollie and Clara again. "I hope to get letters when we get to Boston as we have not heard from you since we left. President Hayes is having a great time in Boston, he was here [New York] the day we arrived." Their American journey ended with a long train trip to San Francisco where they boarded their steamer, *The City of Sidney*, for home.[2] Eight days later, on October 18, they were back in Honolulu, only a day and a night from Hilo—weather and seas permitting.

The Jamaican climate had done nothing to restore Reed to the good health he had once known. But after his return he was not long in rolling up his sleeves and tending to land matters, merchandising, and construction. A serious tidal wave had hit Hilo that summer, but apparently Reed's store and lumberyard were undamaged. He was quite satisfied that Willie had looked after the shop in the manner expected of him during his four-month absence. Nor did Reed's malaise deter him from venturing into a new enterprise. He sized up the local economic situation and decided there was a real need for improved coastal shipping on the long eastern coast of Hawai'i Island. His several years of shipping cattle and hides from Punalu'u to Hilo and supplies on return trips convinced him that maritime service in the region could be bettered, and he was the man to make it happen.

More from the standpoint of profit was the indisputable reality that the new Reciprocity Treaty of 1876 had sparked the development of numerous sugar plantations on all major islands, particularly large and fertile Hawai'i.[3] Most of these plantations had their mills near the coast and needed a way to ship their sugar out to Hilo and receive a wide variety of supplies in return.

Reed saw the need for timely and economical transportion by water between east Hawai'i's mill towns. His timing was on the mark. The "Sugar Boom" had not only created new plantations but also camp communities to house and service the numerous field and mill laborers. Retail and wholesale outlets sprang up and prospered beyond his initial hopes. Reed was familiar with the several landings up and down the eastern coast of the island of Hawai'i. To the north of Hilo were Onomea, Laupāhoehoe, Pāpa'ikou, Pepe'ekeo, Honomū, Hakalau, Pāpa'aloa, 'O'ōkala, Pā'auhau, Koholālele, Honoka'a, and Kukuihaele. Many of these landings were located at the entrances to the large ravines that notched many of east Hawai'i's slopes. To the south of the Hilo port were Keauhou, Pohoiki, Punalu'u, and Honu'apo. Sugar would be shipped from some of these landings, but so would cattle and hides. Early on, sugar was shipped out of Pohoiki, and so were coffee and rubber, and probably *awa* (a narcotic) used to make quinine. The remains of an old coffee mill in the Pohoiki area testify to that product's being carried out on coasters. Vessels other than Reed's also provided services to these many landings. No one coaster served all of them, but probably worked alternate ports.

Reed already had a headstart in the coastal shipping business. He had his own Reed's Landing at Waiākea where coasters could moor and two large warehouses to protect and store incoming and outgoing cargo.[4] The body of water that harbored shallow-draft vessels was first known as Kanakea. It eventually came to be called Reeds Bay, a name that remains on current maps of Hilo Bay. Today Reeds Bay is an official state harbor for small boats and is widely used by recreational vessels of that class.

Late in 1877, Reed moved to purchase from San Francisco a two-masted schooner, the *Fanny*. Built in New England as a Boston pilot boat, the 84-ton vessel, twenty-two years earlier, had made its way to the Golden Gate after a perilous trip through the Straits of Magellan, breaking long-standing speed records. Once Reed had it delivered to the Islands, it was registered under the Hawaiian flag and put into service. Unfortunately its career was cut short when, a few months later, it foundered on a reef off Punaluʻu and was reckoned a dead loss.[5]

During this period Reed turned his attention back to construction. His reputation as a builder of bridges may have encouraged the minister of the interior in 1879 to ask him to make a bid to build a bridge across the Waiākea stream, since, according to the minister, he "had all the material required except for the iron."[6] Reed had already supplied the necessary redwood pilings for this bridge at a cost of only nine dollars. The completion of a bridge across the Waiākea stream enhanced commercial opportunities for Waiākea village, to the displeasure of the many nearby Hilo merchants, including Richardson. Whether Reed and Richardson later parted company is unclear, but it is a fact that Richardson established a landing in Hilo Harbor at the foot of Waiānuenue Street, more or less the small community's business district. Both Reeds Landing at Waiākea and Richardson's accommodated cargo and passengers by means of lighters. Hilo historian Milton George records: "The battle between east and west, between Waiakea or Reed's Landing and the landing started by Richardson . . . was fought to a draw."[7]

Undaunted by the loss of his first coaster, the *Fanny*, Reed entered into partnership with Hilo businessman J. P. Sisson. The decision to take on Sisson as a partner no doubt sprung from Reed's awareness that his own health was declining. In 1879 the two partners bought the 95-ton schooner *Pato* and had it registered under the Hawaiian flag in their joint name. Built in Manila in 1876, the *Pato* was made of teak, ironwood, and mahogany. When sold to Reed and Sisson it had been advertised as having a "full set of good sails, and a new anchor and chain." It had only recently arrived from Oregon, where it had been in service.[8]

There is no evidence that Willie participated in his stepfather's coastal shipping, as he preferred the ranching and lumber business. The sleek coaster *Pato* continued to ply Hawai'i island's several eastern landings for about three years. Then, on November 15, 1881, while tied up at the Pāpa'ikou landing, with no warning the *Pato* sank at her moorings.[9]

Several months before this disaster, Jane's niece, Mary Jones, wrote from her post as a telegraph operator in Jamaica, "We are sorry to hear of Mr. Reed's poor health." It did not improve. Much of 1880 saw him confined to his house, often bedridden. On November 11 of that year, at the age of sixty-six, William Reed died, mourned by his wife, his three stepchildren, and much of the Hilo community. A missionary friend in Honolulu, Maria Forbes, wrote: "My dear Mrs. Reed, How I want to see you & throw my arms around you to mingle my tears with yours and also

William Reed, who died at the age of sixty-six, was a practical and prominent businessman, generous in a warm and quiet way.

to rejoice with you that Mr. Reed's sufferings are over. . . . How glad I am that you could get Mr. Reed at home to die. God was good. I was so afraid that he would never live to reach Hilo. We want to hear from you about the last hours of Mr. Reed. I rejoice that there is so much to cheer us up, that he died *trusting* in the Blessed One."

Mary Jones, whose father, Samuel, had died only months before, leaving Catherine a widow in desperate straits, expressed their family's sorrow: "We grieve to hear of the death of our dear Uncle Reed. His suffering must have been very great indeed. It was a great comfort that you were able to care for him. . . . It was a strange coincidence that Willie's baby was born the same day and in the same house. I am so glad to hear that dear Uncle died a sincere Christian. . . . Many thanks for writing me that Mr. Reed remembered me in his will, it was very kind of him to do so."

The month before he died, Reed had drawn up a relatively simple will, and Mary Jones was the first beneficiary mentioned.[10] He left her "one thousand dollars in money." The residue of his estate was left to his wife, "to have and to hold for her own use and benefit during her lifetime,—in lieu of dower." Upon her death, the residue of the estate was to

Mary Jones was the niece of Jane Stobie Shipman Reed. She was born to ABCFM missionary parents in Jamaica. When Mr. Reed died in 1880, he left Mary, who supported her impoverished mother as a telegraph operator, the grand sum of a thousand dollars.

be divided equally between "my two step-children, Marg‑ man and Oliver T. Shipman." Should they not survive have issue, those children would receive the porti‑ intended for their parents. But, if only one step-child with ٮᴀᵣ. survived Jane, that stepchild and his or her issue should "take two-thirds of said residue, and the other one-third thereof shall vest in William H. Shipman of said Hilo or in his lawful issue if he is dead." The will further stated that William would inherit the whole estate, provided his brother and sister died without issue before Jane, and then only upon her death.

The thoughtful step-father included a clause expressing confidence that his wife "will make the same suitable provision for the education, maintenance and advancement in the life of said Margaret Clara Ship-man and Oliver T. Shipman that I myself should if living."[11]

Willie's "share" may be looked upon as conspicuous by its absence, except for the portion he would receive only in the event of the deaths of other family members. But Willie had already been well taken care of seven years earlier, when Reed wrote him that he had bought out Rich-ardson's share of Kapāpala and was giving it to him. When, in 1876, Kapāpala Ranch was sold by Reed and Shipman to Bishop for $75,000, Willie received half the amount. When the will was probated in 1881, it showed that Reed had left real and personal property valued at approxi-mately $80,000.[12]

Some months before the *Pato* sank, Ollie returned to the Hilo he had left in 1868. After graduating from Knox Academy, he had enrolled in Amherst College in 1873. That school's records show that in 1879 Oliver T. Shipman graduated with a Bachelor of Arts degree.[13] Later the same year he attended St. Louis Law School in St. Louis, Missouri. (The biographical summary Ollie submitted to Amherst College in 1937 states that he did not receive a degree from the school.) He remained in St. Louis until mid-1881, about seven months after the death of his step-father, when he returned to Hilo. In that same year he went to work in the family lumberyard and store, part of the W. H. Reed Estate.

In 1882, the estate, wishing to continue the coastal service estab-lished by Reed, purchased in San Francisco the 95-ton steamer *George S. Harley*. It was put into service under the ownership of The Estate of W. H. Reed, but the following year was reregistered under the name *W. H. Reed*, with the owner shown as O. T. Shipman.[14] Like its two prede-cessors, it was home-based at Reed's Landing.

Only a few weeks after coming to Hawaiian waters, the *W. H. Reed* was caught in a heavy squall off the Puna coast. One man was killed and another seriously injured. According to the report filed by Captain J. H. Robertson,[15] the Chinese cook, Lee Win Wong, had been sitting on top of the galley, something he had been warned not to do. As a result of heavy seas, the "fore-boom jibbed to starboard," knocking the man overboard. Although the engines were reversed and a search conducted, only the cook's hat was found floating on the surface.

The following year, in August 1883, during a severe storm off the cliffs of the Hāmākua coast, the *W. H. Reed* suffered the loss of two anchors, necessitating a trip to a Honolulu shipyard for repairs. Several months later the vessel was chartered by the government to make soundings in the various channels among all the Islands.[16] At the end of the government mission, the Reed Estate saw the handwriting on the wall for small coastal vessels. Larger and faster interisland steamers were proving much more satisfactory, picking up the cargo business upon which the coasters had relied. Furthermore, the larger interisland vessels were accommodating passengers in increasing numbers. Before the year 1884 was out, the W. H. Reed Estate sold the ship to the Pacific Navigation Company, which, after removing its engines and converting it to sail, renamed it the *Ke Au Hou* (The New Era).[17]

# 16

# *The Lands of Lunalilo*

*. . . an area of 64,275 acres, more or less.*

—LAST LINE OF THE DEED FOR THE KEAʻAU TRACT

Eleven months after King Lunalilo's death, the government Boundary Commission issued a certificate "for the Ahupuaa of Keaau, Puna, Hawaii, containing by survey, 64,275 acres."[1] It was not until 1877 that a royal patent for the tract was granted to the William Lunalilo Estate, by decree of Kalākaua Rex. But in Honolulu the Lunalilo Home, that place of rest intended for "the use and accommodation of poor, destitute and infirm Hawaiians" which the late king had provided for in his will, was not ready for construction until 1881. A choice site not far from central Honolulu (the present location of Roosevelt High School) would house the spacious buildings planned for its residents.

The king had specified that the home was to be built and maintained from revenues derived from his personal estate. The three trustees of the Lunalilo Trust appointed by the Supreme Court of the Kingdom as responsible for both construction and management of Lunalilo Home were J. Mott Smith, Edwin O. Hall, and Sanford B. Dole. All were contributors to Hawaiʻi's history in their own ways.[2]

Probate courts are not known for speed and dispatch of wills. Nor did it hasten matters that Charles Kanaʻina, Lunalilo's father, contended "that the will offered for probate is not the Will of the deceased; that at the time of the execution thereof he was incompetent and that the Codicil thereto was not executed according to law."[3] A month later Justice Harris declared the will was valid and admitted it to probate. The court determined that Lunalilo's "estate consists of real and personal property valued at $60,000 in the Kingdom of Hawaii." In light of the many thousands of acres owned by Lunalilo on most islands, such a figure seems unreasonably low, even for those times. When the trustees were faced with the fiscal responsibility of financing Lunalilo Home, they chose the

Money was needed to fund King Lunalilo's request that a home for aged Hawaiians be built. Thus was the 65,000-acre Kea'au Tract sold to provide the funding. The first Lunalilo Home, in use from 1883 to 1927, was built on the present site of Roosevelt High School. (BM)

Kea'au Tract as land to be disposed of for the necessary funding. But they first applied to the Supreme Court of the Kingdom for instructions as to whether they had the authority to lease, rather than sell, "lands belonging to said Estate." On February 7, 1881, the court informed the trustees that they had no authority to lease: "It is the duty of the Trustees to sell this estate, and we do so advise and order."[4]

The tract the trustees had chosen to be sold for funding Lunalilo Home was originally recorded following the Great Mahele of 1848. At that time William Lunalilo was just over fifteen years old. It was undoubtedly his father, Chief Charles Kana'ina, who then spoke up for his young son, a chief in his own right. By the time the young chief ascended the throne, he was the owner of over 33 *ahupua'a* on all major islands.[5]

Like many large land divisions going back to the Mahele, the Kea'au Tract ran from the sea to the mountains. It was shaped like a long, slender piece of pie. The crust of the pie's rim ran along the coast for a distance of about ten miles, and at its midpoint was the small coastal vil-

lā'ena. Traveling upland along the pie's southern boundary, along
couple of gentle bends, the apex was at an elevation of 4,000 feet.
y was the opening of what came to be known as the Thurston Lava
The opposite side of this imperfect triangle was about five miles
, owing to a jagged piece of land pointing west. Much of the land
vered by a forest of ohia trees and brush. In the uplands, where rain
re plentiful, an abundance of large tree ferns were mixed with the
several places ancient lava flows, and some not so ancient, were
he landscape, often leaving only a postage-stamp thickness of
nough to permit growth of vegetation. For the most part, the
pulation was settled in the lowlands, the rest being pretty much
ntry.
etheless, three individuals surmised that the tract had possi-
r economic growth, and ranching was foremost. The trio con-
Willie Shipman, Captain Elderts, and Samuel M. Damon.
ed a *hui* (union, consortium) and decided to bid for the prop-
h was being offered at public auction late in 1881. Willie was
ty-seven years old, married, and the father of two children.
was the son of the well-known missionary, Samuel Chen-
who had married Willie and Mary two and a half years ear-
ten years Willie's senior, had been educated at Punahou,
married. Sam had gone into business in the bank of
ishop in Honolulu, but was interested in enterprises on
Hawai'i island. (He would later become president of Bishop Bank.)
These three diverse speculators made an offer of $20,000 at the auction
and ended up as the owners of the Kea'au land of Lunalilo. Each of
them financed their one-third equal share by taking out promissory
notes for $6,000 with William Hillebrand, a well-known physician and
expert botanist. The terms were 8 percent per annum for three years.[6]
Presumably, each owner had access to limited funds of his own, but
each chose to put up as security his "undivided one-third interest in and
to the ahupuaa of Keaau, Puna, Hawaii." The individual notes carried
the signatures of William and Mary Shipman, Samuel and Harriet
Damon, and J. E. Elderts and wife, Ka'ai, "X her mark." All were dated
January 9, 1882.

On the same day the three principal signatories put their names to a
document that would give each of the parties first right of refusal should
one of them desire to sell. It was "agreed that a bona fide offer in writing
shall be made to each of the other parties . . . before any sale or lease shall
be made to any other or others, of any interest in said land of

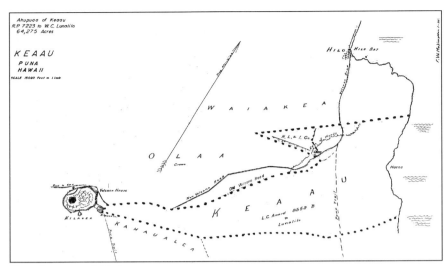

The ahupuaa of Keaʻau

Keaau . . . and other lands." The agreement was acknowledged for the
Shipmans and Elderts by L. E. Swain, Agent to take Acknowledgments
for the Island of Hawaiʻi. It was notarized for the Damons in Honolulu by
Sanford B. Dole, notary in that city.[7]

The deed to the purchase was carefully detailed in the boundaries
certificate of the tract. The state of the art of surveying in 1880 may
have been less than perfect, judging by later standards. Nonetheless,
considering the absence of sophisticated instruments that came later,
surveys of the period have generally held up in boundary disputes. For
fifty years Lahainaluna School had been teaching young men the sci-
ence of surveying. They, and later surveyors from the United States, had
no dearth of work awaiting them as Hawaiian lands were divided, par-
celed, and described in the Western manner. The Keaʻau surveyors were
faced with the problem of rough terrain and often impenetrable vegetation. Lacking the advantage of modern theodolites and given the diffi-
culty in staking in lava, the surveyors often resorted to sighting on
identifiable geographic or arboreal features, and occasionally a visible
artifact. Metes and bounds and degrees and azimuths often gave way to
"by guess and by gosh." Extracts from the surveyors' description in the
deed of the Keaʻau Tract read like a long walk up and down a nature
trail. Conspicuous by its absence is any mention of streams, for none
exist on Kīlauea's slopes.

The description is as follows:

Commencing at the E. angle of the land at a pile of stones on the sea shore at a place called "Keahuakaliloa" . . . 10,900 feet S.E. along the Government Road from the cocoanut grove at Keahou, and running thence along the lands . . . to a large Ohia with an X . . . to the Kaluaike crater, to the E. side of the Puna and Volcano Road . . . to the Pohakuloa koa grove on the Hilo and Volcano Roads . . . 10,230 ft. along the land of Olaa: to "O" cut in the pahoehoe [lava] at a little rise in the road about a mile and a quarter above the Omao woods . . . to "K" cut in the road at Kahalau . . . to "A" cut in the road at a place called Kahooku where some Neneleau trees are growing and where some houses at Kanekoa can be seen in coming down from Volcano; E. 23,810 ft. to a pile of stones by the side (E) of the road a little below Waiuli . . . to a pile of stones at the upper edge of a little strip of woods through which the road runs . . . to a large pile of stones on the lower side of the road at Makaulele, . . . W. 25,800 ft. to a point in the woods where the lands of Olaa and Waiakea join; thence along the land of Waiakea 36,000 ft. to a well-known place called Mawai in the woods on the Hilo and Volcano Road 9,122 ft. along the road from the cocoanut tree at the side of the road: . . . E. 29910 ft. through the Panaewa woods to seashore to point of commencement. Including an area of 64,275 acres, more or less.[8]

A year and a half later, Elderts lost his interest in being a one-third owner in a land venture whose profits, if any, seemed to him a long way down the road. He offered his share to his two partners, and on June 30, 1883, Willie and Sam Damon became coowners of sprawling Kea'au Tract. In the following months the two landowners leased two hundred acres to J. Tucker "between Kahalai and Mano and the Pahoehoe and the Woods, the metes and bounds thereof to be hereafter determined and made part of the lease." Similar transactions affecting small parcels of the tract also took place within the next two years.

Elderts was not happy about pulling out of the *hui*. The way Herbert Shipman, Willie's son and later manager of William H. Shipman, Ltd., recalled his father's telling it, Elderts and Willie had had a falling out. "Elderts went down to Honolulu," related Herbert, "and told Sam Damon that if he wanted to lose his shirt just to stay in this partnership. So Damon offered his third to my father at cost and said he'd loan him the money at no interest, he was so anxious to get rid of it. Then afterwards he changed his mind when Olaa Sugar Company was started, but my father didn't see why he should sell the third back. So that's why we had this big piece." The bottom line was that William and Mary Shipman became sole owners of the Kea'au Tract. Mary was that much closer to realizing her wish for a home on the beautiful Hā'ena shore.

# 17

## *Romance and Revolution*

Clara Shipman, like her two brothers before her, became a resident student at Punahou. She was fifteen years old when she was enrolled in 1873, the same year as a young man named Lorrin Andrews Thurston.[1] Clara graduated as a high-school senior in 1875; he did not, then or ever.

Willie and Ollie Shipman had departed from Punahou for American schooling in 1870, three years before either Thurston or Clara arrived on campus. Her scholastic ability and willingness to study was attested to by a faculty member in a letter to Jane Reed when Clara was ready to move onward and upward. Her education after leaving Punahou was a joint concern of Jane and William Reed. Jane consulted a trusted Honolulu friend, Frank Damon, a Punahou faculty member, about what might be the best course for Clara to follow. In his reply of February 13, 1876, he commented: "It has always been a pet theory of mine that our Island girls and boys should have an opportunity for study and culture in America if possible,—after completing studies here. Knowing Clara's interest in her studies and desire to continue them it would seem best to take some course of study at the East. There she might perfect herself in what she has begun here." Damon then cited the advantages of Wellesley and Smith Hadley colleges. Then Clara's former teacher informed Jane that he was very pleased "with her faithfulness in Latin . . . and I am speaking for the other teachers as well in saying that we always found her a most pleasant and earnest pupil." Clara did go "at the East" but it was to Abbott Academy in Andover, Massachusetts, where she was enrolled in 1876. She is listed among the graduates of the class of 1880.[2]

Lorrin Thurston was born in 1858 in Honolulu, grandson of the 1820 First Company pioneer missionaries, Asa and Lucy Goodale Thurston. He, like Sanford Dole and Sam Damon, would figure in Shipman enterprises, but even more importantly in changing forever the course of Hawai'i's history. His early years were spent in Honolulu, where many of his cohorts later became prominent, for change was in the air.

Some of his youthful playmates had a mischievous streak that also

Clara Shipman was married to Lorrin Thurston in Hilo in 1884. (Courtesy Fred Potter)

characterized young Lorrin. He later wrote of their days as a "gang" swimming in well-known pools in the cool Nuʻuanu Valley, just outside the city. In one fracas with a "rival gang," he defended his brother from a boy he considered a bully. Bully or no, the boy turned out to be Prince Leleiohoku, whose brother became King Kalākaua. Thurston held no grudges and years later recognized the prince as an accomplished composer and patron of music.

When Thurston was ten years old, his widowed mother assumed the position of matron of the Haleakalā Boys Boarding School at Makawao on Maui. There, on the Valley Isle, he made acquaintances who in later years became prominent in a variety of ways. One was the part-Hawaiian Robert Wilcox, who launched the failed scheme to restore the deposed Queen Liliʻuokalani to the throne. Thurston described him as a "chronic revolutionist, I say 'chronic' because it seemed to make little difference to him which side he took, so long as he was heading a fight." Young Thur-

ston recalled his Maui years as being adventurous—not dull in any sense.
Horseback riding to Wailuku, where he later attended school, gave him a
taste for the saddle. And by becoming familiar with and later exploring
Maui's massive extinct Haleakalā volcano, he acquired an interest in that
type of geology which would increase over the years and occupy much of
his later life.

Lorrin's pleasant Maui years ended in 1875 when his mother saw
the advantages of having him attend Punahou and enrolled him as a
boarder. His reminiscences of that period are many and vivid. He had to
work for his spending money, mostly by doing chores for various faculty
members, including the school president, Dr. Edward Church and his
wife, for whom Willie Shipman had once worked for his pocket money.
Lorrin displayed an early appreciation of money and set about to increase
his dollars by ingenious means.

Lorrin was not impressed by the rate of five cents an hour paid to
boys who worked around the school. At that time beans from the algaroba tree were in demand as feed for horses. The boys earned twenty-five
cents a barrel for beans they picked up on the school grounds. It was slow
and tedious work; three or four barrels a day were a great accomplish-
ment. Willie had made the acquaintance of a Hawaiian man who lived in
a humble house below the school grounds. "A brilliant idea occurred to
me," Thurston later wrote. He would pay the man and his children ten
cents for picking a barrel of beans. The price was most appealing to the
young Hawaiian children, who jumped at the chance, and Punahou's
school grounds were soon clear of algaroba beans. But the day of reckon-
ing came when the principal examined Lorrin's bill for twenty-five barrels at twenty-five cents a barrel, which came to the munificent total of
$6.25. The principal suspected the sum was too much for one boy to
amass in a day and asked if he had indeed picked twenty-five barrels the
previous Saturday. The young entrepreneur tried to evade the question by
replying, "They are all out there in the shed, you can see them for yourself." The principal persisted in asking how he could have picked twenty-
five barrels in one day, until Lorrin was forced to disclose that he had
done it with the help of a work crew of native children, which netted
him a profit of fifteen cents a barrel. The principal pondered long and
hard before telling Lorrin that this time he would pay the full amount,
but "I have been paying 25 cents a barrel to encourage habits of industry,
and not to stimulate speculation."

When Thurston left Punahou in 1875, it was not as a graduate but
in response to a letter from the principal, Amasa Pratt to Mrs. Thurston

suggesting that "you transfer your son to other fields of usefulness." It said, in essence, that his presence as a student at Punahou seemed no longer desirable. Pratt cited three indictments against the mischievous descendant of missionaries. The first charge related to the Sunday evening scripture selections that were read by the young boarders. Lorrin sanctimoniously, but with tongue in cheek, had quoted Saint Paul: "But I suffer not a woman to teach. . . . For Adam was formed before Eve." As most of the teachers at Punahou were women, and as Lorrin's selection had "caused undue levity among the pupils," such conduct could not be tolerated. Second, he was guilty of having kicked a bucket of water being carried by a student on a stairway, thus creating an unholy racket as it bounced its way, step by noisy step, to the bottom. If that did not warrant dismissal, Thurston's response to the correction of a composition did. In his original essay, he had used the ampersand throughout in place of the word *and*. As punishment, he was required to rewrite the composition correctly. He did so, but in script so minuscule that one would need a microscope to read it. Apparently guilty on all counts, "though I did not kick the bucket with the intent to knock it downstairs," young Thurston transferred his belongings to the residence of Grandmother Thurston. "Thus I 'graduated' from Punahou," he wrote in his memoirs.

Thurston was fortunate enough to find employment less open to the temptations afflicting a young man with a mischievous bent. A short time before his "graduation" he had been approached by a leading Honolulu lawyer, Judge Alfred Hartwell. The judge was looking for an office boy who could speak Hawaiian and thus act as an interpreter. Thurston possessed that ability. Hartwell pointed out that Lorrin could also study law in the office and "take care of the place." At the time, the young man was not attracted by the offer—that is, not until the Monday after his dismissal, when he had moved into the home of Grandmother Thurston. Then, he quickly informed Hartwell that he had had a change of heart and wished to be his interpreter as well as study law in his office. He was accepted and began his first job at a salary of four dollars a week.

That year, 1876, marked Thurston's entry into the field of law, elementary though it was. It was a move that shaped his career and the future of the Hawaiian government. Many law students of that period in Hawai'i, and also in the United States, got their feet wet by "reading law." Two years later, when he thought he had read enough law and wanted to practice it, he applied for a license to do so. It was granted, and he was permitted to practice in all courts of the monarchy.[3] When he was just thirty years old Lorrin Thurston was appointed deputy attorney general of Hawai'i. For unknown reasons, he gave up that post the same year and moved to Maui, his former home island. There, in its capital of Wailuku, he hung out his shingle and waited for clients. But business was not as brisk as he had anticipated, and when offered a job as bookkeeper with the Wailuku Sugar Company, he took it. Included was the responsibility of being head *luna* (supervisor) to one of the planters.

But the desire to practice law won out over any interest in becoming a big fish on a plantation. Thurston decided to go to Columbia University Law School in New York City to become a more qualified attorney in the Kingdom of Hawai'i.[4] Before making that move, however, he found time to visit the island of Hawai'i, in particular Kīlauea volcano. The trip captivated him, converting him almost immediately to Madame Pele's shrine, and thus to volcanology. Subsequent trips to that nearly virgin area found him more and more drawn to the idea of protecting the region for posterity. He attached himself to a cause that he would pursue and see become a reality: the development of the 200,000 acre Kīlauea Volcano National Park. His attraction to that part of the island of Hawai'i would continue for the rest of his life.

Thurston's enrollment in Columbia in 1880 gave him his first contact with a classmate named Teddy Roosevelt. (Roosevelt, when president, would be helpful to Thurston in his concerns for a Hawai'i national park.) After only one year, Thurston graduated. Presumably his years of reading law and his having been admitted to the Hawai'i bar reduced the required amount of study. He left New York the same year to return to Honolulu, where he immediately became a practicing attorney.

Even though Thurston set up his practice in Honolulu, the Kingdom's capital, he was still captivated by his strong interest in and fascination with Kīlauea. He made trips to the island of Hawai'i as frequently as his work and other demands allowed. In all likelihood, it was on one of those early visits to Hilo that he and Clara Shipman renewed a friendship which had first blossomed at Punahou. Marriage records reveal that on February 21, 1884, Margaret Clarissa Shipman and Lorrin Andrews Thurston were married in Hilo. The groom was twenty-five years old, his bride a year younger. For much of the rest of his long life the Shipman residences in Hilo and Volcano would be Lorrin Thurston's homes away from home.

Thurston's interest in law was complemented by an active interest in local politics. At the time of his marriage, he favored independence for Hawai'i as opposed to the much discussed annexation.[5] He became an active member of the Reform Party, but when it fell apart, he not only

As this example of Thurston's artistic doodling shows, he was fond of practicing penmanship of his initials and also his name. (Courtesy Peter Charlot)

*To have the honor of being present at*
*the* CORONATION CEREMONIES *of*

✦ THEIR MAJESTIES THE KING AND QUEEN. ✦

*The Chamberlain of the Household is authorized to invite*

Mr. W. H. Reed.

*to a seat in the amphitheatre opposite the front entrance*
*of* IOLANI PALACE *on Monday, February 12th, A. D. 1883.*

FULL DRESS.                              11 O'CLOCK, A. M.

The 1883 coronation of King Kalakaua and Queen Kapiolani was a great occasion. This special invitation to Mrs. W. H. Reed (Jane Stobie Shipman) came when the widow was fifty-six years old. A similar invitation to attend the coronation was also extended to her son, William, and his wife, Mary Shipman.

turned toward the prospect of annexation but was involved in organizing its implementation. He had already been elected to the House of Representatives, a legislative body comprised of far more Caucasians than Hawaiians. In 1890 he, along with a number of other up-and-coming young men (and some not so young), were of the opinion that experienced minds, and certainly learned ones, were needed to guide and run the monarchy. Thurston was already on speaking terms with members of King Kalākaua's cabinet and his advisers, which probably accounts for his being appointed minister of the interior in 1887.[6]

What King Kalākaua did not know in 1887 was that his minister of the interior became a cofounder of The Hawaiian League. This was a secret organization comprised of Caucasian men, mostly from the circle of white Honolulu businessmen, and mostly of American background. Their aim was to bring about reform according to their definition of it. Known as the "Committee of Thirteen," they operated in such secrecy that they kept no minutes. It is doubtful that Clara Shipman Thurston, or any of the other wives, was ever privy to the group's goals of stripping the king of his authority and forcing him to sign a constitution favorable to their interests. A few years later, the members of the League would play an important part in the overthrow of the Kingdom, with Thurston playing a leading role.[7]

During the four years in which he was minister of the interior, Thurston also served as a member of the Board of Health and of the Board of Immigration. As minister of the interior he took an activist position in preserving large areas of land on the major islands for public parks. The years before, and certainly after, his marriage continued to find Lorrin Thurston an active member of the inner circle of American businessmen, many of whom had heavy investments in plantations. Slowly, they were drawing a net closer around the ruling monarchy.

Lorrin and Clara Thurston became the parents of a baby boy on February 1, 1888. They named him Robert Shipman Thurston. The first name was in memory of Lorrin's deceased brother Robert, four years Lorrin's senior. The two brothers had always been close. Robert was later described by Lorrin as having been a strong and vigorous youngster. Once, when vacationing at their Uncle Samuel's cattle ranch at Wai'anae, the boys went reef fishing barefooted, as was customary. Robert got a slight cut on the ball of his foot from sharp coral. In three days' time, the wound had become so painful that they traveled forty miles on horseback to Honolulu to see a doctor. The foot had been infected by a poison coral called *kauna'oa*. Three days later Robert was dead from blood poisoning at the age of twenty. Lorrin remained by his side during his last days. His namesake, Robert Shipman Thurston, was a lusty, bouncing baby who gave his parents joy, as well as the satisfaction of perpetuating the names Thurston and Shipman.

Talk of annexation by the United States had been around for decades, but it intensified with the passing of years and increasing American involvement in the affairs of the nation, both economic and political. It was certainly a subject at the dinner table between Clara and Lorrin as the latter became more and more wrapped up in the concerns of his Caucasian clients and the future of the monarchy. With Hawai'i as part of the United States, the sugar planters would be able to reap greater profits through the elimination of any tariff. Pearl Harbor, coveted by the United States but presently unattainable because of Kalākaua's refusal to use it as a bargaining chip, would be another bonus.[8] Thurston was among the clique of haole businessmen who saw annexation as not only a possibility but a goal. In his position as both a member of the House of Representatives and minister of the interior, he had his foot in the door of division.

The Thurstons became the parents of a son, Robert Shipman Thurston, in 1888. (Courtesy Fred Potter)

Kīlauea's protection and park development were the other consuming passions of Thurston, and this new position provided him with the perfect opportunity to implement his dream. One of his first tasks would be to replace the horse trail from Hilo to the volcano. It was an arduous thirty-mile trip that took close to eight hours. For those who wished to break their ride, there was a halfway house at Mountain View and thatched shelters here and there along the trail. The latter offered nothing more than protection from rain, which increased with the elevation. Thurston would have been the first to agree with the Irish sage who said of his own country, "This would be a grand country if only they'd put a roof over it."

Travelers crossed through dense ohia forests and heavy growths of large tree ferns. If the trail was not muddy, it often passed over rough lava flows that were hard on horses' hooves. Thurston's efforts led to a graded and straightened road that not only shortened traveling time but had room for covered carriages in inclement weather. Suppliers of goods welcomed it for the convenience it offered to wagoners and the decrease in the need for bearers.[9] For those who preferred something more comfortable than walking or riding on horseback, a round trip from Hilo could be made in one day by a four-in-hand team of horses drawing a fancy carriage supplied by the Hilo-based Volcano Stables.

The volcano itself offered visitors a spectacular reward, with its majestic mystery and ongoing heaving, belching, and burning. Thurston, the self-appointed promoter of Kīlauea's attractions, was also sufficiently enterprising to see that the already steady flow of visitors could be significantly increased if accommodations were improved. The existing Volcano House, an outgrowth of what had generally been created for, and known as, a halfway house, had grown by fits and starts. It lacked the class and moderate comforts that many world travelers to the volcano expected. Thurston had visions of a modern hotel to provide shelter and comfort at this destination point. To implement these visions he set about obtaining title, as a leaseholder, to the property. In June 1890 he purchased the lease for the Volcano House from Samuel G. Wilder. At the same time he acquired the lease for the existing and somewhat run-down hotel, at Punalu'u. There he could take care of visitors from Honolulu if they came by way of the Wilder Steamship Company to Punalu'u Landing. And if they came by carriage from Hilo, he wanted their stay at Volcano House to be a memorable one. To accomplish this he raised sufficient funds to remodel the old Volcano House, which included adding rooms.[10] It soon became renowned as an attractive hostelry for visitors from countries near and far.

# Wilder's Steamship Co. Ltd.

OFFICE, CORNER FORT AND QUEEN STREETS, HONOLULU.

C. L. WIGHT, President,
S. B. ROSE, Secretary and Treasurer,
CAPT. J. A. KING, Superintendent,
J. F. HACKFELD, Vice President.

Directors: WM. G. IRWIN,
WM. C. WILDER,
WM. F. ALLEN,
GEO. C. BECKLEY.

The above named gentlemen together with the President, Vice President, and Secretary and Treasurer of the Company, constitute the Board of Directors.

# THE POPULAR ROUTE

TO THE

### VOLCANO

IS BY THE

## Wilder's Steamship Co's Steamer Kinau, VIA HILO.

A Good Carriage Road the Entire Distance.

TICKETS FOR THE ROUND TRIP, - - - $50.

Lorrin Thurston's promotion of the Volcano area brought visitors from Honolulu by interisland steamer as well as by land. (*Hawaiian Annual*, 1895)

Whether minister of the interior, owner of the upgraded Volcano House, or practicing barrister, Thurston was never too proud to rough it. In the same year he acquired Volcano House, he and a party of four others made an ascent to the summit of Mauna Loa, 13,650 feet above sea level. The party included Julian Monsarrat, manager of Kapāpala Ranch, and it was from that last vestige of civilization that the party headed up the slopes. They had the good sense to include a Hawaiian guide. "We spent the night at the upper edge of vegetation," wrote Thurston, continuing on to the crater the next morning. "Monsarrat was soon put out of commission by mountain sickness. . . . I wished to go to the floor of the crater [Mokuʻāweoweo] which lay 800 feet below the summit." He made it, but not before he too fainted from altitude sickness. The five spent an uncomfortable night in a tent meant for four, "so cramped that whenever one of the party wished to turn over, all five of us had to turn together." Although it was August 1, the temperature dropped to 18 degrees above zero. Before returning to Kapāpala, the party cut pieces of ice a foot thick from cracks in the surface. "We wrapped it in blankets and took it on mules to Pahala [*sic*] Ranch where it was used to freeze ice cream for our dinner that night." If Thurston was heady over his acquisition of Volcano House, his promotion of a fine carriage road, his trip to Mauna Loa's summit, along with his dreams of a Kīlauea federal reserve, he had every right to be so.

But his domestic world came crashing down around him on May 5, 1891. Clara was in her second pregnancy and ready to give birth. But it was not to be: she died in childbirth. Her second baby, a girl, did not survive her for long. In its next issue, *The Friend* reported: "The death of Mrs. Lorrin A. Thurston was an unexpected and severe stroke of sorrow to her circle of relatives to whom she was particularly dear, and to many other friends. She had been in an unusual degree a solace and support to her young husband in his arduous public duties. Mrs. T. was the daughter of Rev. Wm. Shipman, missionary at Kau, who died in early manhood. She leaves one motherless boy of three years."[11]

In its annual report for 1891, the Hawaiian Mission Children's Society, in observing many deaths which had occurred that year, wrote: ". . . Mrs Clara (Shipman) Thurston, aged 31, another whose loveliness in wifehood and motherhood was valued by those who knew her. When told that the journey's end was near she expressed herself as ready and went quietly across the river. Sweet change from death to life."

The first two months of 1891 were to be landmarks in Lorrin's life. Only a month before his wife died, another death had occurred that would thrust him into the forefront of the movement for annexation and foster a century of unrest. King Kalākaua died suddenly in San Francisco on January 20. The succession fell to his capable sister, Liliʻuokalani, who soon made clear her intention to abrogate the Kalākaua constitution and rule under a new one more favorable to a strong monarchy. The conspirators, now operating more openly, saw in the determined queen an obstacle that must be removed if their interests were to succeed.

Ever the politician, Thurston had shared with his wife, Clara, his views on the need for the overthrow of the monarchy and why it must come to pass. It did, two years after Clara's death, and Thurston was one of the ardent annexationists who brought it about. For two years after the 1893 downfall of the monarchy, Thurston was in Washington, D.C., as minister plenipotentiary for the Republic of Hawaiʻi. He used his time there to press for the annexation by the United States of the new nation. The five-cent blue postage stamp of the Republic of Hawaiʻi bore Thurston's portrait.

Prior to arriving at his Washington post, Thurston stopped off in Chicago for a short visit, primarily to attend the World's Fair on behalf of the budding Hawaiʻi tourist industry. During his stay he met a young lady, Harriet Potter, a member of a large family from St. Joseph, Missouri. Romance bloomed. They were married that year and resided in Washington. The following year their first child, a daughter, Margaret, was born in the nation's capital. A son, Lorrin Potter, was born five years later in Honolulu.[12]

At the beginning of the century, Thurston became publisher of the *Honolulu Advertiser,* a metropolitan daily that, until 1993, continued to be under the management of Thurston family descendants.

Despite his involvement with government affairs and his newspaper, Thurston continued to pursue his interest in Kīlauea Volcano. Along with Professor Thomas Jaggar, a globally renowned volcanologist, he succeeded in establishing the Kīlauea Observatory. Thurston the editor used his journalistic skills to influence congressmen and other key officials in promoting the observatory. With the help of Dr. Jaggar, he was successful in getting Kīlauea declared a national park.

In 1913, in the company of his niece, Margaret Shipman, and his daughter, Margaret (later Mrs. William Twigg-Smith), Thurston came across an immense lava tube near the edge of Kīlauea Crater. As a publicist, he soon ensured that this geological formation became a prominent tourist attraction. The tube is in a crater whose slopes are surrounded and covered by a luxurious forest of tall fern and high-altitude vegetation. Today, Thurston Lava Tube remains one of the popular highlights for visitors, who may walk the developed four hundred feet from one end to the other. Another thousand feet of the tube have been explored but remain undeveloped for visitors. (Coincidentally, the opening to Thurston Lava Tube is only yards from the summit of the Kea'au Tract, owned at that time by William H. Shipman.)

Again with enthusiastic support from Dr. Jaggar, Thurston was instrumental in establishing the Hawaii Volcano Research Association and was its president until his death. Similarly, he was a founder of the Hawaii Visitors Bureau. Nor did he stint in reporting in the columns of his daily paper news of Kīlauea's eruptions, describing the charms of the verdant Volcano area and the beauty of the road from Hilo. Much of this road traversed lands over which Willie Shipman had granted rights-of-way. Thurston remained an active businessman, an investor, and a prolific writer until his death in 1931 at the age of seventy-three. He had outlived his first wife, Clara Shipman, by exactly forty years.

# 18

## Onward and Upward

While Lorrin Thurston was occupied with the political life of the King-dom, particularly altering its government, many people on the neighbor-ing islands were indifferent to, even uninformed about, the changing tide. Willie and Ollie Shipman, engaged in managing their own lives and business affairs, were not caught up in the machinations of their brother-in-law. Nor were they affected by them. The Puna district, with its sev-eral hundred square miles, remained sparsely populated. In 1887 its inhabitants were mostly Hawaiians who lived along the coast and a few ranchers, like Willie and Elderts, who lived slightly inland. When not running the Kapoho ranch, Willie moved in quiet circles, devoting much of his time to his late stepfather's other enterprises, learning as he went along.

Over the next few years Willie would acquire, by government lease or purchase, other tracts of virgin land in the lower Puna and Kapoho areas. By 1883 Shipman & Elderts had formally dissolved. But though Elderts had pulled out of the partnership, he and Willie shared ranching interests around Kapoho.[1] Each of them continued to ranch on his own. Whereas Willie expanded his ranching and land management, Elderts confined himself to ranching on Kapoho lands where he and his family resided. In addition, he found time to serve as deputy sheriff. He died in 1923 at the age of one hundred five, the oldest resident on the island, leaving eight children.[2] Today the *Ohana o Elderts* (Family of Elderts) numbers close to three hundred members, all with Hawaiian blood from Elderts' wife, Ka'ai, and other Hawaiians who married into the family.[3]

Around 1883 Willie, Mary, and their young children left Kapoho and moved to a larger dwelling on Volcano Street (now Kīlauea), then two miles from the center of Hilo. One compelling reason for the move was Willie's taking over the lease of a fish market in the small waterfront section of Hilo.[4] Its Chinese owner had watched his business suffer from competition closer to Waiākea. In no time Willie had converted the pre-mises from a fish market to an outlet for fresh beef from his own cattle

A corner of Shipman's cattle ranch in Kea'au. A spring-fed lagoon was adjacent to grazing lands.

ranch. The move was a wise one. The Shipman Meat Market provided Hilo households with a ready and ample supply of beef at prices they could afford. (It became a cofounder of the future and highly successful Hilo Meat Company, a cooperative of several Hawai'i ranches, of which William H. Shipman would become president, a position he held for the remainder of his long life.) The market was located near the outlet of the Wailuku stream in the business section of Hilo. The side street that ran from it, and which soon attracted other enterprises, later acquired the name it still carries today, Shipman Street.

Still in his thirties, Willie had become recognized as an enterprising individual whose efforts were bearing fruit, a fact that did not escape the eye of public officials. His background and experience led them to appoint him an appraiser of lands. This was soon followed by a place on the Land Claims Commission. In 1887 he found himself on the Puna Road Development Board. In the next two years he was named Executive Inspector of Animals for the Island of Hawai'i and a tax collector for the growing Hilo community.[5]

Willie's duties as a public servant caused no disruption of his own private business operations. When a group of businessmen from Honolulu wanted to open up land in what was to become the 'Ola'a Homesteads, Willie was glad to lease them the hundreds of acres they wanted.[6] There is no indication that he became a major stockholder, let alone a minor one. The same held true for the expansion of the Hilo Railroad Company. This too was financed and promoted primarily by Honolulu investors, such as Benjamin Dillingham, the man behind the successful Oahu Railroad & Land Company. The vice president of the Hilo Railroad Company was Lorrin Thurston.[7] Early in 1900 the Hilo Railroad pushed its way eight miles south to the 'Ōla'a community. There it not only offered access to the 'Ōla'a homesteaders but provided transportation for the Puna and 'Ōla'a sugar companies to haul their raw products to the Hilo wharf. As with the 'Ōla'a land development for homesteaders, if Willie was an investor in the Hilo Railroad Company there is no evidence of it.

While Willie was expanding his ranch holdings, Ollie was profiting from the increasing number of visitors to the volcano. In a partnership with H. Wood, he obtained from the Bishop Estate a lease on the Volcano House, the only hostelry in the area and the only place for hungry

"Downtown" Hilo looked like this shortly after Willie opened his market. At the corner of Waiānuenue and Front Streets is the post office at the right (ca. 1880).

travelers to eat. Wood and Ollie continued their joint management until 1895 when Thurston picked up the lease as part of his plan for the renovation of Volcano House.[8] At that point Ollie decided that he, like Willie, would go into ranching, though on a smaller scale. He leased from the Bishop Estate land amounting to about 35,000 acres between Kīlauea Volcano and Kapāpala Ranch. It extended from sea level to an elevation of 7,000 feet, with ample green grazing land in between. The land was in the *ahupua'a* of Keauhou. Originally, by virtue of the Great Mahele, the entire tract had been the property of Princess Victoria Kamāmalu. Upon her death she left it to Princess Ruth, who in turn willed it to Bernice Pauahi Bishop.[9] The new rancher called it Kuapaawela, the name of a prominent mound on the side of Mauna Loa. Several years later, when Willie bought the ranch from his brother, he named it Keauhou, the name of the *ahupua'a*. (In recent years much of the ranch land has been converted to residential use: the Golf Course subdivision. It is not a Shipman enterprise.)

At about the same time Ollie left Volcano House to start ranching and Willie was doing well with his own ranch, meat, and land affairs, the coffee industry came to east Hawai'i. By 1890 it had not only taken hold, it had taken off. The soil was rich and so was the mainland market. Many eager homesteaders were planting young coffee trees in the thirty-mile corridor between Hilo and Volcano. So were farmers in other portions of Puna and the Kea'au Tract. By 1898 a total of about 150 coffee planters had 22,670 acres of coffee trees in the Puna district. Some plots were as small as 7 acres; others as large as 1,850; most were around 100 acres.[10] Willie and Ollie had modest holdings of only 25 acres, each on his own property. According to Lorrin Thurston, the first planting in the Kea'au area yielded an excellent crop three years later. However, there was a marked decline in the next couple of years. "The third crop," wrote Thurston, "decreased radically and the fourth was a failure."[11]

By the turn of the century, coffee was a dead industry in east Hawai'i. It ended as rapidly as it had started. There were several reasons for the crops taking a nosedive. Foremost, perhaps, was the rainy weather. Then came a blight that attacked the trees. Disease spread to large and small holdings. Aside from these factors, the quality of the coffee could not match that of the Kona district's many thousands of acres planted in coffee, which flourished in the district's drier weather. Nor did the advent of high-quality Brazilian coffee to the United States at a favorable tariff help the situation. The farmers and homesteaders eventually gave coffee growing up as a bad job, many having suffered financially, as did Hilo

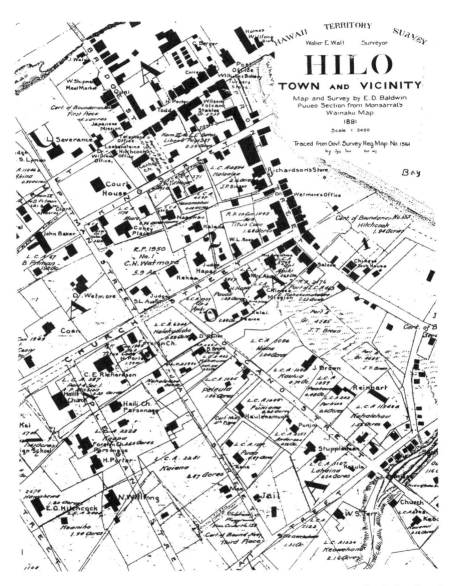

The Shipman Market (in upper left on this 1891 map) was on the left side of Bridge (now Keawe) Street. It faced what later became Shipman Street. By 1916 most Hilo streets were given Hawaiian names by order of a city ordinance.

At the turn of the century, Shipman Street bustled with horse-drawn vehicles. Hilo Market is on the right. Beyond it is the armory, now the National Guard Armory. The two-story white building on the corner of Bridge (Keawe) and Shipman Streets was then Serrao's Winery. Later it became the offices of the *Hilo Tribune Herald*. It was demolished after World War II and is today a municipal parking lot. (Courtesy Carl Rohner)

businesses. Several beautiful homes were abandoned along with the farm lots. One whose losses were minimal was Willie Shipman. Exhibiting a caution typical of him, he had invested a mere 25 acres, and that on land he owned, unlike others who paid rent or lease.

In fact, the failure of coffee led indirectly to Shipman's prospering. The historian Milton George reported, "The gain through the promotion of two large sugar plantations, Olaa and Puna, was enormous."[12] No one gained more than Willie Shipman. As the owner of all the land in the area, he leased to those two plantations the thousands of acres needed to plant cane, an arrangement that continued for another seventy-five years. It was also these two sugar mills which provided employment for many who were adversely affected by the demise of the coffee industry.

Another agricultural enterprise that benefited Willie was the incorporation of a Honolulu syndicate called the Hawaiian Land and Improvement Company. In 1893 it purchased from William Shipman 3,277 acres of land along the Volcano Road for the healthy sum of $18,000. The company's intentions were to subdivide much of it into lots, and also to set out 50,000 orange seedlings, as well as a large quantity of cocoa and

Over the years cattle ranches have played a substantial role in the economy of all the Hawaiian Islands. Many of them are represented by these fifty-six brands. (Courtesy Gordon Cran)

coffee plants.[13] The lots were subdivided, ultimately to Shipman's advantage. But it is doubtful that the projected plantation of orange trees, coffee, and cocoa even got off the ground.

Records of land transactions involving Willie, and to some extent Ollie, fill several pages during the last decade of the nineteenth century and the first quarter of the twentieth. Some were tracts Willie sold off, large and small. One of the latter was three acres sold to the Catholic Bishop of Honolulu for the sum of $120. To Peter Lee, the Norwegian entrepreneur, he sold 54 acres for $1,350. Most other sales in this period averaged around a hundred acres. Willie had the wisdom and instinct to sense what would become profitable in the way of land usage. That he was no speculator he had demonstrated by his restraint in not investing in sugar, coffee, cotton, and even the railroad. Each of these, in time, had drained their investors of their financial resources.

Willie Shipman had stuck to what he loved: ranching. Having made that choice, he broadened his holdings, which were, for the most part, on the Mauna Loa side of Hilo, to the eastern flank of Mauna Kea. In 1890, Willie purchased the lease for the 23,000-acre Puʻu-ʻŌʻō ranch, which became one of his largest cattle ranges.[14] In the same general area of Mauna Kea, and for the same reason, he picked up the sizable Puakala Ranch. The Keaʻau Ranch of 50,000 acres was perhaps less risky, despite poor grazing land, for at least there he already owned 40,000 acres, lock, stock, and barrel. The only money he had to put up was that needed to lease the neighboring 10,000 acres from the government. Of the thirty-eight cattle ranches on the island, Shipman's now ranked among the largest.

While Willie's own world was expanding successfully and fulfilling his expectations, the outside world, at the turn of the century, was experiencing growing pains as it underwent momentous changes.

# 19

## *Into the Twentieth Century*

As calendars changed from the last years of the nineteenth century to make way for the twentieth, so did the world. Russia had annexed Manchuria and South Africa's Boer War had intensified. The Boxer Rebellion threw China into chaos. Vladimir Lenin returned to Russia from one of his many exiles. In Austria the works on the laws of genetics of the Augustinian friar Gregor Mendel had been discovered; they would benefit mankind in many ways, not least of which was increased food production. Also in Austria, a neurologist named Sigmund Freud emphasized sex in psychosomatic medicine. Queen Victoria, an unlikely Freudian fan, died after sixty-four years on the British throne.[1]

In the United States, George Eastman put photography into the hands of young and old with the introduction of his one-dollar Brownie box camera. The first Davis Cup tennis tournament took place and lasted for three days. Times were good, judging by the fact that F. W. Woolworth racked up five million dollars in sales in twelve months from his fifty-nine five-and-dime stores. A gigantic hurricane snuffed out seven thousand lives in Galveston, Texas, and was recorded as the worst natural disaster in North American history. President McKinley died from an assassin's bullet in Buffalo, New York. The population of the United States reached 76 million, of whom over 10 million were foreign-born.[2]

Hawai'i, which had been in a sort of limbo since the formal annexation of 1898, became a nonvoting territory of the United States in July 1900. The Marconi Wireless Company established communications among the Hawaiian Islands. Seven miles of Honolulu's streets were served by electric trolleys. A memorial service was held for Queen Victoria in Kawaiaha'o Church, often referred to as Hawai'i's Westminster Abbey. Maritime disasters reached a high, with eleven vessels becoming total losses in Hawaiian waters or on its shores. One of these was the interisland steamer *Kilauea Hou*, which was wrecked beyond repair on Hilo's beach.[3]

The Hilo Railroad Company extended its lines east to Pāhoa and

Kapoho then south fifteen miles to Glenwood, largely over Shipman lands. The population in the two Hilo districts approximated ten thou-sand, most of whom lived in the city. For the past five years most of the residences and businesses had been serviced by the Hilo Electric Light Company. Coffee was being phased out and sugar was taking over its failed fields. A list of prominent males in Hawai'i (feminism was not in vogue) was published in a book entitled *Historic Honolulu*. It expanded to include those whom it considered outstanding male citizens on the island of Hawai'i. A handsome Willie Shipman, at thirty-nine, was pictured with his full, flowing beard. He was described as "This sterling citizen, whose every thought is for the good of the community in which he reared

It was a handsome Willie Shipman who was elected to the Territorial House of Representatives in 1904. He was fifty years old.

his home and cemented his associations, commands the respect and esteem of his fellow citizens." It added that he also operated the well-established Hilo Meat Company and "has various other interests . . . and has a family of seven children."[4]

Many east Hawai'i residents considered it a foregone conclusion that the Shipman brothers would enter the political arena. They certainly had the qualifications. They were natives of the Territory of Hawai'i, were well-educated, and had demonstrated astuteness in business as well as a commitment to public service. But some who knew Willie intimately wondered if he was eager to become a public figure, especially to seek political office. Willie never did quite follow his sister Clara's advice to be less shy and taciturn, to get out and become part of the crowd. In fact, in his reluctance to become a joiner, he may have fallen just short of being a loner.

Both Shipmans did run for office in 1904, but only after their cousin, James Stobie, had set an example; two years earlier he had run on the Republican ticket for the post of treasurer for the newly created East Hawai'i County. Stobie, now fifty-three, had been born in Quincy, Illinois, and was a relative newcomer to Hawai'i. A nephew of Jane Reed, he was a cashier in the Bank of Hilo. His opponent, H. N. Lyman, was the victor. Many would agree with Stobie that Lyman, a member of the long- and well-established Lyman family, had a distinct advantage over a candidate who was considered a *malihini,* or newcomer. Stobie, who had made his political entry in 1903, made his exit the same year.[5] He never ran for office again.

Both Willie and Ollie had their names on the ballots of 1904 for different offices, and each from a different party. Ollie ran for the Territorial Senate as a fusion candidate of the Home Rule and Democratic parties. Willie was nominated by the Republicans for one of the four seats in the Territorial House of Representatives.[6] The campaign had many of the smearmarks of campaigns past and to come. The *Hilo Tribune* reported that Carl Smith, who may have been a Republican roisterer, sounded off at a GOP rally, criticizing Ollie and his colleague, Frank Wood. Smith made it a point to remind his audience: "They have been brought up as cattlemen. These two gentlemen can conceive of no more beautiful picture than cutting up the lands for alleged benefits of the cattlemen."[7] The results of the 1904 race were encapsulated in a headline in the *Tribune* stating that it was a clean sweep for the GOP.[8] Ollie came in third for the two seats in the Senate. Willie was on the winning ticket and was elected to the House.

Representative William H. Shipman served his community well by focusing on the need for more and better schools for the Puna and Hilo districts. Similarly, he pressed for funds to expand and pave some of Hilo's lanes and streets.[9] But apparently politics and the public spotlight were not to his liking; there is no indication that he ever ran again for public office.

Ollie, on the other hand, did, and was quite successful. In 1905 he ran on the Democratic ticket for county supervisor from Ka'ū. He was elected and continued to serve in that capacity for six years.[10] From 1914 to 1921 he was the tax assessor for the Third Taxation Division of Hawai'i County.[11] In 1924 he was elected Treasurer of Hawai'i County,

"Ollie" T. Shipman was, over the period of a half-century, a legislator, rancher, hotel manager, Hilo businessman, and county treasurer. (Courtesy Petroglyph Press book *The Volcano House* by Gunder Olsen)

The cattle brand of Oliver Shipman left no doubt
as to ownership.

holding that position until his retirement from office in 1939, a successful
Democrat in a Republican stronghold.[12] Oliver's wife, Hannah Naeole,
died in 1907, leaving three children. The following year he married Mary
Keliiwahamana Lo, a resident of Honolulu. They had no offspring.

Socializing was not as easy or comfortable for Willie as it was for
Ollie, and when it did occur the hand and heart of his hospitable wife,
Mary, were in evidence. She not only had the knack of making friends
and entertaining, but Willie saw to it that she had the means, even the
setting. Mary possessed the gift of being a genuinely warm and capable
hostess to many visitors. She also proved to be a competent mother of
seven children. The last of these was Herbert Cornelius, born in 1892.
He carried the middle names of both his father and his paternal grandfather. Some twenty years later he would begin to carry on his father's business interests.

Nevertheless, in 1900 Mary tired of living at the Waiākea house on
Volcano Street (now Kilauea Avenue, where the State Agricultural
Experimental Station is located). She had good reasons. Foremost was
the fact that her seven growing children required more living space; the
house was beginning to bulge. In addition to nine Shipmans, Willie's
mother, Jane Stobie Shipman Reed, was very much a member of the family. It appears that her brother, Alex Stobie, also lived with them. He had
moved some years ago from Quincy to Hilo, where he went into business.
Mary's other reason for seeking a more appropriate domicile was her wish
to get away from land leased by the government. She also considered the
house too far, by two miles, from the center of Hilo.

Mary had earlier admired a semisteepled Victorian residence recently built on Reed's Island by John Wilson, a contractor. Fronted by Reed Boulevard (now Ka'iulani Street) it was perched on a high knoll surrounded by trees and a purling stream. Its two-plus acres included a spacious yard, and its many rooms, reasoned Mary, were intended for a growing family. Servants' quarters nestled under trees near the back of the three-story dwelling. It was also close to downtown Hilo. After examining the property, Willie agreed that it was a good investment for his extended family and, for $13,000, closed the deal with Wilson in February 1901.[13] However, it was a month before he told Mary about it. Meanwhile she continued to urge him to buy the property. He let her fret about it until, one day when she brought it up again, he told her: "Wilson doesn't own that property. We do. I bought it from him a month ago."

The house Willie bought for his wife and seven children is one of the few remaining Victorian mansions in the state, and certainly among Hilo's most attractive. At the turn of the century it was considered an excellent example of the formal style of living. The first residence to be constructed in the exclusive area of Reed's Island, it also expressed opu-

When the new Shipman home was occupied around 1902, it commanded a clear view of Hilo Bay from Reed's Island. It was the main residence of the Shipman family for over seventy-five years. Today it is the home of Barbara Ann Blackshear Andersen and her family.

lence. It was surrounded by the Wailuku River on one side and the Waikapū stream on the other.

The buildings aside from the main complex included stables for horses and carriages, servants' quarters, and a two-story guest cottage. The main house commanded an unspoiled view of the gulch on one side and, from the front of the mansion, a spectacular panorama of Hilo and its bay beyond. A semicircular veranda enclosing the first floor, and four curved bay windows, enhanced the viewing.

The main house included a formal dining room off the pantry that separated a spacious kitchen. On the other side of the kitchen was a dining room for the working men and women. It had access to the outdoors so that the workmen need not remove their shoes. Another adjoining room, once a cheery atrium, was converted to what was called a breakfast room, but it was there that the family took most of its meals. When there were a number of guests, however, the "formal dining room" was used. If the guests were numerous, then both dining areas were utilized. An electric bell, activated by a floor button in the breakfast room, was for the matron, Mary, to summon Ah Mi or other kitchen help as necessary.

The living room, with its Steinway grand piano, was furnished not only with pieces of polished koa, Hawai'i's prized red wood, but also with touches of Far Eastern and Victorian accessories. An adjoining library with a wide variety of books was of special interest to Jack and Charmian London, who were Shipman guests in 1907.[14] (The couple had moored their yacht, *The Snark,* in Hilo Bay and enjoyed the hospitality of the Shipman residence.) A guest room, with attractive koa furnishings, completed the first floor. A sweeping stairway led to the second floor. So did Hilo's first elevator, which filled a space once occupied by a spiral staircase. (The original Otis elevator was manually operated but was converted to electricity several years later.) The upstairs contained six bedrooms and three baths. Like the rooms below, the bedrooms were generously supplied with handmade koa furniture—all, that is, except Caroline Shipman's room: she believed that the house already contained enough koa furniture of all kinds, most of it tailored to complement the interior. A guest room at the top of the stairs had next to it a roomy dressing room that often doubled as a sewing room. Its large mirrored closet was made of Pride of India wood from a tree that had been planted many years earlier by Mary Shipman's mother, Eliza Johnson.

This Reed's Island residence, often referred to as the Big House, was more than a home for the Shipman family. It was frequently the setting where invited guests and many off-island visitors were welcomed and

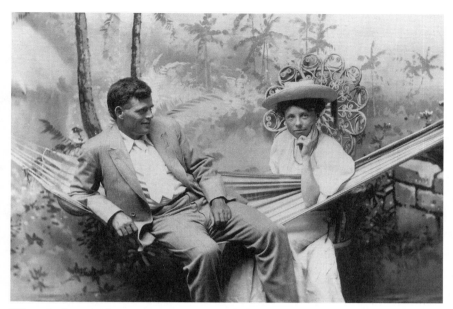

When Jack and Charmian London visited Hilo they enjoyed Shipman hospitality at the Reed's Island residence as well as their Mountain House in Volcano.

made to feel at home. It was a home fit for a queen; indeed, the deposed Queen Lili'uokalani more than once enjoyed Shipman hospitality at their upland Hilo home.[15] Herbert Shipman said he remembered her well, and her own place, facing the ocean, at the circular koa dining table: it is still regarded with pride by Shipman descendants some eighty years later. Two young Shipman female friends, ages eight and nine, had the honor of fanning the queen when she visited. The ladies would enjoy lunch, then "talk forever," but the girls would tire and begin to giggle. They suppressed their laughter as they tried to see how close they could move the fan to the back of the queen's head without touching it.[16] Herbert remembered the former queen not only as an occasional luncheon guest, and someone who played the organ at Haili church with charm, but also as a person who enjoyed a cigar when offered one by Willie from his silver cigar box. The gracious lady was pleased with the privacy of the Reed's Island residence, where her desire to enjoy a cigar would not be frowned upon.

Lili'uokalani must have been impressed by the hospitality and character of Mary Shipman. She once wrote to a young friend: "I know Mrs. Shipman of Hilo very well. She was a very dear friend of my sister [Princess] Likelike,—a very nice woman she is, and as good as she is lovely in character."[17]

About seventy-five years after the Shipmans moved into the Big House, the home was put on the Hawaii Register of Historic Places. Three years later, in 1978, after being carefully scrutinized by the appropriate review committee, it was placed on the National Register of Historic Places. A plaque on the front of the house will testify to this when restoration is completed.

Currently a major work program will have restored the Big House to its earlier elegance—at no small expense. The new owners are Barbara

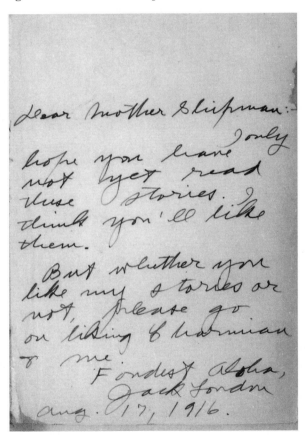

Mother Shipman, as Willie's wife became known in later years, was presented with an autographed copy of his book, *A Son of the Sun*, by Jack London. A picture of the Londons accompanied the book.

Ann Blackshear Andersen and her husband, Gary, who have been the overseers of the final restoration phase.

Much of the old furniture, mostly hand-crafted koa and milo, remains in the home. It includes a well-tooled settee made by the Reverend Shipman back in 1860. The books on the koa shelves in the library are the same ones through which the two visiting Londons browsed. The Andersens have appropriately designated that room the Jack London Library. Many of the dresses and much of the millinery worn by the six Shipman daughters still hang in large cedar-lined closets off their bedrooms, protected from moths and mildew. Many Hiloites retain memories of the grand tours of the Shipman house conducted for charitable causes a few years ago by Roy Blackshear, who periodically resided there with his grandparents and aunts during his adolescence.

It was to the Big House that Jane Reed moved when her oldest son became its owner. Its ample living space was in sharp contrast to the close quarters she had endured in the Wai'ōhinu rectory forty-one years earlier. In 1904, the year she saw her two sons enter the political arena, she died peacefully at the Reed's Island residence at the age of seventy-seven. Always frail and often unwell, Jane nevertheless outlived her first husband by forty-three years and her second by twenty-four. She was buried in Hilo's Homelani Cemetery, between her husbands.

Shortly after acquiring the Reed's Island home, Willie built what came to be called the Mountain Home up in the cool Volcano woodlands. It rested on property he had owned for many years and was the first dwelling of any size to be built in what is now Volcano Village. More than a vacation home and alternative dwelling, it was a welcome haven for friends visiting Kīlauea Volcano. One couple who were welcomed there were Jack and Charmian London. Seeing Kīlauea Volcano was high on their list of activities.

Some years later Charmian wrote of "the pleasant fact that we are the enviable guests of Mr. and Mrs. W. H. Shipman at their volcano residence. . . . Such a breezy household it is; and such a wholesome, handsome brood of young folk, under the keen though indulgent eye of this motherly deep-bosomed woman. Her three-fourths British ancestry keeps firm vigilance against undue demonstration of the ease-loving strain of Polynesian blood she has brought to their dowry." In her book *Our Hawaii*, Charmian wrote, "Jack's first lady of Hawaii is Mother Shipman herself."[18]

Charmian London saw in their hostess one who had been preserved from age and decay by "the tropics wine in her veins." And in William Shipman, Charmian viewed a spouse "in whose contented blue eyes twin-

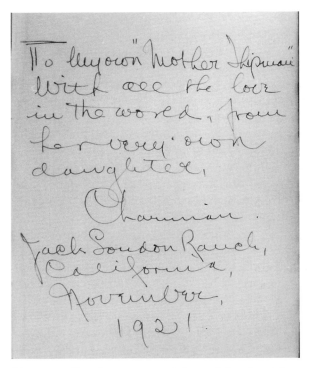

Charmian London expressed her aloha for Mary
Shipman in writing, "To my own Mother Shipman
with all the love in the world, from her very own
daughter."

kles pride in her handling of the family." As for the younger Shipmans, the
writer described them as "models of discipline and courtesy . . . brimming
with hilarious humor, while oftimes their mother's stately silken-holokued
figure is the maypole of a dancing, prancing romp."

Willie left the details of entertaining, of hosting, to his wife, a role
she filled graciously. And she, in general, left the operation of the Shipman enterprises to her husband. Yet not entirely, for Willie acknowledged
that his wife had a firm mind of her own and a good grasp of business.
This was attested to some years after her death by her son Herbert.
Remembering his Hawaiian grandmother, Eliza Davis Johnson, he
observed: "She was quite a general. And so was my mother. Nothing was
impossible to her. She was a much better businessman than my father
was." Once, when Willie had been offered some hundreds of acres on
Hawai'i's northwest coast at the bargain price of one dollar an acre, he

declined it. It was called Waikoloa, and Willie was right at the time in declaring the land remote and useless. But his wife was looking ahead. In recent years it has become known as Hawai'i's gold coast, the price per acre being in three and four digits.

On the domestic scene, Herbert remembered his mother's reputation for making superior mince pies. They were among his father's favorites; but Willie apparently could not or would not bring himself to compliment her. "When she would ask how was the mince pie," said Herbert, "he'd always reply 'Oh, pretty good.' One day when mother was not in a very good mood she announced, 'If you don't say that my mince pie is GOOD I'll never make another one again.' And she didn't. For the next 20 years she wouldn't give in and neither did he. Then they wondered why their children are stubborn."

By 1912 Willie had enough operations going to keep three men busy in management matters alone. But Willie preferred to be his own manager until such time as continued growth dictated otherwise. At the end of the first decade of the new century, he had a slaughterhouse outside of Kea'au that not only served his own needs but those of other nearby ranchers who paid for the service; likewise the Shipman Meat Market, a profitable outlet for beef from his own ranches.

Lands along the Volcano Road corridor brought Willie revenue from rentals and outright sales. His largest lessee was 'Ōla'a Sugar Company, which had a long-term lease for over 8,000 acres of his lands. The Hilo Railroad ran over about twelve miles of Shipman land from Kea'au to its terminal at Glenwood. (A side benefit was that Shipman family members were allowed to ride free over the entire length, which eventually ran forty miles north to Honoka'a and eighteen miles south to Glenwood. The passes were for perpetuity, but perpetuity ended on April 1, 1946, when a disastrous tsunami wiped out much of the Hilo Consolidated Railroad tracks and its numerous bridges.)

Among Willie's own ranch lands was the Kea'au Ranch, located at the base of the Kea'au Tract, which he had acquired a quarter-century earlier. Its many acres ran almost as far as Pāhoa and reached from the sea to a 1,800-foot elevation. The ranch, which Shipman acquired in 1882, was already a going concern, having been started by a *hui* that included Rufus Lyman, Charles Bishop, and John Paty. It was never a high-profit venture because much of its land was covered by brush, small ohia trees, and scrub guava. At best it was mediocre pasturage. Seventy miles of wire and stone fences confined the cattle. It had more than its share of lava holes, traps for horses and cattle, which suffered broken legs. On many of

the lava-based acres the soil was skin-thin. As a result of such poor grazing, the cattle, sometimes labeled as half-wild, rendered second-grade
beef at the most and sold in Hilo at prices well under first-grade beef,
which went to hotels as well as to choosier customers at the Shipman
Meat Market.

In 1904, when Willie's son Ollie II (named after his uncle) was
manager of the ranch, a low, rambling, shacklike hut was built near the
beach. Among other amenities it lacked were indoor plumbing and running water. A second home, which would eventually become known as
the family Beach House, was built in 1908 just yards from the lagoon
where twenty-seven years earlier Mary had told Willie she would like to
have a home someday.

Prior to the construction of the larger and more lavish beach home,
the Shipmans, when visiting at Hā'ena, lived in the primitive 1904 dwelling. For several years Mary had urged Willie to replace "that old shack"
with something she could be proud of. While she was on a European tour
in 1908, Willie had the older building torn down and replaced with a
beautiful six-bedroom house, complete with three bathrooms, a kitchen,
and indoor plumbing. Necessary ten thousand-gallon water tanks were
provided to hold the fresh water pumped from springs at the upper end of
the lagoon. The Beach House was indeed something Mary could be
proud of—and was.

When Mary and her children returned to visit Hā'ena, they got the
surprise of their lives when they saw a spacious green lawn where once
the old shack had been. Instead, Willie's beautiful "monument" to Mary,
as he considered it, stood there in all its glory. Eventually it became one
of the choice Shipman family residences, and is still known today as the
Beach House. In 1937 Herbert Shipman had the well-known architect
Charles H. Dickey redesign and remodel the home into the beautiful
house that today stands by the lagoon. It is now the home of Blackshear
and his wife, Donna.

By the start of the century Willie had acquired a lease for 23,000
acres of the Pu'u'ō'ō Ranch, on the eastern flank of Mauna Kea, near the
6,000-foot level. Here the rancher had five thousand head of cattle living
on rich grasslands, helped by ample rainfall averaging ninety-two inches
a year. Open forests abounded. The ranch at one time had seventy-five
miles of fencing. Later the ranch size was scaled back to 13,000 acres,
then to 6,000.

So satisfactory were grazing conditions that cattle from Kea'au
Ranch were often sent up to Pu'u'ō'ō, a long uphill trek. When these fattened cattle were ready for market, they were returned to Kea'au by the

same circuitous route. The drive would head south from Puʻuʻōʻō, cross the saddle dividing Mauna Loa from Mauna Kea, and, after a couple of days, reach the Kīlauea area. When the Shipman brothers had the ranch at Keauhou the party would stop for a day or so. There the cattle would rest and feed on good grazing land after the trek from Puʻuʻōʻō, which was often over lava flows that offered scant nourishment. Leaving the Kīlauea rich grasslands, the drive then continued down the Volcano Road to Glenwood. The total overland trip had been on forty miles of terrain that often meant rough footing over jagged lava, sometimes up hill and down dale. At Glenwood the cattle were loaded aboard freight cars that carried them to the twenty-acre holding paddock at Keaʻau, a step away from the slaughterhouse. More often than not Willie went with his cowboys on these drives.[19]

Puʻuʻōʻō was a remote though profitable operation. Its isolation may have appealed to Willie as an escape from his Hilo managing duties. Sometime around 1910 he did, however, feel it was important to have a telephone installed. It was quite a feat to string miles of wire up the mountain slope from Hilo, and he probably paid top dollar to get it done.

On one occasion in 1914, a party of young men from Honolulu who wanted to climb Mauna Kea stopped by the Shipman market to ask Willie the best way to go, but were told he was at Puʻuʻōʻō. When they reached him from the market by phone, he invited them to come and join him, saying he would send a horseman down the trail to meet them about halfway. A day later they met the Hawaiian guide on the Puʻuʻōʻō trail. He told them to follow him and led them over the difficult miles to the ranch house. On their arrival Willie noticed the fatigued condition of the hikers, burdened by their packs and worn out by the long trek, and asked the Hawaiian guide why he hadn't offered to carry their packs on his horse. "Because they never asked me to" was his answer.[20]

Seven miles north of Puʻuʻōʻō, and at about the same high elevation, was Puakala Ranch consisting of 5,500 acres of prime forest and grazing land. It was then leased by Willie, but later he bought it. Its cattle, too, were taken to market along the same arduous trail. (After the Saddle Road was built by the military during World War II to provide a relief road from Hilo to Kona, cattle were trucked to Keaʻau once they reached the road.) In 1987 the Nature Conservancy acquired 5,000 acres of Puakala Ranch, which had rich ohia and koa forests as well other environmental treasures. Shipman, long an advocate of the forest primeval, was generous in paring the price for the new buyer. The Shipman Company still retains 500 acres at Puakala.

In 1915 Willie had persuaded other Hawaiʻi cattle ranchers that it

would be to their mutual advantage to form a consortium. It was called
Hilo Meat Company and would serve as an outlet for grading and distrib-
uting beef to Hilo consumers, both wholesale and retail. Among the
larger customers were the Volcano House and other hotels. Shipman
owned 30 percent of the stock, Kūkaʻiau Ranch about 28 percent, and
the remainder was owned by Parker Ranch, Hind, and some smaller
ranchers. William Shipman was its president and remained in that position until his death.[21]

It was also in 1915 that Willie felt the need of an office other than
the back room of his market or the desk in his Reed's Island residence.
There were those who perceived Willie as carrying his businesses in his
hat. But he had obviously outgrown both his hat and his home desk. A
local contractor, Charles Will, was hired to build a one-story concrete
and brick structure at the junction of Wailuku Drive, Kamehameha Avenue, and Shipman Street. It was recognized as the first building in Hilo to
have a sprinkler system to combat fire. The building was a somewhat tri-
angular structure, with its blunt apex facing the bay while its main
entrance looked toward the Wailuku River. It was designated as Number
One Kamehameha Avenue. When completed, it was Shipman's headquarters for the Hilo Meat Company as well as his land and ranch operations. There was just enough space to accommodate three people—
himself, one—sometimes both—of his two sons, and eventually a clerk,
Richard Devine, who didn't join them until 1933.

By the second decade of the century, Shipman's business interests
had expanded to the point where he required more than an office; he
needed an organization that promised stability. He had been his own boss
for many years, while depending on his wife to manage the family and
arrange for entertaining guests. Perhaps it was her business acumen that
persuaded Willie to incorporate his holdings. Much of the Shipman land
was in the joint names of William and Mary. In March of 1923 he had
papers drawn up for the Articles of Association of W. H. Shipman, Limited. The corporation became a stock company of limited liability, and it
allowed the firm to engage in a wide variety of enterprises. Willie saw it as
a vehicle to share and transfer ownership to immediate family members.
The corporation was capitalized for $600,000, and it would remain a
closed family corporation. At the outset a minimal number of stock shares
were distributed by Willie to Mary and to each of their living children.
Also included was Alice Aspelin Shipman, widow of Oliver B. Shipman.
Ollie II, ten years Herbert's senior, had been a veterinarian as well as resident manager of Keaʻau Ranch. He died in 1920 of throat cancer.

Over the years Willie distributed an increasing number of shares to

Richard Devine, Shipman's office manager, recently retired after fifty-three years with the company. (Photo ca. 1945)

the initial stockholders. In this same time frame, those lands which were in the name of William H. Shipman were, by virtue of incorporation, deeded to William H. Shipman Limited. These holdings consisted primarily of the ranches at Kea'au (which also had a commercial dairy), Keauhou, Puakala, Pu'u'ō'ō, and a sizable number of acres leased elsewhere in the Kea'au Tract. In addition, there was Ohialani Dairy at Volcano run by Shipman's son-in-law, Otis English, married to Mary, the eldest daughter of William and Mary.

The year after the incorporation, Mary Shipman thought it high

time she visited the mainland and also took a European tour. She did it in
reverse order, and in style. Her daughter Caroline (generally called Carrie) and son Herbert accompanied her. Her letter to the family from Bal-
boa Heights relayed her impressions (all favorable) of the Panama Canal
and the country on both sides as they traveled to the Caribbean.

Mary was most enthusiastic over their stay of several days in Wales.
She was especially taken with the picturesque mountains and "the grand
bays, something like Pearl Harbor. The Bay of Milford is where our
grandfather [John Davis] came from. . . . Herbert and Carrie went to the
vicar to try and find out some information about the Davises." One day
and two vicars later, they found a custodian of "old books yellow with
age, where we found the names of several Davises. Among them was
John, [who] might be our great-grandfather. And one lady, it must be
Isaac Davis' sister that wrote to him the same month and date. . . . The
cemetery was too overgrown and tombstones too faded . . . to make out
the names."

A visit to England's Lake District provided a welcome respite for
Carrie and her mother. But not for Herbert. Being his father's son, the
cattle rancher in him prevailed, and he took two days off to "go to Perth
to see the livestock show there."

In Mary's letter to her daughter Clara, she provided a good description of those parts of London which captured her interest—the parks, old
homes, and many old and new churches. From Paris she wrote daughter
Margaret that, while in Florence, she and Herbert had enjoyed a play,
"the second time we had seen it." Their tour of France was made more
complete and educational thanks to a friend, a Madame Bina, who acted
as their guide. A Russian play was like nothing they had seen before. The
singing was "very good and some of their tunes are like Hawaiian."

Mary gave no details, but Herbert landed in the hospital while in
Paris and the "minister called to see him." Nor did that unanticipated
setback diminish Mary's enthusiasm for the city. "This is a great place,"
she wrote her family. "Always some place to go every day. All kinds of
amusement, including the opera." But apparently her energy had begun
to flag. "I have a cold, so must hurry and get to bed. The cold weather is
beginning. I will be glad when I get home again. Have had enough of
traveling around and living out of suitcases. I am hungry for *poi* [a popular
Hawaiian staple made of taro]."

# 20

# *Passing the Scepter*

*The old order changeth,*
*Yielding place to new.*

—ALFRED, LORD TENNYSON

The seven years that followed the incorporation of W. H. Shipman, Limited were good years for the Shipman interests and for the family members who saw their shares and dividends increase. Willie kept a firm hand on the tiller and his mind on business. The mainland depression of 1929 had not quite hit Hawai'i, but it was on its way.

Although not a mixer or a hail-fellow-well-met, Willie knew other ranchers in east Hawai'i and was the first to pick their brains. He wanted to learn the best cattle-breeding practices so as to raise and sell prize beef; nor did cattle-breeding journals escape his attention. His love of the land must have come from the genes of his father, who had grown up on an Illinois farm and endeavored to interest his Ka'ū congregation in raising wheat and learning how to live off their land. Willie was far more comfortable in the saddle on one of his ranches than he was in a swivel chair. He was still riding horseback at seventy-five.

But all this came to an end on July 11, 1931, when Mary suffered a paralytic stroke after a long illness. She was beyond help and died two days later at the age of eighty. Services were held at the Reed's Island residence, where Hawaiian songs and *himine* lent their beauty to the ceremony. Hundreds of friends and workers paid their respects in the twenty-four hours she was on view in the formal parlor. Hawaiian attendants with *kahili* (royal standards) stood guard over her body throughout the wake. Interment was at the parklike family cemetery on the Kea'au premises. Her pallbearers were cowboys from Kea'au Ranch. On the day of the services, several Hilo businesses flew flags at half-mast, and the Hilo Public Library was closed for the afternoon. She and her husband had celebrated their golden wedding anniversary two years earlier. Willie was

Bedecked with leis from loving friends and family, Mary and William H. Shipman celebrated their golden wedding anniversary in April 1929.

Son, daughters, and grandchildren helped Willie and Mary celebrate their fiftieth wedding anniversary at Reed's Island in 1929. Mrs. Shipman died two years later. *Front row, left to right:* Virginia Fisher Dennis, Roy Shipman Blackshear, Mary Johnson Shipman, Beryl Blackshear. *Back row:* Florence Shipman Blackshear, Clara Shipman Fisher, Caroline M. Shipman, William Shipman, Mary Shipman English, Herbert Shipman, Margaret Shipman, and Margaret Clarissa English. *Missing:* Eldon Shipman English.

still savoring the memories of that event, celebrated by loving children, grandchildren, and a wide range of family friends from many circles. The widower was determined not to go into seclusion after his loss. But at the age of seventy-seven he was no longer out driving his cattle or surveying his ranches from the saddle. More time was spent in the Wailuku Drive office.

At least a decade before his own death, Willie had, by degrees, groomed Herbert to become manager of the Shipman holdings. After the death of Ollie II in 1920, this sole surviving son moved from the Reed's Island residence to the Kea'au ranch property, where he took over as manager. Aside from a certain amount of seclusion it offered, Herbert also preferred the Kea'au location for the opportunity it afforded to put in hothouses and further indulge his love for flowers and rare plants. Willie took into account Herbert's passion for plants, particularly orchids. He also derived personal satisfaction from Herbert's having earlier rounded out his education after college with a sound course in accounting and business management. Also, Willie was aware of Herbert's interest in attending a livestock show on his first of many trips to Europe. Willie was still very much in charge, but both father and son relied more and more on Dick Devine, their office bookkeeper, to earn his salary as a yet untitled manager.[1]

Dick Devine was the son of the foreman, Daniel Devine, who had been brought over from Honolulu by Hilo contractor Charles Will to construct the Shipman building. Dick had graduated from the then Saint Louis College with a business and accounting background. In 1925 he was hired by Marshall & Henderson, a Hilo accounting firm of which William Shipman was a client. As Dick Devine recalls it: "Mr. Shipman took a shine to me and asked me to come and work for him. I demurred but then Henderson spoke up and reminded me that it was 1933: they were suffering from the depression, and he couldn't afford to keep me any longer. I took the hint and Mr. Shipman's offer."

Devine first did basic bookkeeping for both the Hilo Meat cooperative and Willie's other ranch- and land-related enterprises. Half of his salary was paid by Shipman; the other half by Hilo Meat. Willie was definitely in command; his first lieutenant was Herbert. Both were in and out of the office, often at one of the ranches.

Mr. Shipman, as Devine always called Willie, spent more time in the office in his last ten years. Devine remembers him "as having a gruff exterior, but actually a soft touch. His trademark was his cigar, which sometimes made him appear forbidding, a mask he wore purposely, I think. But he was always good to me. He seldom called me by name, but rather just *haole*. Once he stood over my desk, and barked, 'What are you doing, *haole?*'" Devine explained that he was preparing Shipman's own taxes. "Well, just make sure you put everything in there that should be," Shipman said with a puff on his cigar. Willie's integrity in Hilo had never been in doubt and he wanted it to stay that way.

One special aspect of his work that Willie preferred to do himself was preparing the payroll. Some thirty people, mostly ranch hands, were personally paid by Willie whenever possible. It was Devine's job to go to the Bank of Hilo (of which Willie had been a founder; it later became part of the Bank of Hawaii), and to draw out the amount of cash specified by Willie, so much in one-dollar bills, fives, and tens. Also stacks of nickels, dimes, quarters, and half-dollars. All this currency Willie would

Lili'uokalani, Hawai'i's last queen, was an occasional visitor at the Shipman home. (Photo by Bonnie. HSA)

then divide up and place in appropriate piles for dispensing to his employees.

As Willie grew older he remained the same sort of a loner he had always been, maybe more so. He was not antisocial, but he certainly was no joiner. He had done his share of being a public servant in his younger years. He was not known to have any buddies or cronies. "But if you were a true friend of Willie you were a friend for life and he never forgot you," said Blackshear. Before Mary's death, aside from his businesses, Willie devoted more attention to his wife and children than to being with "the boys."

In time Willie sought still more solitude and found it at the much improved Kea'au Ranch house, where Herbert, now in essence the manager of W. H. Shipman, Limited and Kea'au Ranch, made his home. With Mary gone, the Big House meant less to Willie. He was glad to let his daughters enjoy its setting and comforts. They were also in frequent attendance on their father as he spent his last years between Herbert's "manager's house" and the nearby Beach House, some three hundred yards away, next to the lagoon.

This seven-acre Kea'au property was sometimes identified as Hā'ena, after the once small Hawaiian fishing village that nestled next to the three-acre lagoon. Willie chose to live out his years at the site selected by his young bride, more than a half-century earlier. By 1927, the manager's house had been added on to, and was expanded again in 1937 when Herbert, as residing manager, sought more space for his art collections as well as entertaining and room for more gracious living.

The nearby Beach House was built in 1908 and underwent considerable remodeling in 1937. It was there that the Shipmans gathered to celebrate holidays, birthdays, and family picnics. The lagoon between these two houses provided a typical tropical setting for filmland, and Hollywood shot at least two pictures at the site. The first was Cecil B. deMille's *Four Frightened People,* made in 1933. *Bird of Paradise,* featuring Debra Pagett, Louis Jourdan, and Jeff Chandler, was filmed in 1950. More recently one of the *Hawaii Five-O* episodes was filmed there. Nature was generous in providing not only a marine setting for filming but also trees and birds that could be conjured into a jungle background. Besides the nene there were such tropical birds as mynahs, cardinals, egrets, doves, mejiro, and Chinese thrushes, as well as wild birds and ducks that migrated every year from North America to spend their winters at Hā'ena.

Both residences, as well as their surroundings, furnished the inspiration for Hawaiian songwriter Helen Desha Beamer to compose the haunting "Lei O Hā'ena" (Lei around Hā'ena), one of those Island songs which feature the hospitality and beauty of famous Hawai'i homes.

When World War II reached America, it also came to the island of Hawai'i—with a bang. In the first two months of 1942, troops by the thousands manned beaches, bunkers, hillside outposts, and makeshift air-

Washington D.C.
Jan 14. 1899
1415 - 15th St. N.W.

My dear friend Maud,

What was my surprise on looking over my heap of unanswered letters to find one from you and dated as far back as the 30th of October...

...I am happy to know that you are progressing so well in your studies, and that you seem so hopeful as to your future course.

My best wishes attend you in all your undertakings. Give my best aloha to your mother. I hope you will write often,

Sincerely yours
Liliuokalani

The deposed queen was in Washington, D.C., in 1899, seeking the return of her throne from the American annexationists. She found time to write "Dear Maud" a letter in which she referred to Mary Shipman as a very dear friend. (See beginning of second paragraph.) The former queen's crest is at the top of the page.

strips. Many of the Shipman ranch lands were temporary homes to GI infantry, artillery, and searchlight battalions. Coastal defenses and machine-gun bunkers were constructed and manned adjacent to the Kea'au beach, and inevitably the GIs sought out people to visit. Those local people who knew Willie to be crusty would have been surprised to hear this man in his late eighties chatting with young military men on the roomy porch of his home. Overlooking a spacious lawn and a rippling lagoon, he was reciting history from early missionary days up to Hawai'i's present.

There was a closeness between Willie and Roy Blackshear that lasted until Willie's death. It developed during those weeks when Roy and his grandfather were together at Pu'u'ō'ō Ranch with Herbert. On one occasion, although Willie did not like to have his picture taken, he willingly posed for Roy, who had a new Brownie box camera. That picture, Willie often said, was one of his best.

When Roy lived with his Uncle Herbert for a year, his grandfather also shared the manager's ranch home, and often Roy would ride back from Hilo, where he was in school, to Kea'au with the cigar-smoking Willie and Henry Ha'a, the chauffeur.

Once, when Willie was living with his daughters Caroline and Margaret on Reed's Island, they asked Roy if he would spend the night there, as they were going to a New Year's party and wouldn't be home until late. Roy recalls that it was a most enjoyable evening. Margaret had instructed Roy to have dinner with his grandfather and then, after dinner, ask him to play dominoes, a game Willie loved. Margaret also instructed Roy to let her father win at least two out of three games. The evening went along as planned, and after supper Willie agreed to play three games of dominoes. Willie won the first game, Roy the second, and the third game "went on and on forever," according to Roy. "I purposely played so Grandpa could win," and finally Willie did win it and the two retired for the night. The next morning Margaret laughingly pulled Roy aside. She told him, "I know you played dominoes last night with father, and he won, but I was just in the kitchen with him enquiring about how the evening had gone and he told me 'We played three games of dominoes and I won two of them. I did my best to let the little tyke win the last game but just couldn't do it!'"

When Roy started attending Punahou School at age thirteen, Willie seemed to recall his own youth and experiences when he and his brother Oliver were students there in the late 1860s. He was very much interested in how the school had changed. He would sit his grandson down and ask him questions pertaining to the present life of a boarder at the school. In 1941, the day Roy left Hilo to go to the mainland for the first time to attend New Mexico Military Institute, his grandfather and Henry drove from Keaʻau to the Blackshear home in Hilo to say goodbye and wish him well. Roy took several photos of his grandfather, and then Willie drove away. It was the last time the two would see each other.

In early 1943 Willie knew that he was failing. Twelve long years after losing his wife, he died at the age of eighty-nine, leaving forever the island home that he had been so homesick for when away at school in Illinois. His death did not come as a surprise.

In July 1943, the month Willie died, Roy was returning from college. He recalls:

In June of 1943 I was on my way home to Hawaii after graduating from Military Institute in Roswell, New Mexico. I looked forward to returning to Hawaii as soon as possible so that I could enlist in a war that was now 19 months old. But inevitable delays had me chafing at the bit. Once in San Francisco I learned I could get passage to Hilo only on a space-available basis. It was July 6th before I was assigned to a Hawaii-bound freighter. That night we slipped out of the Bay, beneath the Golden Gate Bridge and headed west into the Pacific.

I was one of twelve passengers, all male. My sleeping quarters was a box-like cabin with six bunks on the top deck. For an undetermined length of time, since we were traveling in a convoy, my bunk would be on the bottom. On the night of Wednesday, July 7th, I finished my supper, read a little, played some cribbage before it got dark, then retired to complete darkness in the rather damp make-shift cabin.

As usual for me, I had no trouble falling to sleep. But sometime in the early hours of Thursday, July 8th, I was awakened from a dreamlike vision of my grandfather. He was standing at the foot of my bunk, wearing his customary felt cowboy hat and he had a contented look on his face. He was saying good-bye to me, smiling as he said it. The vision of Grandpa slowly faded from sight. I shared the experience with my cabin-mates at daybreak, who questioned me as to where my grandfather would have been. I told them I knew he had been in the Hilo Hospital when we had been in San Francisco, so I presumed he was O.K.

The following week, on July 11th or 12th, our freighter reached Maui and the captain told us we would have a four hour layover and anyone who wished to go ashore could do so. I was among the several passengers who decided not to. But while we were tied up there the incident I had experienced came home to me with emphasis, for Lahaina was where Grandpa had been born in 1854.

We sailed out of Lahaina under cover of darkness, headed for our destination, Pearl Harbor. The following morning our vessel was off Diamond Head, always a welcome beacon to people returning to their Hawaii home. After breakfast I was walking along the deck, headed for my cabin. I passed a crew member leaning over the rail reading the *Honolulu Advertiser* which he had picked up the day before in Lahaina. As I passed him I felt compelled to slow down and look over his shoulder. There on the front page I saw the heading of a column which read, 'W. H. Shipman Services Held.' The story said he had died on Thursday, July 8th. When I landed at Pearl Harbor, I immediately called my Aunt Mina Blackshear and she verified it. Grandpa Shipman had indeed said goodbye to me that morning of July 8th in my cabin on the high seas. That vision still remains etched in my memory."[2]

The well-known Reverend Stephen Desha officiated at the Shipman funeral services at the Kea'au home. The main room where the coffin reposed was, as at Mary's services, filled with rich Hawaiian songs, in Hawaiian, from the gifted Haili Church choir. Ranch employees were the pallbearers for the man who had long been recognized as a prominent and successful Hawai'i island rancher. The names of the honorary pallbearers could have been taken from the Who's Who of the community.

Shipman's last will and testament was drawn up in September 1936, seven years before his demise.[3] In the terms of the will, his son Herbert was named executor. It was no surprise that he left the Reed's Island residence to his six children. To his four nieces and nephews he left $500 each, and to the widow of Ollie II, Alice Shutte, he bequeathed $1,000. The rest of his estate, consisting largely of shares in William H. Shipman Ltd., was left to his children in a trust managed by Herbert and the First Trust Company of Hilo. A prize possession was his gold pocket watch, which he left to Roy.

Willie had made it quite clear that he wished to keep intact and in the family the property which "with the aid of my wife I have spent a lifetime in creating and acquiring . . . I am desirous that said property be kept intact and properly managed in the form of a corporation. . . . It is my hope that my children do not sell or hypothecate any share . . . but that each one of them may take and derive pleasure in holding and owning said shares: but should necessity compel any of [them] to sell, dispose of . . . their shares it is my profound and lasting wish that they first give ample notice and first opportunity of purchasing to my other children."

The First Foreign Church of Hilo and Haili Church were each bequeathed $500. No other similar beneficiaries were mentioned. The will clearly stated that "I make no specific bequests to any social service institution, as I have endeavored to contribute to the aid of and assist my fellowman during my lifetime, as well as to promote the advancement of the Christian religion." Willie's missionary parents would have liked that.

Willie had relinquished the reins of management by 1940, satisfied that his scion was capable of running the family business. When in 1943 Herbert took over, he was fifty-one years old. He did indeed carry on the family business, but the family name ended with this bachelor son.

# 21

# *Herbert Shipman: Man of Many Talents*

When Herbert Shipman, the youngest of Mary's and Willie's seven sur-viving children, died in 1976, he had lived through five forms of Hawai'i's often turbulent government. He was born in the twilight of 1892, when the Hawaiian Kingdom was on the eve of a bloodless revolu-tion. It came in January 1893 when Queen Lili'uokalani was overthrown by American business interests living in Hawai'i. No one was more responsible for this long-planned and -plotted event than Lorrin An-drews Thurston, Herbert's uncle by marriage. Herbert's very early years were spent at the Volcano Street residence, then on the outskirts of Hilo, during the reign of the Provisional Government, which was followed by five years of the Republic of Hawai'i. When a lad of only eight, he was aware of the creation (postannexation) of the Territory of Hawai'i by the United States of America. That form of semi-self-rule endured thoughout most of Herbert's adult life. In 1959 Hawai'i became the fiftieth state, and Herbert was able to vote in national elections for the next seventeen years.

In order of their birth, his siblings were Mary, Oliver, Clara, Caro-line, Florence, and Margaret. Mary and Florence married into the English and Blackshear families, respectively, and their offspring remain active in Shipman and Hawai'i island affairs. (William and Mary's first child, Wil-liam Reed Shipman, died at the age of five, the victim of burns from a pot of hot tea accidentally spilled on him.)

When Herbert Shipman agreed to a taped interview for the Watu-mull Foundation in 1972, he was obviously in a relaxed mood—not one of his traits—and revealed unfamiliar sidelights and interests.[1] In the two-day interview he hearkened back to his birth, informing the inter-viewer, "I first met my parents on November 4, 1892 and we've been friends ever since." He was given the name Herbert Cornelius, the mid-dle names of his father and grandfather. His sense of humor, a characteris-tic that many failed to observe in him, surfaced again when he explained, "They gave me the name of Cornelius before I could talk back." He was the first to admit, as close associates charged, that his five doting sisters were responsible for his having "been spoiled rotten."

Herbert was four years old when he first became aware of his Hawaiian heritage. His mother took him to Kona to visit his full-blooded Hawaiian great-grandmother, Kauwe. They also planned to visit Eliza Davis Johnson, Mary's half-Hawaiian mother. This meant a trip of several days by horse and rig to Kona, about a hundred miles distant, on the other side of the island, over what were euphemistically called roads.

"We had a span of horses and a two-wheel rig for the first part of our trip," recalled Shipman. The first night was spent at Volcano, probably at the Shipman mountain house. The next day took them to Kapāpala, where they enjoyed the hospitality of ranch manager Julian Monsarrat and his wife. The following day they arrived at Wai'ōhinu, scene of the pastoral labors of his paternal grandparents thirty-six years earlier. Their

Herbert Shipman was the only surviving son of Mary and William, three others having died much earlier (ca. 1950).

rest for the night was provided by the deep-rooted Meinecke family, whose home was only yards from the former Shipman Congregational church. The remainder of their trip meant leaving the rig and traveling by horseback. It took two more days to reach their Kona destination.

Herbert's memory at age eighty-one was keen enough to recall his only visit to Kauwe. "Little bit of thing, my great-grandmother," said Herbert. "She was blind. Wanted to feel me all over. She was pleased that I didn't cry." Herbert didn't know it then, but it is estimated that Kauwe was about a hundred and four years old, a century older than he. She would have remembered King Kamehameha the Great, perhaps had even seen him.[2]

Living with Kauwe at the time was her lady-in-waiting. Forty years later, on a trip to London, Herbert made it a point to buy a gift for the former lady-in-waiting. The present was fabric from Harrods, and Herbert remembered: "This little frail person, who didn't even wear glasses, made a garment out of it." Like Kauwe, she had lived in the reign of Kamehameha the Great and may well have remembered when he was dying. The woman thought she was about fifteen years old at the time of the king's death. Shipman estimated that she would have been around one hundred and twenty-five years old at the time she made the garment.

Some aspects of chiefdom seem to have been carried down from Kauwe to Eliza and into the Reed/Shipman residence. "Mother Reed," as Jane was often called, was treated by some of the servants as though she were a member of the Hawaiian *ali'i,* and they would sometimes kneel to her. Herbert remembers her reaction to such obeisance: "Get up! Get up! I'll have no such thing," she would scold.

As both Willie and Mary could speak Hawaiian fluently, it was not surprising that as an adult Herbert had a working knowledge of the language, though he was not fluent. He also had an understanding of and appreciation for the worth of Hawaiian medicines. This he acquired from his mother, who firmly believed in the medicinal properties of herbs, Hawaiian fruits, and other native plants and used them throughout her life.

When Herbert was about ten years old, the family moved into their recently purchased Reed's Island "Palace." By then he was already receiving his primary education from Mrs. Kennedy's private school in Hilo for children of the "upper class." There would have been few if any Hawaiians for Herbert to converse with in their tongue. His high-school education, like that of his siblings and father and uncle, was completed at

Punahou; he graduated in 1911. His first trip to the mainland was to attend college at Lawrenceville, New Jersey. He finished his academic studies with a year at the University of Wisconsin.

Herbert's last formal education was perhaps his most important. It would have been at his father's urging that he agreed to take a business course, a step that Willie had found to make the difference between success and failure. Money was no problem, so Herbert graduated from one of the best business schools in the nation, Heald's Business College in San Francisco. After serving in Hawai'i as a lieutenant in the army during World War I, young Shipman came back to east Hawai'i to live with his family on Reed's Island.

He began to learn the operations of the Hilo Meat Company while working in the office, which his father very much headed. But Herbert's strong interest in horticulture kept him out of the office as much as in. Willie knew from his own experience the benefits of a business background, but beyond that he initiated Ollie and Herbert into such ranching essentials as animal husbandry, cattle driving, and the raising and grazing of good beef cattle.

This youngest son never pretended to be the rancher his father and brother Ollie were. Willie, in comparing his two sons, once commented: "Ollie is a hell-for-leather cowboy. He loves athletics and being out in the field. Herbert goes more for fancy flowers, likes to plant and grow things." Herbert also differed from his father in that he had a good Eastern college education. Whereas Willie couldn't wait to cut his mainland education short and come home to his stepfather's Kapāpala ranch, Herbert took his time about shedding the college gown for a cowboy outfit. Whereas Willie had been a rancher from the moment he hit Kapāpala, his young son left room for other interests, of which he had many.

Herbert's education actually did not end with college. He had several areas of interest as a reader, particularly whatever related to his personal interests in orchids, arboreal subjects, animal husbandry, and various types of grasses. Throughout his life he was a member of several societies related to horticulture and similar subjects. He remained a dues-paying member in order to have the benefit of receiving their periodicals, which kept him current and informed. Later in life his peers considered him an authority on the matters of Hawai'i's complex land laws, leases, and land ownership. His parents, too, were quite knowledgeable in this changing field and surely taught him about it.

Such expertise was vital to the growing W. H. Shipman Company, which was very much into land acquisition and exchanges; many involved Hawaiian portions of *ahupua'a*, so its manager had to understand old deeds and new laws.

Brother Ollie's role as manager of Shipman's Kea'au ranch abruptly ended with his sudden death in 1920. Herbert not only stepped in to fill the vacancy, he moved into the manager's remote house and would make it his home for life, despite the retreat ranch of 'Āinahou he created in 1941. Ranch life was to his liking, but not to the degree that it had been enjoyed by Ollie. Kea'au offered Herbert the privacy he loved, but it also afforded him more opportunity to experiment with plants, particularly orchids. This was a hobby that earned him national acclaim and foreign recognition.

A man of diverse interests, Herbert acquired a fondness for and became a respected collector of silver, Asian art, and tasteful paintings

Oliver B. Shipman was the eldest son of Willie and Mary, and the nephew of Oliver T. He died of throat cancer while the manager of Kea'au Ranch and was a recognized athlete.

and furniture. These interests occupied much of his long and sometimes lonely life, alternately filled with travel and self-imposed isolation at Kea'au.

Herbert's longtime chauffeur, steward, footman, dominoes partner, and gofer was Henry Ha'a. (Herbert once told a friend that Henry's Hawaiian surname was "pronounced with a hiccup between the two *a*'s.") It was, friends say, Henry's Hawaiian disposition that enabled him to remain a loyal and friendly servant for the next fifty-five years of Herbert's life. More than once, Herbert used Henry as his punching bag. For example, when Herbert lost a game of dominoes to Henry, he would sometimes express his frustration by throwing them at his placid partner.

Despite Herbert's sometimes irascible behavior toward Henry, the two were close, almost inseparable, companions. They frequently took their meals together. Herbert, who knew a good drink when he had it, would often "strike a blow for liberty" with his manservant. Furthermore, he was proud to show friends his own four-poster bed in a spacious bedroom, and in a corner Henry's single bed, flanked by his special table radio. Such a setup lends support to the assertion that Herbert was actually a lonely man. But he provided a good life for Henry, who accompanied him on some of his journeys to Europe as well as on mainland trips.

## Man of Nature

Of Herbert Shipman's many and diverse interests none surpassed horticulture, a field that fascinated him for most of his life. Early evidence of this emerged in 1907; while a student at Punahou, he developed an interest in raising the *Schilleriana* orchid. His own father observed that he was more often found in a field of flowers than among a herd of cattle.

In 1920 Herbert made the Kea'au ranch manager's house his home. Surrounded by seven acres and a lagoon, he was in an ideal setting to expand his passion for propagating plants. Orchids, say those who knew him then, were his obsession. When his nephew Roy Blackshear was still a schoolboy, his uncle taught him the fine art of raising and planting seedlings. In time, Herbert had a sizable hothouse at Kea'au devoted especially to the cultivation of orchids, and a Japanese gardener whose responsibility was to care for and nourish the prized plants, many of which had come from other parts of the globe. Numerous nurseries on Hawai'i island came to have rare orchids that were made possible by Herbert Shipman. In time he was the recipient of many awards for his contributions to horticulture and conservation. Among those he prized most was one of twelve gold medals awarded by the American Orchid Society, of which he was a lifetime member. He was also an overseas member of the Royal Horticultural Society of London, the Hawaii Orchid Society, which he once headed, the Pacific Tropical Botanical Gardens, the Botanical Society of South Africa, The Pacific Orchid Society, the Hawaiian Botanical Gardens Association, and the Friends of Foster Gardens.[3]

In his lifetime Shipman made several trips to England, usually on matters related to horticulture, particularly orchids. Kew Gardens outside London was one of his favorite haunts, and he became a supporting member of that famous five hundred-acre botanical nursery and park.

Henry Ha'a had the good fortune to accompany Shipman on most of these trips, not only because Herbert wanted his company, but because he had kindled in Henry a genuine interest in plants. Ha'a took to horticulture easily. Although this manservant's formal education had been very limited, thanks to Herbert he became a perfect speller of any and all botanical names. Herbert had instilled in him not only a knowledge of plants but a genuine love for them. It strengthened their unique bond of friendship.

Although a great lover of orchids, Shipman's interest and erudition extended to many other flowers and a variety of bushes, shrubbery, and trees—especially flowering trees. He took special pains to preserve rare trees, even if they required transporting and transplanting, often many miles away. A particular blossoming tree, the *Gardenia remyi*, is indigenous to Hawai'i, yet there are precious few. The tree's first blossoms are yellow; they turn orange, and after that white, sending out the fragrance of the true gardenia. Shipman, concerned about their paucity, made a successful air-layer graft of one of these uncommon trees found on Shipman property. Today it is a tall and full tree adorning an opulent garden in upper Hilo, a gift to a friend.

In the boardroom of W. H. Shipman, Limited there is an elegantly shaped and polished mango wood bowl. Its bronze plaque reads: "Awarded to Herbert C. Shipman as the Conservationist of the Century by the Waiakea Soil and Water Conservation District." His concern for conservation went far beyond saving grasses, bushes, and nutrient plants found on Shipman ranches and other properties. Ranch owners elsewhere in Hawai'i heeded his concerns in such matters and stood to profit from them in ways related to their livelihood.

Preservation and conservation were to Herbert Shipman handmaidens to one another. He considered trees to be among the planet's greatest riches. Woe be to the utility companies if their tree trimmers hacked off a frond or branch that Herbert felt was unwarranted.

If restoration can be equated with preservation, then Shipman deserves the acclaim given him in the November 1965 issue of *National Geographic* magazine. Many years before the article was published, Shipman had become acutely aware that the Hawaiian goose, better known as the nēnē (pronounced "naynay") had all but disappeared. Distant cousins of the wild Canada goose, a gaggle may have found its way to Hawai'i carried by a storm a half-million years ago, some biologists speculate. Hawai'i Island is at least a million years old, and its lava fields would have provided suitable nesting areas, as they do today. But nēnē are friendly, and also delicious, an unfortunate combination for them: 1911 found them almost extinct.

As early as 1918, Shipman, who as a boy had seen the birds flying over family ranch lands, wondered if they could not be brought back. He was soon given a pair as a gift and kept them at his Kea'au ranch home. Nine years later he had a small flock. The Hawaii Territorial Commission on Forestry and Agriculture soon expressed interest and support. Shipman supplied the agency with a few pairs of nēnē, which in turn multiplied, allowing more to be shipped to some of the other Islands.

In April 1946, a disastrous tidal wave swept east Hawai'i's coast, and out of Shipman's flock of forty-three only eleven survived. But, with Shipman determination, Herbert began to restore the flock, now moving breeders to his ranch, 'Āinahou, in the high fields on the slopes of Kīlauea. They took hold, and by 1950 there may have been fifty birds in existence. Shipman expanded his efforts to develop flocks abroad, a goal of the International Union for the Protection of Nature. The same year Sir Peter Scott, honorary director of England's Wild Fowl and Wetlands Trust, sent an emissary to Hawai'i to learn techniques in rearing young nēnē. (Scott, born in 1909, was the son of Captain Robert Falcon Scott, leader of the ill-fated Antarctic expedition who died in the attempt to reach the South Pole before Roald Amundsen. Captain Scott and his men perished on the ice in 1910.) Six months after Sir Peter's emissary arrived in Hawai'i, Shipman sent back with him a pair of his precious birds. Things went awry when it was later discovered that both birds were females. Shipman solved the dilemma by flying to England a proven gander named Kamehameha; nine young nēnē later increased England's nēnē population. As a result of Shipman's help and Sir Peter Scott's program, descendants of these three Hawaiian nēnē have been distributed to breeders in France, Great Britain, the Netherlands, Switzerland, Germany, and, of course, the United States.

Saved from extinction in Hawai'i, the nēnē now number about 550, ten times their number forty-five years ago. Herbert Shipman gladly recognized the invaluable help of government wildlife agencies in Hawai'i for the success in nēnē propagation. But he well deserves the accolades given him for the role he played, many years earlier, in saving the nēnē from the fate suffered by the passenger pigeon. So closely is the nēnē associated with Shipman interests, that the company's logo is a stately pair of these colorful feathered birds. The nēnē has been officially designated as the state bird of Hawai'i.

Sir Peter Scott and Herbert Shipman, who often met in England, continued a correspondence until Shipman's death. In one letter Scott wrote: "We have raised 380 nene so far and it all began with you. We are very grateful to you." Scott was also grateful to his Hawai'i friend for introducing him, and later royalty, to macadamia nuts. "My Dear Herbert," he once wrote, "The macadamia nuts were extremely welcome. They arrived most opportunely the morning that Prince Charles came to stay here, so were able to introduce him to the best nuts in the world. Thank you indeed for the appreciated gift."[4] It was probably through Sir Peter Scott that Queen Elizabeth II was treated to the Hawaiian nuts. Word of Her Majesty's fondness for them reached Herbert Shipman, and for several years he regularly sent her a supply for Christmas. Once he had them delivered to her airplane as it passed through Honolulu.

# W.H. SHIPMAN, LTD.
## KEAAU
## HAWAII ISLAND

Hawai'i's state bird, the nēnē, owes its survival to the efforts of Herbert Shipman. A pair of these still rare birds is represented in the logo of W. H. Shipman stationery.

Each time a quantity of the nuts arrived at Buckingham Palace, a letter of appreciation came to Herbert, always signed by the queen's personal secretary.

One, dated January 11, 1967, acknowledged that "The tins of macadamia nuts which you sent to The Queen have reached her safely. Her Majesty was delighted to receive them. The Queen desires me to convey her very sincere thanks for your kindness in giving them to her and to send you her best wishes for 1967."[5]

## *Herbert in the Eyes of Others*

Arrogant, irascible, authoritarian, and domineering—these and similar adjectives emerge from descriptions of Herbert Cornelius Shipman by many of his associates—he had few truly close friends, nor did he want them—during his long life. Those who knew him best include his close friend Dr. Leslie Weight; a cousin, Mrs. Kapua Heuer; veteran office manager Richard Devine; longtime secretary, Bessie Morita; and his nephew and successor, Roy Blackshear. Maggie Wessel Stearns, young enough to be his daughter, has a heartful of pleasant recollections of him, mostly testifying to his thoughtfulness. These same individuals add that Herbert could be generous, fair, considerate, and thoughtful, though not to excess. They also remember that he possessed a good sense of humor.

Dr. Weight considers his forty-five-year friendship with Shipman as a qualification for judging the man. The acquaintance began when veterinarian Weight treated Shipman livestock on the various ranches. Weight became something of a confidant of Shipman and was included in much of his social life. He saw both the pluses and minuses, the pros and cons, the Jekyll and Hyde in his longtime friend, whom he continued to admire after death.

"He was not an easy man to really know," recalled Weight. "He had few real close confidential friends. I think I was one of them. But he was highly interesting. Very intelligent and well-informed in areas of interest to him. He was handsome, a tall man, over six feet, but well-poised and always well-dressed. He seldom varied from wearing a black-knit tie. He was generous if he liked you. He was well-spoken, authoritative, and demanding. Also very independent and sometimes selfish. He was a complex man."

Weight admired Herbert for admitting that he had been spoiled by his mother and five older and doting sisters. "After all, he was not only the youngest child in the family of six living children, he was also the sole surviving male child of William and Mary Shipman. He possessed a love, an attraction, for the better things in life as he saw them. They included class, high quality, important people, art, flowers, and entertaining. He was a great host."

The retired veterinarian saw Shipman as an expert on special grasses, feed mixes, pasture lands, cattle breeding, and crop rotation. "He is the man who introduced the famed Santa Gertrudis cattle to Hawaii and then advanced cattle productivity by selective cross breeding. Herbert Shipman was always a supporter of wild life preservation, as well as plant conservation. His reputation as a horticulturist, especially in orchids, was international. Also he was recognized as an authority in Hawaiian arboriculture."

On a personal level, Weight saw Shipman as a good, though older, friend. "We had our squabbles; we didn't agree on everything, but we got along fine." He also knew this friend as a lover of Hawai'i's history, a great raconteur, and an accepted source of information related to land matters. "He had a fantastic memory and remained sharp his entire life. And no one ever accused Herbert Shipman of ever having lied. He didn't have to."

A cousin on Mary Shipman's side was equally frank in describing the man she knew well and saw often over the years. Mrs. Heuer recalled Herbert as someone who demanded attention; he liked "important" people. The feeling was mutual. "He had a superiority complex," declared Mrs. Heuer. "He felt he was special and his sisters were partly to blame. But as they got older his sister Margaret would stand up to him. He was often hard to get along with, but I knew him very well and will say that I liked him. He DID have a good sense of humor which helped a lot."

"Herbert and his father were as different as night and day." That is the recollection of Richard Devine, who should know, having been with the company in a management capacity for fifty-three years, ten of which were while Willie was still alive and very much in charge. Herbert took over in 1943, and Devine worked under him for the next thirty-three years.

Devine recognized that Herbert had inherited some of his father's gruffness, faked or otherwise. Like his father, he was not a joiner, though he later belonged to numerous organizations, often to take advantage of acquiring information that interested him. Some of Willie's shyness may also have rubbed off on his younger son, which he camouflaged with a testiness that became his trademark to some people. Whereas Willie was inclined to be blunt, brief, and abrupt, Herbert was an artist with a rapier-like tongue. When the spirit moved him, which was often in later years, Devine recalled he could rip a person up one side and down the other, hardly pausing for breath. "He had an amazingly caustic vocabulary," remembers one friend, who gratefully never had cause to be verbally assaulted by Herbert.

Willie's grandson, Roy Blackshear, has early memories of the man he would someday succeed at the tiller of the Shipman ship of state, memories that go back to the early thirties. There he saw a side of Herbert Shipman that he and many others would remember: "Uncle Herbert could be very strict, very overpowering, very outspoken. When he spoke, one jumped. But I got along with him OK. He had kindness melded with a cantankerous streak." Blackshear also recalls that, while in seventh grade in Hilo, he lived at Keaʻau ranch with his bachelor uncle. His memories of that year are not of Herbert's short fuse but rather of learning orchid cultivation from an expert. "Uncle Herbert also drove me to school in Hilo every morning in his banana wagon and always got me there just as the school bell rang," said Blackshear.

Several years later, when Roy was living in a house on the Keaʻau ranch property, he was distressed to see that the once shimmering lagoon, one of the few remaining royal fish ponds in Hawaiʻi, had been allowed to deteriorate into what would soon be a swamp or, worse yet, terra firma. Blooming hyacinths, water lilies, and *honohono* grass had covered most of the pond. Where these intruders did not cover the water, California grass and small guava bushes did. So neglected had the lagoon become that sand and rocks choked the channel, preventing the fresh, clear springwater from reaching the nearby ocean. Roy felt that with some good hard work the pond could be restored. He mentioned this to Herbert from time to time and in response got only noncommittal grunts.

One day Roy may have been more determined to obtain avuncular approval. He made it a point to say he would like to clean up the pond if he could only get some of the ranch hands to help. Herbert snapped at him, "Who the hell do you think is running this ranch?" "Well, you are," replied an unbowed Blackshear. A few nights later, apparently regretting his outburst, Herbert, who had been playing solitaire, laid down his cards, turned to Roy, and snapped, "When do you want the men?" They were on the job the following Monday. Roy and his father supervised the sporadic work, which turned out to be a massive four-year project. But Herbert Shipman appreciated it and said so after the lagoon had been restored to its pristine beauty.

Others on the receiving end of Shipman's bark, like Blackshear, let it roll off and remained unperturbed. Shipman's testiness, which had been observed by Blackshear while at Puʻuʻōʻō ranch, was a propensity that was part of his style for much of his adult life. However, it was interspersed with acts of kindness and generosity that few people ever knew about but were part of his very private life. Blackshear said that his uncle reserved the right to yell and scream at employees if things went wrong. But if anyone else "downed" them, he unleashed his full rage at that person, who never forgot it.

Mrs. Heuer's observation that Herbert liked "important" people was true only to a degree. He never sought them out but was glad to entertain them, along with others of various social levels. However, the contention that he liked being seen with the high and mighty did not hold when Shipman was on one of his visits to England. He enjoyed a passing but pleasant acquaintance with Prince Philip, thanks to Sir Peter Scott and the nēnē project. "When I was in London I had been invited by Sir Peter Scott to attend a banquet of the Wild Fowl Trust. Prince Philip was there and about the time Sir Peter was about to introduce me, the Prince said, 'Oh, I've met Mr. Shipman. It was at the Honolulu airport,' and he told about my having given him some macadamia nuts for the queen. The prince is a very remarkable person." Then Herbert went on to relate that at a sheep show in Edinburgh the prince and his wife, Queen Elizabeth, were in attendance. "I was asked if I would like to be presented to the queen. I said, 'Naw, she'll never see me again. What's the use?' I saw them as they drove away, she has a most beautiful complexion. As Prince Philip drove by he winked at me."

When, in 1975, Blackshear became vice president of the Shipman Company and its acting CEO, no one was happier than Stanley Hodgins, Hawaiʻi Island manager for the telephone company. Like the managers before him, Hodgins had taken his share of verbal abuse from Herbert Shipman for reasons that might have been an act of God or nature. Not only did the telephone tree trimmers incur the wrath of Mr. Conservationist himself, there was no reasonable excuse for static on Shipman's line or—heaven forbid—for his telephone being out of order for any length of time. Roy heard more than once from Hodgins "How delighted we are now that you're there to keep your uncle off our backs." But Hodgins also observed that if one stood up to Shipman the crusty attitude often dissolved and a warm relationship usually ensued.

Blackshear recalls quite vividly the very first day he took on managerial responsibilities for W. H. Shipman, Limited. His uncle's health was in decline, but not his irascibility. Not that day anyway, though it was observed that he was mellowing with age. On that day Roy saw Henry swing the Cadillac and his boss under the office porte cochere. "Uncle Herbert hadn't been in the office more than a few minutes before he jumped on me about some perceived error in a contract. He simmered down once he was convinced that the error was of his own doing."

One who saw and enjoyed the pleasant side of Herbert Shipman was young Maggie Wessel. A high-school student during the days of World War II, she often clerked behind the soda fountain of her father's downtown Hilo Drug Store. When I was in Hilo as a GI in 1942, I personally remember her as being blessed with a cheerful personality, one that complemented her appearance and also pleased her father's customers. Maggie Stearns' (née Wessel) vivid memories reach back over a half-century. The drugstore was a short block from the Shipman office, and thus convenient enough for Herbert, Devine, and Tony Chang to make mid-afternoon forays to a booth there. It was likely the same booth in which the trio had earlier enjoyed lunch. Maggie recalls that she came to look forward to their visits, and the reverse was also true. "It seemed like I had always known Uncle Herbert, as I called him although we weren't related," she remembered. "He was always very nice to me, often joked with me. Only once did I see him flare up. A man came over and said 'Hello Mr. Shipman.' Uncle Herbert brusquely ignored the man and his greeting. When I asked him why he had been so rude he replied that he just didn't like the man." Maggie ended up scolding her otherwise special customer, giving him a taste of his own medicine. Often after that Shipman would refer, tongue in cheek, to his favorite soda jerk as "Miss Spitfire."

"I saw a lot of the good side of Uncle Herbert," commented Maggie. "He was always very kind to me and we had many a nice chat over his afternoon refreshers." She cited an example of his kindness when she was attending Mills College. As the popular song goes, "May Day Is Lei Day in Hawai'i." It has been a tradition in the Islands for many years to make and share fragrant leis with friends and visitors. Female students from Hawai'i attending school on the West Coast maintained the custom, and Mills College was no exception. Maggie asked her father to airmail a lei to her for the occasion. He grumbled mildly to Herbert about the trouble of getting a lei and then having it airmailed. On April 30, Maggie went to her Mills post office. "There waiting for me was a package with the most gorgeous, fragrant carnation lei. With it was a card saying 'From Uncles Henry and Herbert.' The order of names had been purposely reversed by Uncle Herbert just to be funny." Only later did Maggie learn that the blossoms had come from Herbert's nursery of hybrid carnations. Subsequently Henry Ha'a grumbled to Maggie in a friendly manner that "Herbert had me stay up all night and string that lei. But I told him he'd have to stay up and pour me coffee. He did, too."

Henry Ha'a was probably Number Two on Maggie's hit parade. "He was real fun, very kind, a special person was Henry." Once while at Mills she was thrilled and surprised to receive a phone call from Henry, who, with his boss, was visiting the Bay area. "He was as considerate as Uncle Herbert," she remembered.

Another fond remembrance of Shipman's thoughtfulness to "Miss Spitfire" occurred when her wedding plans were under way. Like many a bride, she hoped for a bridal bouquet that would be special. And a very special one did come to her from Herbert's collection of exotic flowers. He personally selected a number of his rare Singapore plumeria blossoms, then sent them to the famed Hilo flower arrangers, the Ebisu sisters, for the final touch. "The next day," said Maggie, "I carried the most beautiful bouquet that any bride could ever hope for."

Maggie has lasting memories of the outdoor picnics and parties she and her friends enjoyed with young relatives of the Shipman family at the Kea'au beach home, but even more of Uncle Herbert's kindness and sense of humor. "It was a great relationship," she said, "even if he did call me Miss Spitfire."

There are others like Margaret Stearns who had no problem with Herbert's choleric streak. Many are employees of long standing who were often considered part of the Shipman family. Their memories go back many years and are generally quite positive. One is Bessie Morita, until July 1994 secretary to the president of the company. She has been with the firm for forty-seven years, thirty of those while Herbert headed W. H. Shipman, Limited. She would have nothing to lose if she preferred to cast Herbert, now long gone, as a temperamental curmudgeon. On the contrary, she remembers him as "an employer who was very thoughtful, very generous to the people who worked for him." She acknowledges that he was quite capable of giving a person a dressing down, but she herself was never on the receiving end. "If you did your job, what was expected, you could expect to be treated very well."

Bessie recalls that whenever Shipman returned from a trip he had gifts for everyone. "They were good gifts, too. Always something elegant. He bought from the best stores. In Honolulu it was Grossman Moody, and then from his favorite shops in San Francisco." She also remembered the generous checks that came to all employees at Christmas. She spoke

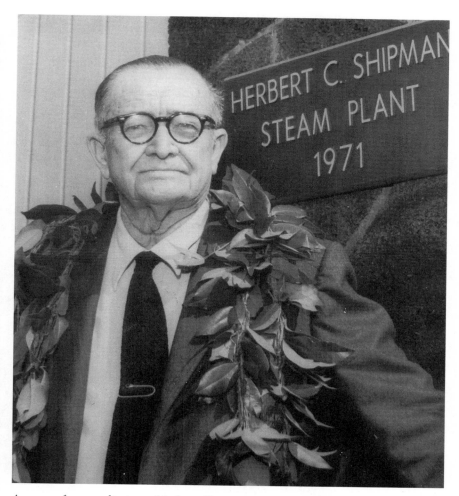

A man of contradictions, Herbert Shipman never married. This dedication of Hilo's electric plant in his name is representative of the many honors conferred upon him. He died in 1976.

with pleasure about the staff lunch hours at the new office of Hilo Meat Company and W. H. Shipman, Limited, on Kekūanaōʻa Street, to which they had moved in 1955, having outgrown the Shipman Street quarters. Herbert always enjoyed eating with the staff, and they enjoyed his sense of humor. "If there had been a big dinner party at his house the night before, he would bring the generous remains of a fine roast. He much preferred to eat with those closest to him than to bother with a business luncheon," observed Mrs. Morita. "Those he avoided as often as possible. But whenever he was visited by a long lost friend or relative he didn't hesitate to invite them to an elegant luncheon or dinner at his own home or at the Hilo Yacht Club."

One of Herbert's close and longtime friends was Francis Ii Brown, sportsman and well-known Hawai'i personality. His Hawaiian heritage once included large parcels of land in the vicinity of the present Mauna Kea Beach hotel. Once, when Brown was hospitalized, he needed a blood transfusion and Herbert was the donor. "Ever after that," said Brown, "whenever I got into trouble I'd say it was that Shipman blood."

## Lord and Master

Herbert closely guarded his privacy and his property, and woe to those intruders who, even unknowingly, found themselves on Herbert's personal domain. Even to be found on the two-mile Shipman dirt road leading from the main highway to the beach residence was grounds for a berating from the lord of the manor.

The author of a private paper entitled "Herbert Shipman, The Man" gives credit to Mr. Shipman as an outstanding conservationist.[6] Then follows this reminiscence: "Kenneth and I went riding on his road. We met Mr. Shipman being driven on the way out by his chauffeur. In his gruff way he asked where we were going. Ken told him we were going to the beach." Shipman replied that they were going no such place, to just turn around and get out. "We didn't do it fast enough," said the author. "So they turned their car around and came after us. . . . So I remember Mr. Shipman in a way that is less than gracious. Poor Mr. Shipman."[7]

Roy Blackshear recalled that once, when Herbert encountered a wanderer on his beach, he angrily asked the intruder just what the hell he was doing on private property. With a cigarette dangling from his lips, the culprit replied he was just looking around. Before the last syllable was uttered Herbert took a swipe at him, knocking the cigarette from his mouth. To the shocked man Shipman shouted: "When you speak to Herbert Shipman you don't do it with a cigarette in your mouth. Now get the hell out of here!"

On a similar occasion Shipman spotted from a distance a man and woman ("hippie types") farther out on the property, near the lagoon. He immediately delegated Roy and Henry to find out why they were there and "tell them to vacate in a hurry." The two deputies fulfilled their errand and returned to the house. But when the couple was observed an hour later on another part of the premises, Roy and Henry proceeded again in their direction, this time with a mission to be accomplished. The offenders' motorcycle was discovered hidden in the grass. It was immediately impounded and wheeled back to the house. When confronted the second time, the couple pleaded, "We were intrigued by the beauty of the place and just couldn't leave." Flattery got them nowhere. Herbert told Blackshear to call the police, meanwhile holding their motorcycle hostage. As usual, when Shipman called the police, or any other authority, the response was not only prompt, it produced results. Three police officers, each in a separate vehicle, appeared posthaste. When the sergeant asked Herbert what he wished them to do with the transgressors, he replied, "Just take their names, give them a good tongue lashing and tell them next time I'll have them arrested." It is doubtful that there was a next time, for Blackshear learned that the man was a professor from the University of Hawai'i (Hilo) and his female "companion in crime" one of his students.

Few individuals other than Henry Ha'a were closer observers of Herbert Shipman than Masaru Uchida and his wife, Yoshie. Shipman sought and bought their services in 1941, being unhappy with his female cook, who had a problem with the bottle. The newlywed couple was at first skeptical about accepting the offer, which included moving into the Shipman beach house as full-time servants. "We wanted to check it out further," said Masaru. "So Mr. Shipman drove us down to his place. Once we saw those beautiful grounds, that nice big spring water pond and everything else, we agreed then and there."

Their relationship was to last forty-three years, but it was not all wine and roses. The couple worked long hours, seven days a week. Their day began at 4 A.M., when they rose to prepare breakfast for the ranch hands, who would show up two hours later. The first chore was to build a wood fire and then cook the rice Japanese-style. That would take as long as an hour. Then the rice had to stand a while. This staple was a favorite of the field workers. By the time the men arrived, the coffee was ready, along with rice, eggs, meat, and fish. Sometimes there were as many as twenty-seven hungry mouths to feed.

Eventually Masaru became the full-time cook and his wife performed the other domestic duties, though still rising early to help make breakfast. There was also lunch, followed by dinner, to be prepared for ranch hands who had worked up a hefty Hawaiian appetite. There were times when Herbert, who may have felt he was considerate, was less than thoughtful of his household help. Masaru has memories of Shipman more than once phoning from distant places such as Kona to announce that he would be home very late for dinner. "Very late" was sometimes close to 2 A.M., but the master was fed, two hours before Masaru and Yoshie had to get up to prepare the first meal of the day.

Vivid, too, were the Uchidas' recollections of social affairs hosted by Herbert. One was a lunch for seventy-four. "We had lots of food to prepare and we did that by getting an early morning start. Thank goodness it was buffet style," groaned Masaru. But there were numerous occasions which called for place settings. Everything had to be, and was, "plus-perfect." Only the finest goblets were used. Shipman's top-drawer silver, from his superb collection, graced each setting, along with the choicest of china. The Uchidas, in preparing the table for such events, usually not more than ten places, often had the help of Herbert's widowed sister, Clara, who lived nearby. But the preparation of the food, serving it, and then the inevitable cleanup, were the jobs of the two Uchidas.

"Many of the guests," reminisced Masaru, "were considered important people." Among them was Lawrence Rockefeller, who once stayed overnight. It was the night of a great deluge. Masaru remembered getting up at four in the morning, and there, sitting in a kitchen chair with a big smile on his face, was Mr. Rockefeller. Rain had found an opening directly over his bed. He brushed off Masaru's concern that he should have called for him so he could have provided this guest with a drier place to finish his night's sleep.

Many other guests came and went over the years: important people, or those who thought they were, and some who could care less. It was always Herbert's pleasure to have his visitors sign their names in a large, green, leather-covered guest book. Fancy gold borders decorated the cover. Between the years 1925 and October 1976, the pages were filled with approximately 4,750 signatures. Many of them were duplicated again and again: these were friends and family members Herbert enjoyed entertaining at the drop of a hat, especially on birthdays, Christmas, and New Year's. His own birthday not only brought out all the old and well-known ranching families, but also a roster of "special" people from elsewhere in the Islands.

Among the genuine "greats" who signed in was Amelia Earhart, who was in Hawai'i seeking the $10,000 prize for the first person to fly solo between Hawai'i and California, which she won.[7] Sir Peter and Mrs. Scott came, as did Franklin D. Roosevelt, Jr., when he was in the military, and Cyrus McCormick of the reaper family. Stage and screen personali-

"Haena, the birthplace of Herbert Shipman, is situated at Keaau, where the hala groves dance in the wind, and where abide two dancing women, Haena and Hopoe. There also, is Kanikaa, the wave (so the old Hawaiians say) on which the Princess Laiekawai surfed. The song tells of the beautiful orchids which seem like companions to Herbert. The orchids are dampened and kept fresh by the waters of Waikoolihilihi. As the lei is worn [on] neck or breast, the Hawaiian compares it to the encircling arms of a child—thus, *Ka Lei O Haena*, beloved child of Haena." (From the notes of Helen Desha Beamer.)

ties included Cecil B. deMille, Lauritz Melchior, Cole Porter, Edward G. Robinson and his wife, Henry Dreyfuss, Paul Newman, and Janet Gaynor. Hawai'i-related business chiefs were Matson Steamship CEO Randolph Sevier, Hawaiian Airlines founder Stanley Kennedy, and Lorrin P. Thurston of the *Honolulu Advertiser*. Parker Ranch scion Richard Smart left his signature, but not as often as his ranch manager, Hartwell Carter, who appears to have come quarterly.

From the neighboring islands came such landed gentry as Wilcox, Baldwin, Podmore, Damon, Moody, Allen, Alexander, Wodehouse, Waterhouse, Caldwell, and Stibbard. Locally, the Otis English family were regulars, along with the Devines, the Leslie Weights, and the Heuers. Lillian Matson Roth signed with a flourish, but not as often as forestry conservationist William Bryan, whose fancy monogram decorates many pages. The Chief of Naval Operations, like John Hancock, left a signature (along with his title) that could not be mistaken. Botanist Horace Clay came, and so did artist Gustave Ecke and his wife, Tseng-yu Ho. The pages carry the personal signatures and often the comments of Hawai'i poet laureate Don Blanding, architect Charles W. Dickey, painter Lloyd Sexton, and Hawaiian baritone Charles K. L. Davis, a Shipman cousin. Two Scobies, relatives of Jane, came from O'ahu. Musical Hawaiian names like Kekaulike Kawananakoa, Solomon Kauinui, and Kekaha Kulani add to the poetry of the pages.

Every state in the union seems to have been represented during that half-century, and foreign visitors were frequent. The British consul signed in along with representatives of the British Embassy in Washington, D.C. Visitors from China, Hong Kong, Thailand, Japan, and Korea left compliments and comments in their own languages. A particularly unusual guest was a maharaja from an Indian state. "How can we ever forget him?" asked Yoshie. "He had seven or eight men-in-waiting, but somehow we were able to feed them all."

During World War II the Shipman beach property was ringed with defense units. One consequence was that the Uchidas were all too frequently on call to serve visiting military brass, some uninvited. They have no memory of enlisted men being entertained, although Blackshear does recall some. A few of the brassier brass invited themselves at the oddest hours. When one high-ranking officer drove up shortly after midnight, Herbert instructed Masaru to "serve him a real stiff drink so maybe we can get rid of him." Like a number of others, he had intruded on Shipman's privacy and worn out his welcome.

The green guest book contains comments ranging from the superb to the supreme, from the paramount to the unparalleled. "A place where the true spirit of old Hawaii moves and breathes" said it for many guests. From another: "The grandeur is indescribable." An appreciative visitor told Shipman, "Your Chinese art collection is a joy," and a horticulturist wrote that he "enjoyed the exquisite beauty of the Shipman orchids." "Haven't had a better time in all my life," penned a gracious guest. Another appreciative individual summed up the sentiments of many with: "The best vision of old Hawaii I will ever see."

These many transient guests saw the best side of their host. There is no indication that any of them knew Herbert Shipman as other than genial; only his close associates were privy to a less hospitable Herbert. The housekeeper and cook were among those who sometimes suffered from Herbert's sharp tongue. But their memory is dim on that score, recalling instead the frequent occasions upon which their master had gifts for the whole family, including the three Uchida children, who were born and raised in the Shipman house. For the three female Uchidas there would be gifts of attractive jewelry, while the father and son were recipients of equally suitable gifts. Once Herbert brought back from Holland a Dutch girl's costume for one of the Uchida granddaughters. She was four years old and had her picture taken wearing the colorful costume. Herbert considered the picture so beautiful that he had it framed and put it on his office desk, where it remained until the day he died.

When a birthday of one of the Uchida children, and later grandchildren, rolled around, it was Herbert's pleasure to have that child as his luncheon guest at the exclusive Hilo Yacht Club, a privilege out of reach for most Hiloites, young or old.

In the early 1960s, with the approval of the Shipman board, Herbert divided some of the company's property into one-acre residential lots. He then donated to his veteran employees one lot each, deeded in their name. He also gave them the opportunity to buy at a very low price additional adjacent lots if they wished to expand their premises. The Uchidas did so, increasing their lot to five acres, on which they planted a grove of macadamia trees and other plants. By 1965 the couple had built their own house, moving from the beach house in which they had cooked—and cleaned—for twenty-four years. Every year after that, until he died, Herbert Shipman would spend most of New Year's Day at the home of these servants, enjoying with other visitors the food, festivities, and aloha that is part of every Japanese New Year. He preferred it to invitations from those who meant less to him.

The seven-day-a-week schedule went on year in and year out, but the hard-working Uchidas did not complain. First, they appreciated having their two girls and boy raised in the family workplace, with its pleasant surroundings. The first break in their schedule came in 1972, after thirty-one years of continuous service, when Shipman arranged for his two household servants to take a first-class, five-week vacation to Japan. All expenses were paid, and nothing was too good for them. Included was a trip to Bangkok, which "Mr. Shipman insisted we take. He wanted us to enjoy ourselves as much as we could. And we did," said Masaru.

On another vacation the Uchidas were scheduled to make their first trip, by plane, to the mainland. All arrangements were made and tickets in hand. Herbert drove them to the airport. Pan American would fly them to Honolulu for an overnight stopover, then on to San Francisco. But when they arrived at the counter, they were informed that their tickets didn't allow for a stopover, which had been prearranged. When Shipman was informed of their dilemma, he immediately went to a public telephone and called Pan American headquarters in New York. He obviously had good relations with the company, for Pan American had earlier included him as an honored guest on its maiden clipper flight to the Philippines. "When he came back to us he was all smiles," remember the Uchidas. Whoever he had talked to gave the travelers carte blanche. But the timing was so close that the steps to the plane had to be relowered to take on the two passengers. Worse, the bays under the belly of the plane had to be reopened to load the Uchida luggage.

Other treasured memories of the Uchidas are Herbert's showing up a couple of hours before dinner "to tell us not to bother cooking tonight. 'Let's all go out and have a good meal at the Hilo Lagoon restaurant.' And 'all' meant all of our family of five."

On many occasions the man of the house would tell the Uchidas to drop everything and get ready for a three-day camping trip. He had it all arranged to spend that time on one of the fabulous beaches of the Parker Ranch, eighty miles to the north, tent and all supplies courtesy of Parker Ranch and Hilo Meat Company.

After the Kea'au Ranch had ceased operating came days when Shipman would tell the Uchidas to get ready for the hundred-mile trip to have lunch at the five-diamond Mauna Kea hotel. There they could lunch and relax while enjoying the spectacular sight of Maui's Mount Haleakalā, which beckoned in the distance across the Alakahiki channel. There being no more ranch hands to feed, thus no more predawn awakenings for Masaru and Yoshie.

Once, when Herbert was mentally calculating the family-owned property on different parts of Hawai'i Island, he chuckled to recall that the Shipman family owned a church on the Kona side—and he was not even a churchgoer. It was the Lanakila Church in Kainaliu and had been built as a Congregational church by Mary's father, William Johnson, then a young man, on Johnson's land. "The old missionary there at the time, Reverend Paris," said Herbert, "tried to prevent him from building it. He just put all sorts of things in the way of my grandfather Johnson. But grandfather was successful and when it was completed he named it Lanakila, which is Hawaiian for victory. An apt name. The property was left to my mother, she being the oldest living child; she in turn willed it to her children, including me." In recent years the Shipman heirs donated the property to the church congregation. It remains an attractive and well-maintained New England–style place of worship.

It is doubtful that Herbert ever thought he had any hobbies as such; his interest in such subjects as foreign grasses and horticulture he viewed as an integral part of his life, despite the fact that he showed an interest in orchids while still in high school. Yet, an overview of his life shows that he was more interested in collecting orchids and objets d'art than he was in acquiring friends. Orchids seem to have been his first love, and a lasting one. As a collector of rare species, at no small output of time and money, he gained endless pleasure and considerable knowledge. Other flowering plants followed.

Nor did he limit himself to flowers. Shipman had not only the eye of a good and appreciative artist, but also the acumen of an appraiser for other fanciful items, those which are to be admired rather than put to functional use. He knew what he liked and was willing to pay for it. As a result of his admiring, then acquiring, articles that caught his eye, the Kea'au home assumed the aura of a combined museum-art gallery. On his many trips to the mainland or abroad, he focused on good glass and silverware. He was especially fascinated by silver. Place settings, gravy boats, platters, candlesticks, jewelry, bowls, candelabra—anything made of silver caught his fancy. He also preferred his silver and glassware in pairs when possible.

His early European prints decorate the hallway of the Shipman headquarters. His rare collection of early, and some modern, Asian art, mostly ceramics, have found sanctuary in Hilo's Lyman Museum. Like that of William Randolph Hearst, who filled his San Simeon palace with art and some boxes unopened for years, the Kea'au house had at the time of Herbert's death several unopened treasure chests.

Shipman's taste for furniture was less lavish, but not pedestrian. He inherited his appreciation of good furniture from his parents, and perhaps his missionary grandfather. Back in 1879, when William and Mary lived at Kapoho, a ship was wrecked off the coast. A pair of captain's chairs floated ashore and were salvaged by Willie. Herbert so admired them that many years later he had sixteen copies of them made out of koa wood for the board of directors' room of the Hilo Meat Company. The koa came from the Puakala Ranch high on the rain-forest slopes of Mauna Kea.

Herbert never talked about the ones that got away. But one piece he sought did elude him and revealed another quirk of the man of many moods. He knew of an attractive table that stood in the vestry of Haili Church. His artistic taste compelled him to own it. He approached the chairman of the church board, expressed his wish to acquire the table, and stated that money would be no object. (It never was when Herbert

Shipman coveted art or orchids.) The chairman carried Shipman's request to the board, which decided that it appreciated the table as much as Shipman did and declined the offer with thanks. The chairman, carrier of the bad news, was never forgiven. Those who know maintain that Shipman never spoke to the man again.

# 22

# Community Pride and Prejudice

## Local Affairs

Shortly after World War II, the poorly paid workers in the sugar and plantation fields and factories of Hawai'i pressed for higher wages and improved working conditions. There were bitter and prolonged strikes and lockouts, and all the plantations on all islands were affected.[1] One that vigorously resisted was the big 'Ōla'a Sugar Company; its tactic in 1948 was to create a lockout that lasted sixty-two days and had negative economic effects on its many employees, the plantation operations, and the broad Kea'au community. 'Ōla'a was in danger of being crippled financially, for the union had dug in and was as stubborn as management about capitulating.

Most of the 'Ōla'a lands under cultivation were leased from W. H. Shipman, Limited, and Herbert Shipman was the landlord. So if 'Ōla'a went under, the Shipman company stood to lose a very lucrative lease arrangement. When an agreement was finally reached, tensions between the two sides eased and plantation work resumed. But Herbert Shipman was unforgiving, for labor had not only won many of its demands, but he felt that it had created such ill will in the community that it would take years to restore a balance. He was understandably apprehensive about the profit picture and visualized a negative way of life for the sugar industry in Hawai'i.

The manager of 'Ōla'a Sugar at the time of the work stoppage was Billy Williams, a member of the old school of labor and management. Williams and Herbert Shipman had been friends for a number of years. In the eyes of Williams, labor's action was completely unjustified, and he let Herbert know it. He also placed most of the blame on a young 'Ōla'a laborer named Yasuki Arakaki, who was at the forefront of ILWU local 148.[2] Arakaki was a community leader, active in the Puna Hongwanji Buddhist Mission and president of the 'Ōla'a PTA. He was correctly described as a militant labor leader, and one respected by his fellow field and factory coworkers. Williams' dislike for Arakaki was personally conveyed to Shipman, the result being a strong hostility toward Arakaki on the part of Herbert himself. Shipman was one of the many managers who did not share labor's satisfaction over the gains it attained as a result of the strike. He took it out on Arakaki personally, and they had some unpleasant run-ins.

But eventually Shipman had a change of heart toward the young "rabble rouser" and supported his campaigns for local community betterment. This about-face came to pass only when Williams was replaced in 1950 by young Frank Burns, a manager of a different ilk. 'Ōla'a was still out of step and behind the times, and Burns knew it. He not only held a more enlightened view toward labor, he was farsighted enough to realize that mechanization, so essential to production and profits, was the only way to go. But Burns also knew that labor's acceptance of such a radical move was equally essential. He had no trouble convincing Arakaki of the merits of and need for modernization; Yasuki saw the handwriting on the wall and took the issue to his fellow union members. It was either mechanize or shut down. Labor was convinced and backed management's decision. Burns was grateful for labor's acquiescence. Unlike Williams, this latter-day manager went to Shipman with praise and appreciation for Arakaki's positive role and the union's cooperation.

From that day forth, Shipman regarded Arakaki not only as a community leader but also as a friend—that is, as much of a friend as Shipman ever allowed. Some time later, when the 'Ōla'a elementary school needed adjacent Shipman land to expand its playground, it was PTA president Yasuki Arakaki who made a request for help, and it was Herbert Shipman who saw that five acres of land were donated. Later, when the government-funded school gymnasium was completed, it was named and is still called the Shipman Gym. At its dedication not only was Herbert feted, but the Shipman sisters and other members of the family were honored and welcome guests. Today it remains an appreciated and widely used facility.

Herbert's involvement in the 'Ōla'a community was reflected in his support for the Hongwanji temple, one of whose pillars was Arakaki. When a columbarium was being built on the attractively landscaped temple lawn, Shipman expressed interest in its progress. When he observed that the workers were installing a single-basin, second-hand sink, he objected, maintaining that the columbarium and temple deserved something better and more functional. "Go down to the American Factors supply house," he ordered, "and get the best one they have and charge it to me." When he noticed that the urn compartments were resting directly on the cement floor, he was equally adamant about bettering the situation. He directed that the small metal containers be placed about thirty inches above the floor and that their base be made from the best Philippine mahogany available. He also stipulated that attractive wood-grain sliding panels be used under the mahogany counter tops—all to be charged to him.

The reverse was true when the workers wanted to replace the old wooden *butsudan* with a factory-made one from Japan. (This structure, encasing a statue of Buddha, was about five feet tall, with three sides exquisitely carved and gilded. Even the gold gilt canopy is a work of Asian art.) Because it had been invaded by termites, the young men reasoned it must be replaced; after all, it had been in use for almost a century. Herbert minced no words—he seldom did—in telling the workers: "You young fellows just have no appreciation for things that are old. Well, this artifact was hand-crafted by Japanese artisans a long, long time ago. It is not replaceable but it is repairable. Just forget about getting a factory-made model. Instead get this one restored and let me know what it costs."

For the rest of his life, Shipman, never a churchgoer, was carried as an honorary life member of the Puna Hongwanji Mission. Today, under a large and beautifully shaped monkeypod tree on the temple's front lawn, is a bronze plaque stating: "This tree planted by Herbert Shipman, December 16, 1963." In 1976 the mission celebrated its seventy-fifth anniversary. A board meeting of the W. H. Shipman Company considered what the company might do to commemorate the mission's role in the history of the Puna district. Vice president Roy Blackshear suggested they donate to the mission the Shipman land on which the temple stood. It had been leased to the mission for one dollar a year ever since its inception three-quarters of a century before. This agreed upon, Blackshear, acting on behalf of his uncle, who was near death, presented the deed to the land to the mission's president. Herbert was very pleased when Blackshear told him about the gift presentation. Five days later the mission's benefactor died.

Even with mechanization, the ʻŌlaʻa Sugar Company was not a money-maker. Board member and landlord Herbert Shipman had an idea why, with the exception of the war years, there was such a poor fiscal return. He well remembered his mother many years before saying that the word ʻŌlaʻa was to the Hawaiians an extremely sacred word and a revered place, one with religious connotations. Mary Shipman had long deplored the word being associated in any way, sense, or manner with a commercial enterprise. Having the school carry the name was all right; having the village post office carry the name ʻŌlaʻa was all wrong: it smacked of secularism. But having ʻŌlaʻa associated with a strictly for-profit venture was downright sacrilegious. When the plantation first called itself ʻŌlaʻa, Mary Shipman predicted it would never make money. She was right, except for those war years when sugar was at a premium.

As a coowner with her husband of most Shipman lands in the early 1900s, Mary Shipman's name appeared on a great many of the leases. Herbert recalled: "My mother wouldn't sign the lease with the sugar company because she said it was a sacred name. It would bring bad luck to use Olaa with a money-making business. It was tabu to the *kahuna* [priests] and she said it [the plantation] would never make money. Henry's father, who had kahuna powers, said the same thing, and he was considered very psychic."

When Herbert became a director of the sugar company, one of the first things he did was press for a name change from ʻŌlaʻa to Puna. He met with no resistance from his board colleagues, who agreed that, aside from the war years, the company had been a loser. Later he often chuckled when pointing out that after being renamed the company became more prosperous.

But Herbert Shipman didn't stop there. The post office still needed to be rechristened. He opted for it to be named Keaʻau, after the small fishing village that later became the Shipman beach property. This meant dealing with the bureaucracy, and if handled at a local level would surely take many months. To avoid glacier-like progress, he forged ahead by making a personal trip to the nation's capital, there to present his case for Keaʻau. He came away a winner. ʻŌlaʻa was relegated to oblivion, and the postmark "Keaʻau, T. H." soon appeared on all outgoing mail.

After that it was just a step for the Territorial Department of Education to approve a name change to Keaʻau Elementary School. Businesses could do as they pleased; if they wanted to lose money by using ʻŌlaʻa, they could go ahead. But over the years Keaʻau gradually replaced the sacred ʻŌlaʻa on many signs and buildings. Herbert's stubborn streak, combined with his love of Hawaiian lore, was, as many saw it, a factor in successfully bringing about the changes. Several of his associates frankly asserted that "his ornery disposition and cussedness" helped free the process from what would otherwise have been "Pacific paralysis." Herbert would have been the first to agree.

The civic and civil interests of Shipman (some labeled him uncivil) were not confined to Kea'au but included Hilo, where for many years the Shipman business was conducted. An avid and early promoter of electric service, Herbert served for decades as a director of the Hilo Electric Light Company. When a large and modern generating power plant was put into service, it was dedicated as the Herbert Shipman Generator.

Only his checkbook, his treasurer (Richard Devine), and the beneficiaries know of the several community-wide charities Herbert supported, and without fanfare. The director of the Hilo Boys Home, Father Louis, wrote in Shipman's guest book: "Mr. Shipman is the best friend the Hilo Boys Club has." A colleague close to Shipman in matters of business and community welfare asserted that "people will never know what a generous man he was because he never wore his giving on his sleeve." The business community of east Hawai'i knew him as a fiscally sensible pioneer as well as a valuable member of certain civic groups.

Although Herbert Shipman presented a reclusive appearance to many, those close to him saw that when the spirit moved him he could become a convivial person. Nor was this side of him confined to being a warm host at Kea'au. His circle of friends was not as limited, at least geographically, as many imagined. He was socially and "agriculturally" close to many Hawai'i Island families engaged in ranching or other related enterprises. They included the Hinds, the Greenwells, the McCandlesses (one of whom went to Congress), the Eben Lows, and, of course, those from the quarter-million-acre Parker Ranch. Despite being separated by as much as one hundred miles or more, these families had long been associated socially, and Herbert Shipman was not one to break with tradition.

## 'Āinahou—New Land

When, in the late 1930s, Shipman sensed that the nēnē had a better chance of survival in highlands, he took steps to acquire a mountain home for his small flock and, while he was at it, another home for himself, his father, and, if necessary, his five sisters. Herbert had a sixth sense which told him that war with Japan was imminent, that the Japanese military would indeed attempt to invade the Hawaiian Islands, and that the island of Hawai'i would not be bypassed. He also knew that this big island which was his home offered a better chance of escaping and hiding from enemy invaders than any of the other Islands. The place he chose

was on the isolated eastern slope of Mauna Loa, for which he had successfully negotiated with Bishop Estate for a long-term lease of their land.
The entire tract totaled 6,374 acres, and the land surrounding it was
owned by the Hawaii National Park (HNP). It was two miles in from the
Chain of Craters Road, which led from the Kīlauea Volcano to the sea
and was reachable by a not too smooth gravel road. The area was called
'Āinahou, "new land."

The region was known by those who, over the years, had traversed
the old Keauhou Trail that ran between the ocean and the volcano, zig-
zagging its way over the precipitous Halina *Pali*. Originally a footpath, it
had served the Hawaiians and others traveling to or from the coast. It
reached an elevation of 4,000 feet. Midway it crossed the 'Āinahou property. It had gradually become a horse trail, and by 1870, when William
Reed ran Kapāpala Ranch, it had been developed into a wagon road. It
was no easy task to negotiate the hairpin turns on the steep *pali*. In Reed's
time, in addition to the Punalu'u pier farther south, he used the Keauhou
landing to ship out hides and meat and bring in necessary supplies. Others, such as the Volcano House, brought in lumber from Honolulu to be
hauled to its highland destination.[3] When interisland coasters gave way
to the larger vessels of Samuel Wilder's steamship line, the Keauhou
landing proved a convenient stopover for visitors to and from Kīlauea,
though it never had a population like Punalu'u. Although some recent
maps show the Keauhou trail as a jeep road, it is under the jurisdiction of
the National Park Service (NPS) and is used by hikers and park personnel moving its horses to fresher 'Āinahou pastures.

The isolation suited Shipman for more than one reason. He was not
entirely wrong in sensing the approaching clouds of war and the threat of
a Japanese invasion. He first had the ranch house designed by profession-
als to include accommodations for his sisters and his father as well as
himself. It was finished in July 1941 and sat at an elevation of 3,000 feet.
He named it 'Āinahou, after the area. It consisted of a story and a half
with ample rooms that had generous windows. The bedroom closets were
cedar-lined. Some called it a modest mountain mansion. Despite its size,
it remained an inconspicuous building blending into the landscape,
much of which was covered by patches of trees and shrubs. The climate
was perfect for Herbert's rare collection of camellias. Beyond that, 'Āinahou was able to boast of blue-ribbon begonias, fuchsias, and many varieties of roses.

At first there was no electricity, so Coleman lanterns and kerosene
had to suffice. Wartime curfews required covering the windows with blan-

kets after dark, especially if a card game was under way. Later Herbert installed an automatic-start gasoline generator, and thereafter there was light at the flick of a switch. Water came from two huge metal tanks, fed from a rain catchment system and capable of holding more than a half-million gallons. Other tanks supplied water for his cattle, the horse corrals, and for irrigating the many exotic plants, mostly grasses and trees, which he had imported. Telephone service was out of the question, as it would have required eight miles of line running from Volcano Park headquarters to the ranch; and that was just the way Herbert Shipman wanted it.

When, six months after the house was completed, the war with Japan became a reality, Shipman reckoned that if the enemy landed and confiscated his Kea'au beach property, the hidden house in the middle of nowhere, partly obscured by high ohia trees and various types of brush, would serve the Shipman family well. Although the need to hide never arose, the house was a peaceful retreat for the bachelor businessman and rancher. He was not deterred by the distance of thirty miles from Kea'au and thirty-seven miles from his Hilo office. Nor did he let it interfere with his duties as head of the Puna District Selective Service Board, a position he held for twenty years.

During the war 'Āinahou was a working ranch; its several hundred head of cattle supplied meat for the military on the island. It continued as a profitable venture for another twenty years, its beef going to Hilo outlets, particularly the Hilo Meat Company.

When the spirit moved him, Herbert found 'Āinahou the ideal place to entertain carefully selected friends, often men only—men of "importance" as a rule. His colleagues and cronies would come up on Saturday, drink to each other's health, eat well, and enjoy one another's company. After the war Herbert used 'Āinahou less as a retreat and more as a social setting for entertaining special guests, as well as many others who did not consider themselves special. A rather ponderous 'Āinahou guest book contains the names of several hundreds of persons who were invited by Shipman between 1945 and 1965. Like those he entertained over the years at Kea'au, they range from small children (usually of family employees like the Uchidas and the Moritas) to adults of all ages and ethnic origins from near and far. Here, as at Kea'au, they came from most states of the union, as well as England, Scotland, Wales, Japan, Australia, India, Trinidad, Sweden, Tahiti, and the Philippines. The names of Blackshear, English, Fisher, Shipman, and other family members abound. Always welcome were friends and relatives from distant places, as were the friends of Henry Ha'a.

The guest book shows that a brigadier general was being entertained on the same day as Dick Devine, among other Hilo friends. Joan Crawford left her autograph, and Janet Gaynor wrote that it had been "a divine afternoon." Sir Peter Buck, who proudly carried his Maori title, Te Rangi Hiroa, visited with his wife at least twice.[4] Also from the Bishop Museum came well-known Marian Kelly and Pacific archaeologist Kenneth Emory. Dignitaries from Tokyo expressed their pleasure in exquisite Japanese calligraphy.

When one young guest, being asked to sign the guest book, said he had already done so on a previous visit, Herbert countered: "But you didn't do it today. Sign it!" On page after page in the bulky book are compliments penned by guests, testifying to the beauty of the site, the view that stretched out below them, the joy of being there, but mostly their gratitude for the hospitality of their host. One appreciative individual reflected the view of many others in writing after her name, "This visit to Ainahou is about as close to paradise as I ever expect to get."

Shipman always saw to it that his guests had the best cuisine that a ranch could offer. Shipman beef was guaranteed. The outdoor lanai had three barbecue pits, which were not there for decoration. Being a bachelor, Herbert had become an excellent cook over the years. He had a collection of hundreds of cookbooks from all over the world and enjoyed nothing more than using them in his kitchen experiments, be it at Kea'au or 'Āinahou. Downslope from the sheltered cooking and eating area was a panoramic view that extended five miles to the sea. Herbert was always happy to share it with his guests. If one tired of the house, relief and relaxation were to be found in the surrounding gardens and greenhouse. Some gardens were confined by low rock walls; others stood by themselves, galaxies of color from foreign as well as local flowering plants. Grapevines crawled up trellises to the second-story balcony. An overall peace and quiet prevailed, broken only by the chirps and singing of birds and the ever-present call of the nēnē.

Kīlauea Volcano became active in 1969, particularly along the rift that bordered the Chain-of-Craters Road, more specifically, the upper-east rift zone, where eruptions occurred near the Pu'uhuluhulu and Alai craters. Although several miles upslope from the ranch, the flows moved closer and closer toward 'Āinahou. In a few months Mauna Ulu, a satellite shield on Kīlauea, came to life, grew steadily larger, and soon covered both of these craters as well as several miles of the Crater Road and a portion of the road leading into the ranch. Sulfuric gases combined with light volcanic rains began to corrode and rapidly rust away the cattle fences. Cinders thrown up by the eruption and carried by the wind clogged water systems and cattle troughs. All this sounded an alarm to Shipman as well as to HNP officials and rangers. The wise thing to do, reckoned the ranch owner, was to evacuate all personnel. The nēnē could take care of themselves.

Shipman's lease with Bishop Estate stipulated that he could terminate it without penalty if volcanic flows threatened. While Shipman was considering this option, the National Park Service expressed a desire to acquire all of ʻĀinahou ranch, thus providing a park unbroken by any private land ownership. Bishop Estate was willing to sell the land to the Park Service should Shipman give up his lease. For reasons of his own, Herbert dug in his heels and decided he wasn't interested in letting the NPS obtain the lease, which still had some years to run.

A letter from the Hawaii National Park superintendent in 1969 to his superior stated: "Mr. Shipman is an influential man—difficult to handle. He has been particularly anti-NPS in the past but seems to have mellowed."[5]

A slightly later correspondence between two park officials showed no improvement in terms of an accord. Wrote the HNP official to another decision maker: "The old man operating the ranch on leasehold is a cantankerous, politically potent curmudgeon. Getting older, he has softened."[6]

In 1971 it was still touch and go. The Board of Trustees of Bishop Estate wrote the HNP: "The National Park Service requests that you do not contact their lessee, Mr. Shipman, who is very influential in the State of Hawaii, is friendly to the National Park Service and works very closely with many conservation groups; consequently he is in a position to be very helpful or quite a hindrance."[7]

A turn for the better occurred later, perhaps as the lava flow became more of a threat. Park officials wrote to their higher-ups: "Recent eruptions of Kilauea have sent lava flows to within one-quarter mile of the ranch. Mr. Shipman has removed his caretakers, apparently fearing a lava flow may inundate the area. Mr. Shipman has informally indicated he . . . is interested in terminating his lease. He has also indicated sale of the ranch to the National Park service seems appropriate."[8]

A satisfactory arrangement was negotiated. Shipman terminated his lease with no penalty, and Bishop Estate sold the property in fee simple to the Park Service. For the improvements Shipman had made on the property, he received $150,000 from the Park Service.[9]

Stories still make the rounds among park personnel that, later,

Shipman regretted having terminated the lease, especially after the threat of lava flows diminished considerably. Instead of reproaching himself, he took it out on individuals connected with the park, but in the lower echelons. For example, shortly after the Park Service acquired the property, they installed a female caretaker on the premises. She related that Shipman went out of his way to ignore her and extended no courtesies to her. The young lady's mother found out that Shipman had mistaken her daughter for a member of the park staff. Once that matter was cleared up, the air also cleared and civility was restored.[10]

For several years after HNP became the owner of 'Āinahou, little use was made of the property other than that the nēnē received tender loving care and park horses a happy grazing ground. The ranch house and adjoining grounds fell into disrepair. This neglect was reversed in mid-1993 when park officials saw that the property offered great potential for programs focusing on educational and cultural themes. The Volcano Art Center and the Volcano Community Association lent support in building a bridge that would involve adjacent communities and groups in the park's aim to utilize the long-neglected ranch more fully. A new roof has been installed and other immediate structural deficiencies corrected. Future plans include installation of a water system, inside toilets, a generator for power, and remodeling to provide a room for assembly and dance groups. The Shipman company has already contributed generously to the cost of some of the recent major repairs. Volunteer help and HNP support is planned for ongoing improvements. Herbert Shipman, said one park official, would be delighted.[11] It is also safe to say that his grudge against the park dissolved in due time.

# 23

## *Rite of Passage*

Never one to run to doctors when he wasn't feeling well, perhaps Herbert Shipman expected them to come to him, like his barber. He was beset by high blood pressure, asthma, and diabetes, which understandably cramped his style, but his faithful servant, Henry Ha'a, continued to give him the best of care and companionship. Although he traveled less as he grew older, Herbert still made visits to the office, with Henry at the wheel of the Cadillac. Nor were his social contacts dropped. But in 1976 his diabetes took its toll: he had to have both legs amputated above the knee. Solitude proved to be good therapy in his last year, a year in which he suffered excruciating pain from the surgery and other illnesses.

In his last months special recognition from the Hawai'i County Council in the form of a lengthy resolution brought Herbert some cheer. After the council had extolled several specific Shipman contributions, it resolved "That Keaau Park be renamed Herbert C. Shipman Park in honor of a man who has achieved success in all aspects of his community, business, and humanitarian endeavors. . . ."[1]

Herbert entered Hilo Life Care Center, albeit most reluctantly, in mid-1976, where he died in October. He was eighty-four years old, six years younger than his father had been when he died. Services were held at the Haili Church and his ashes were buried in the Kea'au family cemetery. He was the last of the Hawai'i male Shipmans to bear that surname.

In his will Shipman requested that the bulk of his fortune go to the H. C. Shipman Foundation, to be established after his death.[2] He was generous in death as he had been in life. A pre-will statement revealed that he had already made generous contributions to the Girl Scouts, the Hawai'i Island Humane Society, and the Henry Obookiah School. He left ample sums of money to his former servants and certain employees of W. H. Shipman, Limited. To his faithful friend and companion, Henry Ha'a, he left $25,000 and all his pets. Nieces, nephews, grandnieces, and grandnephews were all remembered with monetary gifts. Herbert felt that, as his four living sisters, whom he truly loved, had been well provided for by their parents, and by their aunt Caroline J. Robinson, it was not necessary to add to their estates. His sisters understood this and wholeheartedly agreed with him. Two hundred shares of voting stock in W. H. Shipman, Limited, were willed to his nephew, Roy Blackshear. The remaining estate, including Shipman stock and personal assets, became part of the H. C. Shipman Foundation. Herbert specified that the foundation be managed by three trustees and that it "be operated exclusively for religious, charitable, scientific or educational purposes, including the encouragement of art and the prevention of cruelty to animals. . . ." It went on to specify a number of activities and interests the foundation could *not* support, including those political. The will also noted that anyone who claimed to be an offspring would receive one hundred dollars. There were no takers.

At the request of the executors, every item of value in the Manager's House was itemized, given a number, and later appraised. Herbert's

Florence Lukini Shipman on the day of her wedding to Roy C. Blackshear.

art collection was considerable. Such a rabid lover of silver was he that he never got around to opening some of the boxes he had bought. The task of itemizing and numbering was assigned to Masaru Uchida, and it took him two months, working eight hours a day, to complete it. Once he had finished the contents of one room, it was sealed and only he was allowed to reenter it. Following the appraisal, members of the family were allowed to purchase items at the appraised prices. Articles not bought by the family were then made available to selected persons and interested parties. Shipman's Asian art collection, valued at $116,000, was given to the Lyman House Museum. Pieces as old as 1300 B.C. from China, Korea, and Japan were included and are now on display in the Herbert Shipman Chinese Gallery of the museum. Two rare archaic bronze vessels dating back to the Shang Dynasty of the fourteenth century B.C. were later donated to the Honolulu Academy of Arts.

Herbert Shipman also left behind many memories, which came to light in the Watumull oral interviews. It has been observed by some of his lifelong friends that he possessed a remarkable memory, which served him well in recounting past Hawaiian history. His sharp sense of recall included the history of several other established families engaged in ranching and other major enterprises. His memories of visits by Queen Lili'uokalani never dimmed, though he was quite young at the time she was a guest at the Reed's Island residence.

He enjoyed recollecting for his listeners trivia of a half-century ago. For instance, the time his father, in the downtown office of Hilo Meat Company, suggested to one of his workers, named Allen, that it was about time the floor was swept. Herbert would have had apoplexy at the response Allen gave Willie: "There isn't much use doing it, it'll only get dirty again."

One subject that never surfaced in any of Herbert's recollections was reference to a love life. He may have had one, but if so he never mentioned it. The only information on the matter, precious little, comes from two of his last remaining friends, now oldtimers. Individually, each said that he thinks there was once a young lady in Herbert's life and that she lived in Kona. One of these older associates heard it rumored that she had died young, and that with her death died any further interest in the affairs of the heart for Herbert. "But let me tell you," knowingly remarked this older source of information, "more than one eligible young, and some not so young, women had their caps set for him. They had marked him for a real catch."

# 24

## The Shipman Sisters

William and Mary Shipman loved all their children and encouraged them in whatever endeavors they wished to pursue. The two sons, armed with a good education, followed their father's business interests. The five daughters (Mary, Clara, Caroline, Florence, and Margaret), like their brothers, began their elementary education in the Hilo private school of Mrs. Laura Kennedy.[1] When the girls reached adulthood, their parents gave each of them a lot in Hilo with a dwelling already on it. However, three of the girls married and later had homes of their own, whereas Caroline and Margaret, who remained single, continued to live in the Big House.

Mary Mikahala, the oldest, was born at Kapoho Ranch in 1879. But she was reared in the Waiākea residence on Kīlauea Avenue that Willie had acquired around the time he became a third owner of the Kea'au Tract. When still a young lady, she married Otis English (a distant cousin) and took up housekeeping in Volcano Village. The couple spent their lifetime in that community, where Otis operated the Ohialani Dairy and made daily deliveries to several Volcano residents. They had two children, Margaret and Eldon. Mary, like her brother Herbert, was blessed with a green thumb and a love of flowers. She was known for her pompon dahlias as well as new types developed through cross-pollination. Her garden was a kaleidoscope of colorful flowers that she knew would thrive at the higher and cooler altitude of Volcano Village. Mary English died in 1963 at the age of eighty-two.

Clara Shipman, who was born in 1885, was named not only after her aunt, Clara Shipman Thurston, but also her great-grandmother, Margaret Clarissa Shipman of Illinois. After attending Mills College, she married Harold Fisher and they moved to Hā'ena, near the Kea'au Ranch home, where they built a house on a twenty-acre parcel her father had given them. It was on this land that Fisher began what would be the largest poultry farm on the island. During the early part of World War II he supplied the military with fresh eggs and poultry, but when importation of

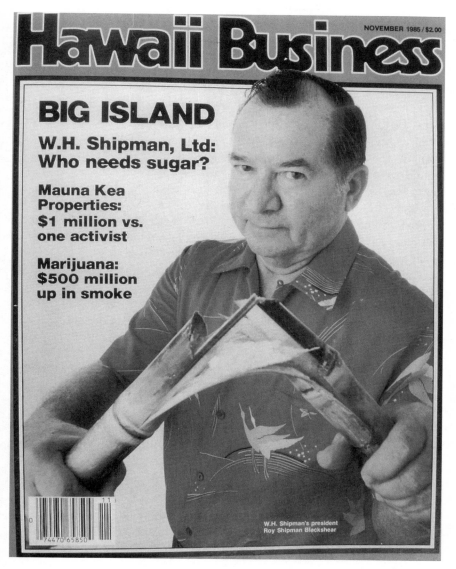

# Hawaii Business

NOVEMBER 1985 / $2.00

## BIG ISLAND

### W.H. Shipman, Ltd: Who needs sugar?

**Mauna Kea Properties: $1 million vs. one activist**

**Marijuana: $500 million up in smoke**

W.H. Shipman's president
Roy Shipman Blackshear

Roy S. Blackshear, Shipman scion and president of W. H. Shipman, Limited. Here he breaks a stalk of sugarcane, foretelling the future demise of that crop. Except for Willie's brief entry into sugar planting around 1880 and the leasing of Shipman lands to sugar growers, the family never entered into what was once a major industry.

chicken feed from the mainland was curtailed, he disposed of the business. Harold died in 1945.

Clara has been described as an outgoing woman and was renowned for the hospitality she extended to the many soldiers who were stationed near the Keaʻau (Hāʻena) home. She soon became known to the servicemen as Aunty Clara, who treated them to her fresh pies, cakes, fried chicken, and biscuits with honey. She became a mother to so many of the island's military men that after the war several kept corresponding with her, and some who later returned to Hawaiʻi with their wives made it a point to visit "Aunty Clara," who had so graciously opened her home to them. In those postwar years, Clara Fisher had a steady stream of visitors, whom she welcomed with true Hawaiian hospitality. One of those visitors was the well-known composer Helen Desha Beamer, who had become enchanted with the Hāʻena setting, with its legend of the goddess Pele and her sister Hiʻiaka. The result was the song "Lei OʻHaena." In her later years Clara often obliged Herbert by acting as hostess at social gatherings at his nearby residence. She also derived pleasure from fishing off the rocks that fronted the property.

Clara and Harold had two children. One, a boy, died at birth, and daughter Virginia lived until 1992. Clara suffered a stroke that brought about her death in 1977 at the age of ninety-two. A nurse who attended

The 488-acre Shipman Industrial Park proved a boon to Hilo businesses as well as to W. H. Shipman, Limited.

her said: "Judging from all the visitors she had daily she was truly loved by many. I wish I had known her earlier."

Caroline, born in 1886, was generally known as Carrie, not only to family members but to a great number of island-wide acquaintances. She too was a Mills College student, and it was there, at 5 A.M. in the morning of April 18, 1906, that she was shaken out of bed by the devastating earthquake which resulted in the San Francisco fire. Four days later she penned a nine-page letter to her parents in which she graphically described the damage suffered at Mills by "a terrific earthquake" and how only days later Mills students spent their time, under the direction of Mrs. Mills, cutting and sewing clothes for the thousands of victims. Carrie described the whole school as having been "turned into a clothes making establishment."

Carrie's letter was written with the clarity of a competent journalist and the compassion of a caring social worker. She described the hair-breadth escape of a girl companion whom a chimney falling on her room missed by inches. On a much larger scale, she told of the pall of smoke

A century ago the present Shipman Street area was a trading ground and market for fishermen and fruit and vegetable growers from miles around. The Greco-Roman designed building in the background is the earlier Hilo Public Library.

A Mediterranean-style building for the Shipman headquarters in Kea'au also houses interesting art.

that covered San Francisco and the total destruction of homes, many in the city's poorer section. "Where all the beautiful buildings once stood it is now a mass of charred ruins," she wrote her parents. "The Call, the Chronicle, the Examiner, the Merchants' Exchange, the Mechanics' Pavilion, the Columbia Theatre, the Emporium, the Palace, the Occidental and St. Francis hotels, and City Hall, are only a few of the buildings burned. The banks are all gone . . . the insurance companies are probably ruined." Mills College facilities also suffered from the quake but were spared the fires. "But our losses are nothing compared to other localities." Carrie's sympathy went out to the "Thousands thrown out of their houses, especially the poorer classes, and they had to fight their way through the smoke and flames down Market Street to the ferry, or fly to the hills with nothing besides what they had on their backs. People who were once wealthy were placed on a common basis with the poor, and only with a satchel of little things they were trying to save from the flames. . . . Some families got separated, which must have been awful. Martial law was enforced, preventing many people from Oakland from leaving. I cannot begin to tell you of the sad stories of the people. They are too many and too awful."

Although it is said that Carrie had many suitors, she preferred the relative comfort of the Reed's Island home and the freedom to do as she chose. Unlike her sisters, she chose to work, and is remembered for having been a capable librarian at the Hawai'i County Public Library and an

A staff of six carries on the business of W. H. Shipman, Limited. *Left to right:* Thomas T. English, Roy S. Blackshear, Donna Blackshear, Robert Cooper, Bessie Morita, and Fred Koehnen.

ardent advocate for an even larger library. When she retired, she returned her retirement checks, saying others were more needy than she.

Caroline Shipman was also known for her involvement in community affairs. Even in her retirement years, she, with her sister Margaret, became forces to be reckoned with. The renaming of streets and acting on zoning requests did not escape their attention; Many subsequent changes were frequently the result of input from these two sisters. The beautification of Hilo, particularly tree planting and park development, were high on their list of community responsibilities. Despite such public exposure, Caroline, like her sisters, shunned publicity.

Her last years found her busy as a competent archivist and self-appointed historian of the Shipman family. Over three hundred family letters that recently came to light are partly the result of her preserving family records. She made sure that copies of her brief history of the Shipman family were sent to all nieces, nephews, and grandchildren so they could appreciate their heritage.[2] These younger people remember "Aunty

Ever since incorporation in 1923, the Shipman board has been comprised of members with Hawai'i roots. The 1993 members are: *seated:* Joan Shipman Blackshear-Leech, Beryl Blackshear Walter, Roy Shipman Blackshear; *standing left to right:* Eldon Shipman English, David P. Young (deceased), Eldon S. English, Jr., Richard Devine, Fred Koehnen, Douglass Adams, and Thomas T. English. Missing are William R. Walter and Robert E. Cooper.

Carrie" not only as a gracious lady but also as a stickler for good manners, proper living, and a good education. Like her sister Clara, Caroline's full life lasted until November 1978, when she was ninety-two. Her love of literature was passed on to her nieces and nephews, and the many books in the Shipman family library testify to her good literary taste.

The fourth daughter, Florence Lukini, was born in 1888 and followed her sisters in attending Mrs. Kennedy's private school. After graduating from Punahou in 1908, she too attended Mills College. Although all the Shipman sisters demonstrated artistic talent in one way or another, Florence—or Flossie, as her siblings called her—enjoyed oil painting. Her interest in the medium included painting flowers, birds, and scenery on Oriental trays, baskets, place cards, and greeting cards. Her biggest canvas was a garden scene painted on a three-panel, five-foot screen complete with a design in the style of the 1930s.

Like her mother, Florence was friendly and did not hesitate to strike up conversations with people from all walks of life. In 1915, while visiting at Pu'u'ō'ō Ranch, she met Roy C. Blackshear when he and a number of friends stopped off before climbing Mauna Kea. They were married in 1919, and the day before the wedding she wrote, "I am so excited I can hardly write this in my diary." Her husband, a native of Arkansas and Texas who had earned a degree in pharmacy from the University of California, was employed in the Benson Smith drugstore in downtown Honolulu. While dating prior to their marriage, Florence had moved to Honolulu, where she taught kindergarten. Following their marriage in Hilo, Roy was employed as a pharmacist by the Hilo Drug Company until he bought the Standard Drug in 1937. Florence and Roy had two children, Beryl Kalaninohea and Roy Shipman Blackshear. Until she died at the age of eighty-two in 1972, Florence enjoyed her hobbies of antiquing and collecting everything from bottles to rocks.

Margaret Beatrice, born in 1891, was the last of the five daughters of William and Mary Shipman. She too was Punahou-educated. In addition to attending Mills College, she was also a student at Dana Hall, back east. She was considered the tomboy of the family, ever ready for horseback riding, fishing, golfing, stamp collecting, and working with leather. Like her sisters, she had a talent for arranging flowers, most often dried, working with coconut blossoms and fronds, and other exotic tropical plants found around Hilo.

When World War II broke out, Margaret volunteered her services, and because of her fluency in Japanese and pidgin English she was taken on by Mutual Telephone Company as a censor. Whenever a phone conversation bordered on restricted subjects, she would tactfully cut in and, if necessary, terminate it.

Margaret, like her sister Carrie, was quite happy to remain unmarried. The two sisters were frequently hostesses to numerous friends and family members. Holidays at the Big House, such as Thanksgiving and

Evidence of early Shipman influence in rural Illinois occurs in this postmark of the town of Shipman.

Shipman, Illinois, endures in the present-day town post office and highway sign.

the Christmas season, were festive family events, and the two sisters not only supplied exquisite decorations but also a bountiful board to satisfy all tastes and appetites. A warm relationship was enjoyed with Jack London and his wife, Charmian, a relationship born when all the girls attended Mills College. The Shipman sisters frequently visited the couple at their California residence, and in turn the Londons were always welcome at the Big House.[3]

Also like Carrie, Margaret found and made time to be an outspoken citizen of her community and an activist on behalf of Hilo beautification. Nor did a full schedule keep her from enrolling in a plumbing class at the Hilo Community College when she was in her eighties.

Brother Herbert, the next child after Margaret, would jokingly complain about being bossed around, not so much by the four older sisters but particularly by Margaret. When a friend once remarked that he should be grateful not to have a nagging wife, Herbert replied: "That's what you think. I have five sisters who henpeck me from all sides."

When Margaret died in 1992 at the age of eighty-nine, it was the end of an era of Shipmans as well as the surname, though the two nephews, Eldon Shipman English and Roy Shipman Blackshear, do carry it as a middle name. Later generations have also used the name in that way.

All five Shipman sisters were honored in their lifetimes for their contributions to their community. Their wartime service as Grey Ladies and occasional USO work are among the activities for which they were long remembered. In March 1974 the Hilo Women's Club showed special recognition to the living sisters, all of whom were charter members. The certificate of recognition presented to each saluted them as being "a powerhouse behind community-oriented activities and a force to be reckoned with when Hilo's welfare was threatened." A published account of that date cited the sisters "for their support of all types of cultural ventures that would enhance the quality of life here."[4] The community was reminded of the sisters' 1922 crusade against billboards, for protesting construction of a fish-canning factory near Hilo's waterfront, for advocating regular rubbish pickups, and for proposing and planning park sites. Many of these efforts and accomplishments were unknown to the community, for individually and as a family the sisters avoided the spotlight. Today they are still remembered for their past achievements. Examples of their ongoing community concerns are the Caroline Shipman Foundation and the Margaret Shipman Foundation, both of which still continue to function as benefactors to the larger community, particularly in the areas of social work and the advancement of individual well-being.

All of the sisters are buried in the parklike family cemetery near the Kea'au residences.

# 25

# A Kama'āina Company That Cares

In the early 1950s the economy of Hawai'i began a slow change marked by a gradual decline from agriculture. Sugar and pineapple, long reliable mainstays, showed signs of slipping, despite—or some say because of—unionization. The cost of doing business was draining many *kama'aina* (older, well-established) firms. Ranching was not spared. Beef prices were dropping and operating costs increasing. The Shipmans soon recognized that they were land-rich and money-poor.[1] A cash-flow problem became very real, for cash was needed to continue to run the ranches, pay the employees, and keep W. H. Shipman, Limited on a profitable basis. A 1932 survey of all Shipman property showed that the company owned 71,000 acres of land. Little change had taken place in the last twenty years. One solution was to sell off unproductive acreage. It was an opportune time to do so, for Hawai'i's postwar years saw an increase in population, accelerated by admission of Hawaii as a state in 1959.

One of Shipman's earliest and largest sales was to a Honolulu businessman, Rudy Tongg. An entrepreneur in many fields, Tongg bought several thousand acres, which he converted into rural subdivisions between Kea'au and Volcano.[2] Of the Kea'au Ranch property, always marginal at best, 9,000 acres went to the Watumull Land Company and provided that many house lots for Paradise Park. In this particular sale to Watumull, Herbert Shipman withheld 104 acres near the coast, in an area known as Maku'u. He did so out of respect for a small Hawaiian *heiau* on the property, as well as other archaeological sites and the belief that an ancient burial ground exists there. Small caves have been discovered along the shoreline and elsewhere on the 104-acre tract, which remains undeveloped today, bisected only by the abandoned Old Government Road.[3]

On the coastal area known as King's Landing, Shipman parted with an additional 2,000 acres.[4] The Mauna Loa Macadamia Nut Company now owns 3,000 acres of former Shipman Kea'au Ranch land. After Herbert Shipman's death, 5,000 acres of fee-simple land at Puakala Ranch were sold to The Nature Conservancy. Even before he died more than 50,000 acres in the Puna District had been sold off.

Roy Blackshear said that the company more or less decided to get out of ranching in 1972 when their lease on Pu'u'ō'ō Ranch was about to expire and was up for bid. The immediate family, Herbert and his five sisters, discussed the pros and cons and decided not to invest any more money in the operation. When the lease went to Parker Ranch for a whopping $65,000 rent per year, the family were glad they had held off. "From that point on," said Blackshear, "we decided to phase out ranching. It no longer interested the younger family members since our know-how was in land management and development." He pointed out that, since then, their income has come from rentals, leases, and land sales. Eventually all the Shipman ranches—Pu'u'ō'ō, Puakala (with the exception of 500 acres), Keauhou, and 'Āinahou—were sold or converted to other uses. Ranching on Kea'au land was discontinued.

Two years before his death Herbert reached out to his nephew, Blackshear, and had him invested as vice president. Roy came to the job with good credentials and a Hawai'i Island background. He had behind him twenty-three years of managerial experience with the Hawaiian Telephone Company in Honolulu and Hilo. That had been preceded by an education that included graduation from Punahou, following in the footsteps of his mother, aunts, uncles, and grandfather Shipman. After two years at the New Mexico Military Institute, Roy returned to Hawai'i and enlisted in the air force for the duration of World War II. In 1948 he graduated from the University of Hawai'i with a B.A. degree in business administration.

When, in 1976, he became the company's third president in fifty-three years, Blackshear knew that the times dictated he be more than a caretaker. He had seen the need for a change in direction and, along with others in the company, helped bring it about. Although affairs were running smoothly, plans were made to develop a new shopping center in Kea'au and also an industrial park of several hundred acres in the indefinite future. All was well in Kea'au—for a while.

But in January 1982 an unanticipated blow fell on W. H. Shipman, Limited. Blackshear was at his Kea'au Beach home watching the evening news on television. He was practically jolted out of his chair when the newscaster announced that American Factors, owner of Puna Sugar Company, was shutting down the plantation: it was becoming a millstone to it, the lessee. Blackshear knew that this could gravely affect Shipman profits, for Puna Sugar leased 8,000 acres of Shipman land, which accounted for 70 percent of its income. Some long-term damage was averted by the fact that the American Factors' lease still had ten more years to run, so revenues were not entirely or sharply truncated. Later, arrangements were made with American Factors to terminate its lease prior to 1994, and Shipman was satisfied with the terms.

Blackshear has said that the demise of the Puna Sugar lease may have been the best thing that could have happened to the Shipman firm, as the abrupt alteration in their scheme of things prodded them to find new uses for their land. They established two goals. The first was to speed up the development of a shopping center on Shipman land in Kea'au. The location was ideal, at the intersection of two main highways. In addition, the Hilo population was shifting in that direction; also, the Puna population had nearly doubled in the last decade. A well-planned shopping center would, they reasoned correctly, attract people from outlying areas and increase Kea'au's population. This goal was met with the completion of Kea'au Town Center in 1982, the largest shopping mall in the Puna district.

The second goal was to press for development of an industrial park consisting of over four hundred acres. Ten years earlier the company had developed plans and applied for such a complex, but it had been shelved for re-zoning and other reasons. In 1984, Shipman dusted off the plans, hired outside planning consultants and engineers at a cost of over $90,000, and resubmitted the revised proposal to the State Land Use Commission. Testimony from Hilo businesses that saw advantages in an industrial area with reasonable rents helped to sell it. Also brought into focus was its proximity to the Hilo International Airport and Hilo harbor, and its location only six miles from Hilo's business center on a four-lane divided highway. This time the commission approved the reclassification of 372 acres out of a total of 488 on Shipman land, all less than a mile from the village and Kea'au Town Center.

Once the permitting and re-zoning process was approved by the County of Hawai'i, the W. H. Shipman Industrial Park went ahead without any major hitches. It consisted of 22,000 feet of county-dedicated, wide, paved, illuminated, and curbed streets. Telephone and electrical service and county water were provided to all lots. Over $2.6 million alone has gone into a drainage system that includes seventy dry wells. All told, $10 million has been spent by Shipman to date on approximately one-third of the park. Development will continue until all 488 acres are completed.

The long-delayed dedication of W. H. Shipman Industrial Park was an event waiting to happen. By mid-1993, about twenty major Hilo businesses had their warehouses and/or wholesale outlets and offices in sizable modern buildings. The present occupants of the park, which employs over three hundred people, have a choice of renting the land or purchasing it outright. Market studies indicate that the complex still has healthy prospects, and 325 more acres are slated for the park's development.

Mid-1993 land holdings of the company were 18,000 acres. Of these, 15,500 were in and around Kea'au. Twelve hundred more were in the Volcano area, and 500 on Puakala Ranch. A business building consisting of 7,000 square feet in Honolulu, opposite the Catholic cathedral on Fort Street, is also Shipman property. It is the only off-island property the company has. Formerly owned by the Watumull Company, it became Shipman property as partial payment for Watumull's Paradise Park acquisition.

For the future, Shipman has somewhat ambitious but realistic plans. Its major objective is the development of a cohesive master plan that will serve the full range of residents in the Puna District for the foreseeable future and beyond. Residential opportunities include land that borders South Hilo. (Residential growth in Hilo is already expanding its boundaries.) Of considerable interest to the many hundreds of people who commute from the Puna area to Hilo is Shipman's plan to assist Hawai'i County in easing commuter traffic on the Pāhoa Road to Kea'au Junction. A new Kea'au community would provide such necessary facilities as schools, parks, government facilities, and police and fire stations.

Far from being a complacent caretaker executive, Blackshear has concentrated on planned development for a community that is expected to expand in the Puna district for years to come. He is looked upon as a leader, and one who has already paid his dues. Even more than his uncle, Blackshear has been a consistent participant in civic affairs. He has served as president of the Hawaii Island United Way (1973); Hawai'i Island chapter of the Hawaii Visitors Bureau (1984–1985); Hawaii Island Chamber of Commerce (1985–1986); and the Navy League, Hilo Chapter (1989). The Girl Scout Council of the Pacific cited him for "outstanding service" in 1979; The Professional Secretaries International, Hilo Chapter, named him their "Executive Director of the Year" in 1989; and the Boys and Girls Club of Hilo named him "Member of the Year" in 1988 and feted him with a roast in 1993. Blackshear was a member of the Trade Mission from Hawai'i Island to Taiwan and Hong Kong, led by former Mayor Herbert Matayoshi. He serves as a trustee of the Lyman House Memorial Museum and is past director of the State Chamber of Commerce and Hawaii Visitors Bureau. His name is among the thirteen most influential men of Hawai'i Island, and in 1985 *Hawaii Business* carried his picture on its November cover and featured his story. Following the death of his uncle, he was named, in Herbert's place, an honorary director of the Puna Hongwanji Mission, a position he values greatly.

Blackshear's care for environmental preservation can be seen in his stewardship of the family beach estate in Hā'ena, as that part of Kea'au was recorded on early maps. Protecting and fostering the general environment is his ongoing concern. The planning for the 5,000-foot frontage of the Shipman Industrial Park provided for a 30-foot-thick buffer of trees that completely hides the tract from busy Highway 11: only a modest and low-key masonry sign at the entrance indicates the park's presence.

The *kama'āina* company has been wise in surrounding itself with capable consultants in economics and planning, persons knowledgeable in aiding the company for future development. Internal support and guidance over the years have come from a ten-member board of directors comprised of seven family and three nonfamily members. The 1994 officers and other directors are Blackshear, president; Eldon S. English, first vice president; Fred J. Koehnen, second vice president; Tom English, treasurer; Joan Shipman Blackshear-Leech, secretary; Richard R. Devine, Beryl Blackshear Walter, David P. Young (Maui), and Douglass S. Adams. Deceased directors are the five Shipman sisters and Herbert, and Margaret English and Virginia Fisher Dennis of the fourth generation of Hawai'i Shipmans.

Although the firm is recognized as a player in Hawai'i Island today and tomorrow, the family itself, over the years, has continued to maintain a low profile. The combined Shipman characteristics of shunning the limelight and being benefactors to the community reflect the motto found in the family coat of arms, *Non sibi sed orbi,* "Not for ourselves but for the world." The chief recipients of this largesse have been educational and humanitarian organizations too numerous to mention. Blackshear's forebears made possible many of these financial contributions.

The Shipmans of Hilo and their life-style were accurately described by the well-read Honolulu raconteur and newspaper columnist Sammy Amalu. The occasion was Herbert's eightieth birthday, celebrated at Hilo's Yacht Club, and, according to Amalu, attended by everyone who was anyone. Wrote Amalu of Herbert and the family:

> When he was born, Hawaii was still a monarchy. Queen Liliuokalani was in the last few months of her short and troubled reign. And he was born into one of Hawaii's most prominent families. But not a family that was given over to ostentation.

It was a quiet family, not one to show off its wealth nor to make that wealth obvious to everyone. If you knew them you knew they were rich. They acted rich, but they did it with dignity, with grace and a refinement that is seldom seen anymore. There was never any need for flamboyance. Where everyone else was trying to reach, they had arrived a long time ago. They were the Shipmans of Hilo. What else need be said.

Herbert Shipman's fondness for collecting rare items of interest rubbed off on his successor and nephew, Roy. For instance, in the United States there is a growing interest in antique telephones. A national organization of collectors of these old instruments meets annually, and many members display and sell their rare wares. Blackshear started collecting these items when employed by Hawaiian Telephone, often picking up discarded and unappreciated equipment. From the national annual antique collector conventions he attends, he often ships home another piece of telephone nostalgia. Today the Blackshear antique phone collection rings a bell among the nation's winners. He is also a collector of Hawaiiana in many forms; his beach house is part art gallery.

Herbert Shipman's dream and subsequent efforts to save the nēnē from extinction have also been continued by Blackshear. Not only does he support the program of raising nēnē in captivity on the Shipman Keaʻau Estate, he has kept in touch with England's Wild Fowl and Wetlands Trust. In 1990 he was invited by the Trust to attend a reception at Highgrove, then the home of Prince Charles and Princess Diana, to honor those who have been instrumental in the survival of the nēnē. Blackshear carried a congratulatory letter from Governor John Waihee and a koa plaque from the state recognizing the Trust for its efforts over the years to save Hawaiʻi's state bird from extinction. The presentation was made in Prince Charles' garden to Lady Scott, widow of Sir Peter Scott. The plaque hangs in a place of honor in the administration offices of the Wild Fowl and Wetlands Trust in Slimbridge, England.

Roy Blackshear's interest in the nēnē has extended to a recent hobby. For over two years he has been studying silk-screen painting under accomplished Hilo artist Jane Chao. One of his works, of which he is justly proud, is a striking picture of two noble nēnē that appeared on his 1992 Christmas cards. Such concerns and interests would reassure the two previous and long-gone company past presidents that the Shipman traditions are being carried on as the company moves into its seventy-second year.

## Postscript

After two decades as head of the W. H. Shipman, Limited, Roy Blackshear retired as of June 30, 1994. The seventy-year-old grandson of the company's founder will continue as head of the company's executive committee and president of its board of directors. In looking forward to retirement, he observed, "Each day I continued to work beyond age seventy was one day less of retirement."

His plans for the future are flexible, but he looks forward to pursuing such hobbies as painting and photography. In the latter field he has been a blue-ribbon winner and had many photos published in national periodicals. He admits that he will find it hard not to continue to add to his rare collection of old telephones, phonographs, and antique radios. Nor does he intend to lose sight of his interest in the future of the company he helped to make such great advances over the past twenty years.

In recognition of Roy Blackshear's many contributions to his island home, the Hawaii Island Chamber of Commerce adopted a resolution focusing "on his outstanding service." It took cognizance of the preservation of Hawai'i's state bird, the nēnē, and his having been a dedicated member and longtime community and public service leader.

Replacing Blackshear as head of W. H. Shipman, Limited is Robert Cooper, who has been with the company for a decade as Shipman manager of its land development projects. There is every reason to believe that the goals set by Blackshear will be realized. Cooper is the first nonfamily member to head the seventy-one-year-old company.

# APPENDIX: GENEALOGIES

Although there were several siblings of both sexes in the first seven generations, only the male Shipman parent of the next generation is shown. Numerals preceding a name denote generation: b.=born, m=married, s=single, n.i.=no issue, d=divorced. Data as of March 1994.

THE SHIPMANS OF HAWAI'I:
(1)  Edward b.?–1697 (Hull, England)
     ar. America 1639
(2)  William 1656–1725
(3)  Stephen 1699–1747
(4)  Stephen 1721–?
(5)  Stephen (Capt.) 1750–1834
(6)  Reuben 1791–1864
     m. Margaret Clarissa Bulkley 1791–1867
(7)  William Cornelius (Rev.) 1824–1861 (Hawai'i)
     m. Jane Stobie 1827–1904
       (8)  William Herbert 1854–1943
       (8)  Oliver Taylor 1857–1942
       (8)  Margaret Clarissa 1859–1891
(8)  William Herbert
     m. Mary Elizabeth Kahiwaaialii Johnson 1852–1933
       (9)  Mary Mikahala (m. English) 1879–1963
       (9)  William R. 1880–1885
       (9)  Oliver B. 1883–1920 n.i.
       (9)  Clara (m. Fisher) 1885–1977
       (9)  Caroline 1886–1978 s.
       (9)  Florence (m. Blackshear) 1888–1972
       (9)  Margaret 1891–1980 s.
       (9)  Herbert 1892–1976 s.
       (9)  Two sons died in infancy

ENGLISH FAMILY:
(9)  Mary Mikahala
     m. Otis Eldon English* 1878–1951

---

*The mother of Otis English was Harriet Shipman, who married George English in Illinois. Harriet's father, James, was the brother of Rev. Cornelius Shipman.

(10)  Margaret Clarissa 1907–1986 s.
(10)  Eldon Shipman 1912–
      m. Martha Bon Durant Taylor 1908–
      (11)  Charlotte Mary 1941–
            1st m./d. Northrup H. Castle, Jr. n.i.
            2d m. Carlton Ferreira
      (11)  Eldon S., Jr., 1942–
            m. Elna Kate Weight 1943–
            (12)  Oliver Calder 1972–
            (12)  Christopher Shipman 1975–
      (11)  Martha Lynn 1943–
            m./d. William G. Simmons
            (12)  Michael William 1973–
      (11)  Patricia Dale 1944–
            m. James Austin Maglothin
            (12)  Ronald Keith 1971–
            (12)  Martha Lee 1973–
            (12)  Catherine Jean 1974–
            (12)  James Eldon 1978–
      (11)  Susan Margaret 1946–
            m. Gerald Dean Thompson
            (12)  Douglas Eldon 1967–
            (12)  Michele Suzanne 1969–
            (12)  Donald Paul 1974–
      (11)  Thomas Taylor 1948–
            m. Kathleen Marie Cullen 1949–
            (12)  Jennifer Anne Kamalalehua 1972–
            (12)  Margaret Elizabeth Mikahala 1977–
(9)  Oliver B.
    m. Alice Aspelin n.i.

FISHER FAMILY:
(9)  Clara
    m. Harold Fisher
    (10)  Robert died in infancy
    (10)  Virginia 1915–1992
         1st m.d. George Selman
         (11)  Gayle 1937–
             1st m./d. Robert Adams
             (12)  Douglas 1958–
             (12)  Rebecca 1959–
             (12)  Heather 1959–
             (12)  Melinda 1962–

            (12) Katherine 1963–
                 2d m./d. Bice n.i.
                 3d m./d. Lingua n.i.
      (10) Virginia
           2d m./d. Al Biehl n.i.
           3d m./d. James Dennis n.i.

BLACKSHEAR FAMILY:
  (9) Florence Lukini
      m. Roy C. Blackshear 1891–1981
      (10) Beryl Kalaninohea 1922–
           m. William B. Walter
           (11) Thomas Blackshear 1945–
                m./d. Joan Libby Carpenter
                (12) Thomas Andrew 1971–
                (12) Sarah Kalaninohea 1972–
           (11) William Roy 1948–
                m. Adella Paterson
                (12) Anja Kalaninohea 1979–
                (12) Dominique Rosemarie 1981–
                (12) Keala Claire 1985–
                (12) Whitney Jean 1987–
           (11) Douglas Bruce 1950–
                m. Elizabeth Naomi Moku
                (12) Kaiinaokapuuwai Margaret 1974–
                (12) Douglas Moku 1976–
           (11) David Joseph Shipman 1953–
                m. Lois Okomoto
                (12) Charlotte Ruth 1979–
                (12) Rebekah Sachiko 1982–
      (10) Roy Shipman 1923–
           1st m./d. Grace Jones
           (11) Barbara Ann 1950–
                m. Gary Andersen
                (12) Christian Blackshear 1974–
                (12) Melissa Kealalaina 1976–
           (11) Joan Shipman 1951–
                m. James B. Leech
      (10) Roy Shipman
           2d m./d. Jacqueline Guilbert n.i.
           3d m. Donna Pope
  (8) Oliver Taylor
      1st m. Hannah Naeole, died 1907

  (9)  John, moved to Napaville, Calif.
       4 sons, 1 daughter
  (9)  Frank, dentist, Lamoni, Iowa
       sons, 2 daughters
  (9)  Jane
       m. Thomas Lindsey n.i.
(8)  Oliver Taylor
     2d m. Mary K. Lo n.i.
(8)  Margaret Clarissa
     m. Lorrin A. Thurston
       (9)  Robert Shipman 1884–1940
            m. Evelyn Scott
            (10)  Robert Shipman, Jr., s. 1923–1946. Lost at sea.

GENEALOGY OF MARY KAHIWAAIALII JOHNSON
(First two generations, using a count of twenty years per generation)
  (1)  Kainakuawalu (m) m. Oheleluiakamoku (f)
       b. ca. 1750
  (2)  Nahulanui (f) m. Kaukamoa (m)
       b. ca. 1770
  (3)  Kauwe b. ca. 1792–1896
       m. John Davis
  (4)  Elizabeth Davis 1825–1913
       m. William Johnson
  (5)  Mary Elizabeth Kahiwaaialii 1852–1933
       m. William Herbert Shipman

Note: Kauwe's grandparents came from Luaehu, Lahaina, Maui. Figuring a generation to be twenty years, that would have been around 1740. They located at Manuka, in South Kona.

Kauwe's full name was **Ka-uwe-a-Kanoa-akaka-wale-no-Haleakala-ka-uwe-ke-kini-o-Koolau,** which roughly translates, "Cry of cries of Kanoa in mourning [for a beloved Maui queen], cries heard from Haleakala to the Koolau mountains."

# *NOTES*

Much information has been derived from letters written by one member of the Shipman family to another. This is especially true for chapters 2–14. Also, letters to or from a nonfamily member, but to or from a Shipman, have been drawn upon liberally.

## *Abbreviations*

ABCFM  American Board of Commissioners for Foreign Missions
BM       Bishop Museum
DLNR   Department of Land and Natural Resources
HCMS   Hawaii Children's Mission Society
HEA     Hawaii Evangelical Association
HSA     Hawaii State Archives
HL       Houghton Library at Harvard University. (Custodian for records of ABCFM.)
RSB     Roy Shipman Blackshear
SLC     Shipman Letters Collection
UHH    University of Hawai'i-Hilo, Library
WCS    Rev. William Cornelius Shipman
WHS    William Herbert Shipman, son

## *1  1854—A Year to Remember*

1. Ralph S. Kuykendall, *The Hawaiian Kingdom*, vol. 2, title page.
2. Neville Williams, *Chronology of the Modern World*.
3. John Clements, *Chronology of the United States*.
4. Kuykendall, 2:4–6.
5. Ibid., pp. 13–14.
6. A. Grove Day, *History Makers of Hawaii*, p. 68.
7. Gavan Daws, *Shoal of Time*, p. 83.
8. Ibid., p. 162.
9. Ibid., pp. 124–128.
10. Maxine Mrantz, *Hawaiian Monarchy*, p. 18; Kuykendall, 2:115–117.
11. Daws, pp. 147–150.
12. Lahaina Restoration Society, *The Story of Lahaina*, pp. 3–16.

13. Ibid., p. 23.

14. Daws, *Dream of Islands*, p. 71ff.

15. Lahaina Restoration Society, p. 8.

16. Ibid., p. 9.

17. Ibid.

18. Ibid., p. 11.

19. *Historic Hawaii*, July 1990.

20. Lahaina Restoration Society.

21. Letter from Charlotte Baldwin to husband, Dec. 24, 1854, Van Dyke Collection.


## 2   *Who Were the Shipmans?*

All Shipman genealogical information from 1653 to 1961, including relevant early American history, is extracted from *The Shipman Family in America*, published by Mrs. Rita Shipman Carl, Mrs. Angela Shipman Crispin, and Mr. and Mrs. William Henry Shipman. Copyright 1962 by the Shipman Historical Society.

1. "Why You Have a Family Tree and What It Means," paper, source and date unknown.

2. Daws, *Shoal of Time*, p. 79.

3. *The Name and Family of Shipman*, pp. 2–6.

4. *The Shipman Family in America*.

5. Glastonbury Historical Society, letter to author, Nov. 13, 1991.

6. Pike County (Ill.) Atlas, 1872.

7. History of Pike County, p. 741.

8. William H. Shipman, son of William Cornelius, went to court with his sister Clara and brother Oliver to obtain title to the property that had been in their father's name. The Illinois court ruled against them.

9. Pike County Court House land records.


## 3   *The Making of a Missionary*

1. History of Hadley Township, 1872.

2. Pike County (Ill.) Circuit Court file.

3. Historical Society of Quincy and Adams County (Ill.).

4. HL 101, Faculty member of Mission Institute.

5. Superintendent of Mission Institute.

6. HL 98, WCS letter of application to ABCFM.

7. HL 94, WCS letter to Rufus Anderson.

8. HL 95, WCS letter to Pomeroy.

9. HL 96, Statement from Howe St. Church trustees.

10. HL 97, Goodrich to ABCFM.

11. HL 100, Whipple to Pomeroy.

12. A major island in Micronesia named by a New England sea captain for Gov. Caleb Strong of Massachusetts. Today it is known as Kosrae. (Source: Rev. Eldon Buck, Hilo.)

13. HL 102, WCS to Treat.

14. HL 105.

15. Daws, *Shoal of Time*, pp. 61, 63, and 64.

16. Ibid. p. 62.

17. *Missionary Album*, by count.

18. Ibid., p. 17.

19. Daws, p. 105.

## 4   Love and Commitment

1. Extract from Aberdour Parochial Register, 1840.

2. Certified document from the Aberdour, Scotland, parish, Sept. 28, 1835.

3. Marriage certificate from Waverly Congregational Church.

4. Rev. Weller to Rev. Whipple, ABCFM.

5. Cowles to Pomeroy, March 2, 1854, ABCFM.

6. *Boston Evening Traveler*, June 5, 1854, Boston Public Library.

7. Diary (1850–1865) of George Driver, Essex Institute.

8. A. A. Lawrence Papers (diary), Boston, 1854.

9. The *Chasca* was built in Medford, Massachusetts, in 1848 by James Curtis. She weighed 659 tons and had three masts, three decks, and a square stern (Peabody Museum).

10. Missionary Album, p. 13.

## 5   Assignment to Paradise?

1. Minutes of Hawaiian Evangelical Association meeting in Honolulu, May 1855.

2. Ibid., p. 7.

3. Ibid., p. 2.

4. Rev. Shipman's letter to Anderson.

5. Rev. Paris' 1849 station report, HMCS.

6. Rev. Shipman's 1857 station report, HMCS.

7. Marian Kelly, *Majestic Kau*. Report #80–2, pp. 11–13.

8. *Journal of William Ellis*, p. 133.

9. Samuel Clemens, *Letters from the Sandwich Islands*.

10. Alphons Korn, *The Victorian Visitors*, 1958.

11. In *The Polynesian*, 1849–1850, titled "Tour of the Islands," in thirteen installments. The anonymous author was identified only as "Sailor."

## 6   Man with a Mission

1. Rev. Shipman's 1856 station report.
2. Letters from Rev. Paris to Rev. Chamberlain, HMCS.
3. Hawaii National Park Library.
4. HEA minutes of 1858.
5. Rev. Shipman's 1861 station report.
6. Marian Kelly, *Majestic Kau*, pp. 11, 12.
7. Isabella Bird, *Six Months in the Sandwich Islands*.
8. Daws, "Evangelism in Hawaii: Titus Coan and the Great Revival of 1837," 69th Annual Report of the Hawaiian Historical Society, 1960.
9. A. Grove Day, *History Makers of Hawaii*, pp. 60, 68.
10. Fr. Reginald Yzendoorn, *History of the Catholic Mission in the Hawaiian Islands*, pp. 79, 80.
11. Ibid., p. 56.
12. Daws, *Shoal of Time*, pp. 102, 103.
13. Ibid., p. 103; Day, p. 68.
14. HEA, 1854 Minutes.
15. HEA, 1857 Minutes.
16. HEA, 1855 Minutes.
17. Rev. Shipman's 1861 station report.
18. Eldon Buck, former missionary in Micronesia. Interview with author.
19. HSA, copy of the Act.

## 7   God Writes Straight . . . with Crooked Lines

1. Rev. Shipman's 1857 station report.
2. Ibid.
3. Arrival of wheat in Kaʻu, station report.
4. State Land records.
5. Ibid.
6. Rev. Shipman's 1859 station report.
7. Rev. Shipman's 1859 station report.
8. Rev. Shipman's 1860 station report.
9. Rev. Shipman's 1855 station report.
10. Rev. Shipman's 1860 station report.
11. Salary increase request.
12. Ibid., 1861.
13. Shipman's statistics re suspensions, etc.
14. Richard Henry Dana, Jr., *Two Years Before the Mast*.
15. Ibid.
16. Ibid.
17. Ibid.

18. Ibid.

19. Postmaster, Thrum's 1884.

20. Road supervisor, Virginia Hanson, former Bishop Museum archaeologist.

21. HSA, file copy.

22. Rev. Shipman's 1861 station report.

## 8   Transition

1. Mrs. Lucy Wetmore to her sister, Dec. 25, 1861, HL.

2. Ibid.

3. *Pacific Commercial Advertiser,* Dec. 19, 1961.

4. Ibid., Jan. 2, 1862.

5. HEA.

6. Department of Public Instruction, Jan. 1, 1862, HMCS.

7. Mrs. Wetmore to sister, Dec. 25, 1861.

8. Rev. Gulick's 1863 station report.

9. Paris re ministerial association.

10. HEA re Female Seminary.

11. Jane to Anderson, July 26, 1862.

12. Ref. to Volcano shelter, old shed. *The Story of the Volcano House,* by Gunder E. Olson, p. 24–26.

13. Marie Pogue to Jane Shipman, Feb. 4, 1862.

14. Richard Henry Dana, Jr., *Two Years Before the Mast.*

15. Jane to Anderson, July 1862.

16. HEA minutes of June 24, 1862.

## 9   Hilo, Crescent Moon

1. A. Scott Leithead, "Hilo, Hawaii: Its Origins and Patterns of Growth, 1778–1900," pp. 40, 42.

2. Peter H. Buck [Te Ranga Hiroa], *Vikings of the Sunrise,* p. 91.

3. *The Journals of Captain James Cook,* p. 605.

4. Captain George Vancouver, *Voyages of Discovery to the North Pacific Ocean,* p. 3.

5. Rev. Stephen Desha, Sr., *The Naha Stone,* Hawaii Nature Notes, February 1952.

6. *Journal of William Ellis,* pp. 212 and passim.

7. Ibid., pp. 238ff.

8. James Macrae, *With Lord Byron at the Sandwich Islands in 1825,* p. 46.

9. Rev. E. Bloxham, "Visit to the Sandwich Islands in 1825," *Hawaiian Annual of 1924,* pp. 66ff. Bloxam's given name is also recorded as Richard and Rowland. His brother Andrew was also on the Byron expedition.

10. Ibid., p. 72.

11. Milton C. George, *The Development of Hilo, Hawaii, T.H.*, p. 9.

12. J. M. Lydgate, "Hilo Fifty Years Ago," *Hawaiian Annual*, 1923.

13. Ibid.

14. George, p. 21. Also, Marian Kelly, Barry Nakamura, and Dorothy Barrere, *Hilo Bay, a Chronological Study*, p. 97.

15. Lydgate, p. 105.

16. Caroline Shipman, *Extracts of the Shipman Family*.

17. HSA, Probate of Rev. William C. Shipman, 1862.

18. Ibid.

19. Leithead, "Hilo, Hawaii," p. 63.

## 10   Enter William Reed

1. Historic Research Associates, Belfast, Northern Ireland.

2. HSA, copy of letter.

3. UHH microfilm.

4. DLNR, Liber 13.

5. Lydgate, *Hawaiian Annual*, 1926, pp. 101–108.

6. Patricia M. Alvarez, *A History of Road and Bridge Development on the Island of Hawaii*, pp. 15–17.

7. LM, Shipman/Lyman letter collection.

8. UHH microfilm, Coan.

9. All information related to the will, probate, and distribution of the property of Reuben and Clarissa Shipman is from the Illinois State Archives; also, researcher and genealogist Jean M. Kay and Donna Pursley of the Pike County (Ill.) Recorder's Office.

10. Letter from Jean M. Kay, Jan. 27, 1933.

11. Laws of Oahu College, 1867–1868.

12. Punahou School, Commemorative Issue, 1841–1941.

13. Ibid., p. 286.

14. RSB, oral interview.

15. Letter from Mary Judd, Punahou archivist, April 15, 1992.

## 11   Notes from Knox Academy

1. Knox Director of Communications to author, April 20, 1992.

2. Ibid.

## 12   Lunalilo

1. James Trager, *The People's Chronology*, pp. 527–528.

2. Ibid.

3. Daws, *Shoal of Time*, p. 209.

4. James K. Ahloy, chairman of the William Charles Lunalilo Trust, paper entitled "A Royal Legacy," Feb. 21, 1991, p. 1.

5. Ibid.

6. Charles de Varigny, *Fourteen Years in the Sandwich Islands*, p. 250.

7. Peter Galuteria, *Lunalilo*, p. 28.

8. Ibid., pp. 22–23.

9. Ibid., pp. 44–47.

10. SLC.

11. Ahloy, p. 5.

12. Ralph S. Kuykendall, *The Hawaiian Kingdom*, 2:254–257.

13. Ahloy, pp. 6–7.

14. Ibid., p. 7.

## 13   *Kapāpala Ranch*

1. Henry Whitney, *Hawaiian Guide Book of 1875*, p. 2.

2. Daws, *Shoal of Time*, pp. 124–128.

3. DLNR, Liber 13, p. 56.

4. HSA, Lyman correspondence.

5. *Hawaiian Gazette*, date unknown.

6. L. A. Henke, "A Survey of Livestock in Hawaii," pp. 8–9.

7. Ibid., p. 22.

8. In her report (*Majestic Kau*, p. 37), anthropologist Marian Kelly describes the 1868 event as "the most disruptive and best recorded of the early historic volcanic disturbances."

9. LM, Letters from Titus Coan to J. D. Dana, April 11, 1868.

10. Father Louis Yim, former archivist of the Honolulu Catholic Diocese, in a letter to Bishop Joseph Ferrario, July 31, 1883; also, an 1867 report of the Mission Catholique, Eglises et Chappelles, diocesan records.

11. LM, Frederick Lyman's report of the quake.

12. *Hawaiian Gazette*, April 26, 1868, p. 4.

13. SLC, Rev. Shipman's remains were later interred in the Shipman/Reed plot in Hilo's Homelani Cemetery.

14. DLNR, Liber 48, Oct. 20, 1976.

15. Ibid., Dec. 29, 1976.

16. This marked the beginning of the C. Brewer Plantation. It is now called Kau Sugar and is still a C. Brewer operation. At this writing it is the last operating sugar plantation on Hawai'i Island.

## 14   *Expansion*

1. HSA, "The Descendants of John Davis," Cartwright Collection.

2. BM, Pukui Collection, genealogy book no. 29.

3. Daws, *Shoal of Time*, p. 34; also Charmian London, *Our Hawaii*, pp. 263–265.

4. Daws, pp. 34–40.

5. Ibid., p. 44.

6. SLC.

7. Genealogy of Tutu Kauwe, paper by Beryl Blackshear Walter et al., 1967.

8. Caroline Shipman, "Extracts of the Shipman Family."

9. Day, *History Makers of Hawaii*, p. 65.

10. SLC.

11. Kuykendall, *The Hawiian Kingdom*, 3:56–59.

12. *Hilo Tribune Herald*, Sept. 24, 1923. "Oldest Resident of Hawaii Dies. Aged 105," front page; also, *Hawaii Tribune Herald*, Aug. 14, 1986, Lifestyle section.

13. HSA, Correspondence index.

14. Ibid.

15. Ibid.

16. Ibid.

17. William A. Simonds, *The Hawaiian Telephone Company Story*, p. 18.

18. E. S. Baker, "A Trip to the Sandwich Islands," *Hawaiian Annual*, 1877, pp. 38–39.

19. SLC, letter from Judge Lyman to Jane Reed.

## *15  Business at Large*

1. HSA, Ship arrivals and departures.

2. Ibid.

3. Kuykendall, *The Hawaiian Kingdom*, 3:46–48.

4. Hawaii Territory Survey, 1891 map of Hilo Town and Vicinity.

5. Data and correspondence from Mifflin Thomas, author of *Schooner from Windward* (Honolulu: University of Hawai'i Press, 1983).

6. HSA, Correspondence index, Reed.

7. Milton George, *The Development of Hilo, Hawaii, T.H.*, p. 27.

8. Mifflin Thomas.

9. Ibid.

10. Probate of Reed's will. Shipman files and author's collection.

11. Ibid.

12. Ibid.

13. Letter from Amherst archivist, May 12, 1992.

14. Mifflin Thomas, letter to author.

15. Captain Robertson's report of Oct. 11, 1882; Mifflin Thomas.

16. Mifflin Thomas.

17. Ibid.

### 16   The Lands of Lunalilo

1. DLNR, Liber 13.
2. Ahloy, "A Royal Legacy," p. 14.
3. SLC, Hawaiian Land and Improvement Co. file.
4. Ibid., p. 3.
5. HSA, Land index.
6. SLC, Hawaiian Land and Improvement Co. file, pp. 15–17.
7. Ibid., Kea'au tract deed, pp. 12–13.
8. Ibid.

### 17   Romance and Revolution

1. All references to Lorrin Thurston's early years, and much of his adult life, have been taken from *The Writings of Lorrin Thurston*, edited by Andrew Farrell and published by the Honolulu Advertiser Publishing Company in 1936.
2. Letter to author from Andover Historical Society, April 14, 1993.
3. Day, *History Makers of Hawaii*, p. 121.
4. Ibid.
5. Kuykendall, *The Hawaiian Kingdom*, 3:348ff.
6. Day, p. 121.
7. Daws, *Shoal of Time*, p. 243.
8. Ibid.; also Kuykendall, 3:9.
9. Day, p. 121.
10. Gunder Olson, *The Story of the Volcano House*, p. 44.
11. *The Friend*, May 1891.
12. Author's interview with Thurston Twigg-Smith, grandson of Lorrin A. Thurston, April 1993.

### 18   Onward and Upward

1. HSA, Correspondence index; also various DLNR records.
2. *Hilo Tribune Herald* 9/24/23, p. 1.
3. *Hawaii Tribune Herald* 9/14/86. Lifestyle section.
4. Leithead, "Hilo, Hawaii," p. 61.
5. HSA, Correspondence index.
6. Leithead, p. 6; see also J. Stacker, *Hawaiian Annual*, 1913, pp. 82–90.
7. Paul T. Yardley, *Millstones and Milestones*, pp. 281ff.
8. Olson, *The Story of the Volcano House*, p. 44.
9. Dorothy Barrere, ethnohistorian.
10. George, *The Development of Hilo*, p. 24.
11. *The Writings of Lorrin Thurston*.

12. George, p. 24.

13. *Commercial Pacific Advertiser*, undated clipping, ca. 1895.

14. HSA, Correspondence and ranch indexes.

### *19   Into the Twentieth Century*

1. Trager, *People's Chronology*, pp. 622–638.

2. Ibid.

3. Mifflin Thomas, *Schooner from Windward*, p. 99.

4. HSA, *Historical Honolulu*, ca. 1910.

5. *Hilo Tribune*, Oct. 30, 1993, p. 6.

6. Ibid., May 21, 1904.

7. Ibid., Nov. 1, 1904.

8. Ibid., Nov. 15, 1904.

9. Report of the 1905–1906 Territorial Legislature.

10. *Men and Women of Hawaii*, 1921, vol. 2.

11. Ibid.

12. Ibid.

13. Caroline Shipman, "Extracts of the Shipman Family," p. 17; see also documents of the transaction.

14. Charmian London, *The New Hawaii*, p. 165.

15. SLC.

16. RSB.

17. SLC.

18. Charmian London, *Our Hawaii*, p. 265.

19. Author's interview with Richard Devine, 1993.

20. Ibid.

21. Ibid.

### *20   Passing the Scepter*

1. Most of the information in this chapter came from oral interviews with Blackshear and Devine in 1992 and 1993.

2. RSB, written statement, May 24, 1993.

3. SLC, will of William H. Shipman.

### *21   Herbert Shipman: Man of Many Talents*

1. All Herbert Shipman's recollections are extracted from a two-day oral interview conducted by Katherine Allen in July 1971 on behalf of the Watumull Foundation. The complete interview is recorded as an eighty-five-page publication in the Hawaii State Archives.

2. Herbert Shipman thought that Kauwe was 103 years old at the time. This

would indicate that his great-grandmother was born ca. 1793. King Kamehameha, who, it is estimated, was born ca. 1758, was about thirty-five years older than Kauwe.

3. A nine-page paper, "Facts and Information About Herbert Cornelius Shipman," provides a considerable amount of data and biographical information about Herbert Shipman's career. It is undated and was authored by Gar Clarke. It can be found in the Hawai'i Volcanoes National Park Library, Biography file no. 22.

4. SLC.

5. Ibid.

6. Persons who provided information and are quoted are, unless otherwise noted: Roy Blackshear, Richard Devine, Dr. Leslie Weight, Kapua Heuer, Masaru and Yoshie Uchida, Bessie Morita, Carl Rohner, Yasuki Arakaki, John Cross, and Margaret Wessel Stearns. Personal interviews with all were conducted by the author.

7. Undated monograph by Brenda Lee.

8. Fred Goerner, *The Search for Amelia Earhart* (New York: Doubleday, 1966).

## 22 Community Pride and Prejudice

1. Daws, *Shoal of Time*, pp. 363ff.

2. This and subsequent information is derived from the author's interviews with Arakaki in 1993. Blackshear also contributed to the subject.

3. Olson, *The Story of the Volcano House*.

4. Sir Peter Buck was the director of the Bishop Museum from 1936 until his death in 1951.

5. Hawaii Volcanoes National Park files.

6. Ibid.

7. Ibid.

8. Ibid.

9. Ibid.

10. Ms. Zoe Thorne.

11. Daniel Taylor, HNP Chief of Resource Management.

## 23 Rite of Passage

1. Hawaii County Resolution no. 516, March 3, 1976.

2. *Honolulu Advertiser*, Nov. 16, 1976.

## 24 The Shipman Sisters

1. Unless otherwise noted, all information was provided by Roy Blackshear.

2. Caroline Shipman, "Extracts of the Shipman Family," 1971.

3. Charmian Kittridge London graduated from Mills Seminary (then so-called) in 1896.

4. *Hilo Tribune-Herald,* "Shipman Sister Saluted for Long Community Service," March 17, 1974, Lifestyle section.

## 25  A Kama'āina Company That Cares

Information on the Shipman Industrial Park and future plans for W. H. Shipman, Limited, comes from personal interviews with Blackshear and a paper he wrote on the subject in May 1993.

1. Interview with Richard Devine.

2. *Honolulu Star-Bulletin,* Oct. 19, 1945, p. 4.

3. Ned D. Ewart and Margaret Luscomb, *Archaeological Reconnaissance of Proposed Kapoho-Keaukaha Highway,* Bishop Museum Project no. 89, p. 25, December 1974.

4. Paper entitled "The Puna Coastline," believed to be by Brenda Lee, undated. Typed information at top of page reads: "Contributions of a Venerable Native to the Ancient History of the Hawaiian Islands, pages 24 & 25, by M. James Remy."

# BIBLIOGRAPHY

Ahloy, James K. "A Royal Legacy: The William Charles Lunalilo Trust Estate." Paper presented to the Hawaiian Historical Society, February 21, 1991.

Alvarez, Patricia M. Monograph. "A History of the Roads and Bridges on the Island of Hawaii." 1985.

Ashby, Gene. A Guide to Pohnpei: An Island Argosy. Micronesia: Rainy Day Press, 1987.

Bird, Isabella L. Six Months in the Sandwich Islands. Reprinted, Honolulu: University of Hawai'i Press, 1964.

Buck, Peter H. Vikings of the Sunrise. New York: Frederick A. Stokes Company, 1938.

Clemens, Samuel L. Mark Twain's Letters from the Sandwich Islands. Edited by A. Grove Day. Honolulu: University of Hawai'i Press, 1966.

Clements, John. Chronology of the United States. New York: McGraw-Hill, 1975.

Crawford, David, and Lena Crawford. Adventures in the South Pacific. VT: Charles Tuttle, 1967.

Dana, Richard Henry, Jr. Journal: Twenty-Four Years After. Los Angeles: Ward Ritchie Press, 1964.

Daws, Gavan. Dream of Islands. Honolulu: Mutual Publishing, 1984.

———. Shoal of Time: A History of the Hawaiian Islands. New York: Macmillan, 1968.

Day, A. Grove. History Makers of Hawaii. Honolulu: Mutual Publishing, 1984.

Desha, Rev. Stephen A. The Legend of the Naha Stone. Adapted by L. W. DeVis Norton. Hawaii Natural History Association, vol. 11, no. 3, 1950.

de Varigny, Charles. The Victorian Visitors. Translated by Alfons Korn. Honolulu: University of Hawai'i Press, 1958.

———. Fourteen Years in the Sandwich Islands. Translated by Alfons Korn. Honolulu: University of Hawai'i Press, 1981.

Ellis, William. Journal of William Ellis. Reprint of London 1827 edition and Hawaii 1917 edition. Honolulu: Advertiser Publishing Co., 1963.

Evangelism in Hawaii: Titus Coan and the Great Revival of 1837. Gavan Daws. 69th Annual Report of the Hawaiian Historical Society, 1960.

Galuteria, Peter. Lunalilo. Honolulu: Kamehameha Schools, 1991.

George, Milton C. The Development of Hilo, Hawaii, T.H., or A Slice Through Time At a Place called Hilo. Ann Arbor, MI: The Edwards Letter Shop, 1943.

Hawaiian Almanac. Thomas G. Thrum. Honolulu, 1875–1924.

*Hawaiian Annual.* Thomas G. Thrum. Honolulu, 1925 on.

*Hawaiian Gazette.* Newspaper, Honolulu. 1865–1918.

*Hawaii Tribune Herald.* Newspaper, Hilo.

Henke, L. A. "A Survey of Livestock in Hawaii." Research Report No. 5. Honolulu: University of Hawai‘i Press, 1929.

*Hilo Bay, a Chronological History.* Ed. Marian Kelly, Barry Nakamura, Dorothy Barrere. Bishop Museum, Department of Anthropology. 1981.

*Hilo Tribune.* Newspaper.

*The Journals of Captain James Cook.* Vol. 3. Hakluyt Society. London: Cambridge University Press. 1967.

Kuykendall, Ralph S. *The Hawaiian Kingdom.* 3 vol. Honolulu: University of Hawai‘i Press, 1947, 1953, 1967.

Leithead, A. Scott. "Hilo, Hawaii: Its Origins and Patterns of Growth, 1778–1900." Senior thesis, University of Hawai‘i, 1974.

London, Charmian. *The New Hawaii.* London: Mills and Boon, 1922.

———. *Our Hawaii.* New York: Macmillan, 1922.

Macrae, James. *With Lord Byron at the Sandwich Islands in 1825.* Extracts from his diary. Hilo: Petroglyph Press, 1972.

*Majestic Kau: Mo‘olelo of Nine Ahupuaa.* Ed. Marian Kelly. Department of Anthropology Report No. 2. Honolulu: Bishop Museum, 1980.

*Missionary Album.* Sesquicentennial ed., 1820–1970. Reprinted, Honolulu: Hawaii Mission Children's Society, 1969.

Mrantz, Maxine. *Hawaiian Monarchy, the Romantic Years.* Honolulu: Aloha Graphics and Sales, 1974.

*The Name and Family of Shipman.* Media Research. N.p., n.d.

Olson, Gunder. *The Story of the Volcano House.* Hilo: Petroglyph Press, 1984. Facsimile edition of 1941.

Shipman, Caroline. Monograph. "Extracts of the Shipman Family." Hilo, 1971.

*Shipman, Herbert Cornelius.* Oral interview by Watumull Foundation. Kea‘au, 1971.

*The Shipman Family in America.* Ed. Mrs. Wayne A. Carl (Rita Shipman), Mrs. Egerton Crispin (Angela Shipman), and Mr. and Mrs. William Henry Shipman. Copyright by The Shipman Historical Society, 1962.

Simonds, William A. *The Hawaiian Telephone Company Story.* Honolulu: Star-Bulletin Printing Co., Inc., 1958.

Thomas, Mifflin. *Schooner from Windward: Two Centuries of Hawaiian Interisland Shipping.* Honolulu: University of Hawai‘i Press, 1983.

Thurston, Lorrin A. *The Writings of Lorrin Thurston.* Honolulu: Honolulu Advertiser Press, 1936.

Trager, James. *The People's Chronology.* New York: Henry Holt and Company, 1992.

Vancouver, Captain George. *Voyages of Discovery to the North Pacific Ocean.* London: G. G. Robinson, Paternoster Row and J. Edwards, Pall Mall, 1798.

Williams, Neville. *Chronology of the Modern World.* New York: D. McKay Co., 1967.

Yardley, Paul T. *Millstones and Milestones: The Career of B. F. Dillingham.* Honolulu: University of Hawai'i Press, 1981.

Yzendoorn, Fr. Reginald, SS. CC. *History of the Catholic Missions in the Hawaiian Islands.* Honolulu: Honolulu Star-Bulletin, Ltd., 1927.

# INDEX

Bold numerals in the index indicate illustrations.